NURSING CHURCHILL

NURSING CHURCHILL

WARTIME LIFE FROM THE PRIVATE
LETTERS OF WINSTON CHURCHILL'S NURSE

JILL ROSE

AMBERLEY

First published 2018

Amberley Publishing
The Hill, Stroud
Gloucestershire, GL5 4EP

www.amberley-books.com

British Library Cataloguing in Publication Data.
A catalogue record for this book is available from the British Library.

ISBN 978 1 4456 7734 7 (hardback)
ISBN 978 1 4456 7735 4 (ebook)

Typesetting and Origination by Amberley Publishing.
Printed in the UK.

Contents

List of Illustrations

Unless otherwise indicated, these photographs and images belong to the estate of Doris Miles. My thanks to the copyright holders of numbers 2, 10, 33 and 34 for permission to use these images. Despite my best efforts, I am unable to ascertain the copyright holder(s) of numbers 1, 14, 17, 20, 22, 27 and 28, which are in my mother's collection, as well as numbers 19 and 32. To the best of my knowledge, numbers 25, 29 and 38 are in the public domain and can be used without further permission.

1. The signed photograph that Winston Churchill gave to Doris, March 1943.
2. Doris Miles in 1942; portrait by Angus McBean (© Houghton Library, Harvard University).
3. Roger Miles RNVR, 1942.
4. Doris and Roger at St Peter's Church, Vere Street, 8 January 1942.
5. Roger with his best man, his brother Richard Miles RNVR.
6. Wedding guests:Ranald Handfield-Jones (H-J), Barbara Ward (later Lady Jackson), Richard Miles, Jill Hippisley, Ted Miles, May Clayton Greene.
7. Doris and Roger's marriage certificate, January 1942.
8. Doris and Roger with Timo the dog, 1942.
9. May Clayton Greene with George and Doris, 1918.
10. William Henry Clayton Greene FRCS, with Zachary Cope and Arthur Dickson Wright (Courtesy of Imperial College Healthcare NHS Trust Archives).
11. Polly Guy with George and Doris, 1928.

12. Roger's mother Annie Jones at her graduation from Aberystwyth University, 1903.
13. Doris in charge of a stall at the local fête, Jersey, 1936.
14. Roger as Clytemmnestra in *Agamemnon*, Bradfield College, 1934 (courtesy of Bradfield College).
15. Roger and Richard, 1937.
16. May Clayton Greene with Hector, the Chow dog she rescued from occupied Jersey, 1940.
17. Sub-Lieutenant George Clayton Greene RN, 1939.
18. Doris, George and May, 1940.
19. Doris with Jill Hippisley in London, 1941 (Courtesy of Juliet Fitton).
20. May, St John Ambulance volunteer, 1941.
21. May, George and Doris in London, 1942.
22. Doris receives her Gold Medal for Excellence in Nursing (Courtesy of Imperial College Healthcare NHS Trust Archives).
23. Doris' Registered Nurse Certificate, June 1941.
24. Cartoons drawn by Doris, included in her letter of 16 January 1943.
25. Winston and Clementine Churchill returning to 10 Downing Street, June 1943.
26. HMS *Tartar*, in which Roger served in the Mediterranean campaign, 1942/1943.
27. Winston Churchill with President Franklin D. Roosevelt in Casablanca, Morocco, 22 January 1943 (Courtesy of the Franklin D. Roosevelt Library archives).
28. Jack and Joan Suchet's wedding, 23 January 1943 (Courtesy of David Suchet).
29. Bearded Roger, 1943.
30. Winston Churchill's temperature chart, 18–24 February 1943.
31. Dorothy Pugh, circa.1937.
32. Doris's notes on the condition of The Patient on the night of 22 February.
33. Postcard showing Chequers in the Second World War (Courtesy, Chequers Trust).
34. Doris's signature in the Chequers' Visitors' Book, 15 March 1943 (Courtesy, Chequers Trust).
35. Inscription in *War and Peace*, given to Doris by Clementine Churchill, March 1943.

Foreword

I was not on this earth in 1943 when my grandfather Winston Churchill contracted pneumonia. He was largely nursed by Doris Miles, the daughter of a former Dean of St Mary's Hospital, Paddington, Harry Clayton Greene. It is her letters to her husband Roger, who was serving in the Royal Navy – and the Arctic Convoys – that form the greater part of this book. The letters are delightful, but it is the section when she spent nearly four weeks nursing the wartime Premier that render her letters of historical significance.

I did know well most of the players in a drama which, without Nurse Miles's skills, could have had such a much worse outcome – not just for the Prime Minister personally and our family but for the whole Western World. I was born in 1949 to Christopher and Mary Soames (née Churchill), who briefly appears in these pages, sharing her worry about her father's health. Indeed my mother's books, *A Daughter's Tale* and her life of her mother Clementine, are quoted in the book.

I vividly remember my grandfather who was in his eighties during my childhood so all my memories are of him as an old man. But my grandmother Clementine was a large and continuing presence in my childhood and indeed on into my teens when I used to regularly have tea with her. For the first eight years of my life, my family lived at Chartwell Farm, in the valley next door to Chartwell itself, where my grandparents spent increasing amounts of time during their old age. Every day that they were there, my brother Nicholas and I were taken to visit them: we swam in the pool constructed by my grandfather and took tea with him on the terrace overlooking the Weald of Kent, a beautiful view that he never ceased to enjoy painting.

But it is a considerable sadness to me that I never knew my grandfather when he was at the height of his extraordinary powers. So reading Doris's letters it is a joy to hear my grandfather coming alive: his charm, his felicitous turn of phrase and his immense intellectual curiosity all shine through this account of his perforce intimate relationship with his nurse who, during the long dark watches of the night, strove to bring down his fever and to bring the pneumonia under control. Doris Miles always identified her patients by their disease: thus in the Prime Minister 'we have a congestion of the right base and a haemolytic strep infection.' Meanwhile in his turn the patient wanted to know every detail of his treatment. He evidently deployed his famous charm on Nurse Miles whose duties included taking a sleeping pill to him on a tray at the end of dinner. I love her story of hearing a group of men talking through the closed door to his bedroom at Chequers; she assumed it was a friend telling jokes ('lowies') to her patient, but closer inspection revealed it to be my Grandfather reading aloud a speech he was due to deliver, to his trusted lieutenant Antony Eden. Her descriptions of Chequers where she accompanied him while he convalesced, boost my very early memories of that rather strange and ugly house. I spent a Christmas there in 1954 when my grandfather was once again Prime Minister after the war. I was four years old and I vividly remember being very frightened by the creaking floorboards in the room in which I slept, supposedly haunted by the ghost of Lady Mary Grey who spent two years locked up at Chequers after Elizabeth I became Queen in 1558. So it is lovely to be able to flesh out my memories of the house with Nurse Miles's fresh and enthusiastic descriptions of what was and still is the British Prime Minister's official country residence.

Pneumonia is not as life threatening now as it was in the early days of rather primitive antibiotic treatments back in the 1940s. In fact it was a sobering reminder of just how dangerous was 'the old man's friend' when Edward Fitzroy, Speaker of the House of Commons, died of the same strep pneumonia that he contracted at the same time as his Prime Minister.

Churchill almost certainly picked up the infection from all the travel he was doing early in 1943, flying around the Mediterranean in unheated Liberators – spending hours in the freezing cold draughts that filled the back of those very basic aircraft as he travelled to the all-important conferences, first in Casablanca and then in Cairo. It was air travel at its most basic, but the conduct of the war left the PM with no choice but to travel in these levels of discomfort – and at considerable risk to his health.

Aside from the historical interest of Nurse Miles's weeks of tending Churchill, her letters represent a document of increasing interest to what life was like for working women during the years of War. Sadly it is a one sided correspondence as Roger Miles's letters to his wife have not survived. But here is a young couple separated in the early months of their marriage for long months by a cruel if necessary war. Her hopes for a future together and her great love for her husband shine through these pages, as does her very dated deferral to him on matters like income tax, insurance and finding a home. Doris was certainly not leaning in ....

Jill Rose, Doris and Roger Miles's daughter, has done a good job at painting in the background and historical context to the letters. They also use a delightfully dated lexicon of language used by girls of Doris's background at this time. Her descendants are 'jolly lucky' to have such a document in their family.

Emma Soames, 2018

Author's Note

Nursing Prime Minister Winston Churchill in February and March 1943 was a defining experience in the life of my mother, Doris Miles. By the end of her long life she could remember very little of her past, but she knew that she had once been Churchill's nurse. She told everybody about it. A mention of Churchill was one of the few things that stirred her memory and stimulated her interest. My brother even named his dog 'Winston' because he knew Mum would like it.

In the more than fifty years since his death in 1965, there has been a steady stream of books and films about Churchill, and the interest shows no sign of abating. He was chosen as Greatest Briton of All Time by popular vote in a BBC poll. It is important that his unique place in history be remembered for, as Boris Johnson wrote, 'Churchill matters today because he saved our civilization'.[1]

My mother was already old and had long been widowed when I discovered that she still had in her possession a cache of letters that she had written to her husband Roger (my father-to-be) while he was serving in the Navy during the War. The correspondence covers her time nursing the Prime Minister in February and March, 1943, as well as her life in the preceding months and immediately afterwards. 'Dearest, you would laugh if you could see me now,' she wrote on 23 February.

> I'm in the PM's study, sitting in that odd-shaped chair he sits in for his photographs, and using a blotter stamped 'First Lord, Cabinet Room' on the outside. An enormous desk, surrounded by telephones with different coloured receivers, pots of glue, pens, paper etc.,

and maps of the world round the walls. The study is next to his
bedroom, and there is a connecting bell, which usually goes off with
a loud buzz about 2 A.M., just as I am getting my head down.

As I transcribed what she had written, I would ask her to explain
and clarify certain things contained therein. Already her memories
were fading, but she told me what she could. I then set the letters
aside and thought little more about them for the next sixteen years,
returning to them only after my mother's death.

Recently, as I have compiled her letters for this book, I realise
with regret that there is so much more that I could have and should
have asked her. I have lived abroad almost all of my adult life,
and my parents' past was seldom a topic of conversation on my
visits home. My father died too soon. He rarely talked about his
wartime experiences, but perhaps he would have elaborated if only
I had shown more interest. I wish I could remember more of my
grandmother's reminiscences instead of the few tattered, tantalising
scraps of memories which are all that I have left.

I have been unable to find any information about some of my
parents' friends. If any readers recognise the name of one of their
relatives I would be delighted to hear from them.

It is one of life's bitter ironies that we seem to become interested
in our forebears only when it is too late, for when they are able
and want to tell us their stories we are too young and too centred
on our own lives to listen and remember, and heedless of the fact
that they will not be with us always. From my personal experience
this is particularly true for people of my own 'Baby Boomer'
generation, whose parents and grandparents lived through the most
momentous times of the 20th Century. Truly we don't know what
we've got till it's gone. I have dug around to find out as much as
I can about my family to flesh out my own recollections of what
I was told, but sadly there is so much more that I will never know.
Who is Beetle? What were the policemen doing in the bedroom?
Why did Pamela break off the engagement?

I have written this book for my parents' grandchildren and great-
grandchildren, because one day, when I am long gone, they will
want to know Doris and Roger's story.

Acknowledgements

With loving thanks to my family for their help and their enthusiastic support, particularly my cousin Elaine Moore, and my nieces Lindsay and Thea Maclean. My sister Vicky Stevens, whose command of the English language rivals Churchill's, has given me invaluable assistance and advice. Special thanks to my husband Allen for the hours he spent reading and editing my drafts, for his imaginative suggestions and astute observations, and for his patience and support during the many months that I was writing this book.

My thanks to the owners of Dorothy Pugh's diary for permission to publish extracts, to Helen Warren for sharing her wartime memories, and to the family friends who have helped fill in the gaps in what I know of my parents' story: Juliet Fitton, Amanda Godman, Cynthia Helms, Robert Pugh, Marie Ridder, David and John Suchet, Gill and Robin Teague.

I am very grateful for the interest and the courtesy shown to me by the people who I contacted in the course of doing my research: Penelope Baker, Archivist, Exeter College, Oxford; Caroline Bell, Churchill War Rooms Museum; Zac Goldsmith, MP, and his assistant Charlotte Cox; Dr John Mather, Secretary of the Churchill Society of Tennessee; Rodney Melville and Peter Jones of the Chequers Trust; Diarmuid O'Keeffe and Philip Spracklan, HM Treasury; Christy Perry and Peter Campbell Smith of St Andrews, Cheam. I deeply appreciate the consideration shown by the Rt Hon Boris Johnson MP for making time to read and comment on my work.

In particular, I owe a huge debt of gratitude to the following people, who have been so encouraging and so willing to share their time and expertise with me: Kevin Brown, Archivist of St Mary's Hospital; Richard Langworth CBE, Senior Fellow, Hillsdale College Churchill Project; Philip Reed, OBE, Emeritus Director of the Churchill War Rooms Museum; Andrew Roberts, author of *The Storm of War* and *Masters and Commanders*; Professor Allister Vale MD of City Hospital, Birmingham, the leading authority on Winston Churchill's health.

Thanks to the team at Amberley Publications: Jon Jackson, Shaun Barrington, Hazel Kayes, Nicola Embery, Cathy Stagg and their colleagues.

I am enormously grateful to Emma Soames, who honours my parents with her gracious foreword. By honouring them we recognise the millions of men and women whose struggles and sacrifice allowed our generation to grow up in peace and freedom.

Above all, my thanks to my mother for writing her wondeful letters, to my father for preserving them, and to both of them for being such super parents!

Prologue

At 3 o'clock in the afternoon on Thursday, 8 January 1942, twenty-five-year-old Doris Clayton Greene married Roger Miles at St Peter's Church, Vere Street in London. Doris was a nurse and Roger a house surgeon at St Mary's Hospital, Paddington, where Doris's father Harry had formely been senior consultant surgon. Roger's father, the Reverend Edwin 'Ted' Miles, led the prayers.

It was a cold, bright day. The bride wore a fur coat that she had borrowed from her mother May, with a spray of lily-of-the-valley pinned to the lapel. She was attended by her best friend Jill Hippisley, another St Mary's-trained nurse. May was as beautiful and elegantly dressed as always. Harry Clayton Greene had died when Doris was a little girl, and it was his former house surgeon and friend Ranald Handfield-Jones (always known as H-J) who walked her up the aisle. Roger's best man was his younger brother Richard, a sub-Lieutenant in the Royal Navy. Despite the austerity of wartime, everyone had made a big effort to look smart for this special occasion. Doris's brother George Clayton Greene, an engineering officer in HMS *Renown*, was unable to attend the ceremony as he was away at sea on active service. On their marriage certificate Roger's 'Rank or Profession' is shown as 'Doctor of Medicine'; there is merely a small line through this space for Doris's occupation.

Roger's brother-in-law John Gilbert loaned the newly-weds a car and enough petrol to take them as far as the little Surrey town of Hindhead, where they spent a relaxing honeymoon in the peace and quiet of the Devil's Punchbowl Hotel, enjoying long rambling walks through the wintry countryside, far away from the clamour of London.

An ordinary enough event, but Doris and Roger lived in extraordinary times, for these were the darkest days of the Second World War, when the eventual outcome was far from certain.

Act One

In the late summer of 1939, Doris had been cruising with friends in the Mediterranean, little realising that it would be many years before anyone could enjoy such carefree activities again. After all, Prime Minister Neville Chamberlain had promised 'peace for our time' just a year earlier, in September 1938, after meeting with German Chancellor Adolf Hitler in Munich following Germany's annexation of the Sudetenland area of Czechoslovakia.

One of the few who had long foreseen the coming military clash was Winston Spencer Churchill. 'You were given the choice between war and dishonour,' he railed when Chamberlain returned from Munich. 'You chose dishonour and you will have war.'[1] In a speech to the House of Commons he deplored the abandonment of Czechoslovakia and the abrogation of Britain's moral authority.

Churchill had been a soldier, a war correspondent, and a Member of Parliament since 1900. Although he had been out of office since 1929, he had remained on the back benches, a powerful voice of dissent in British politics. Even at the tender age of nine the young Winston had shown himself to be a thorn in the flesh of those in authority. His headmaster noted in his school report that he 'is a constant trouble to everybody and is always in some scrape or other.'[2] Nonetheless, the head continued, 'he has very good abilities,' and noted his prowess at history, writing and spelling.

For ten years, between 1929 and 1939, Churchill was politically isolated, focusing much of his attention on painting and writing. He grew more and more alarmed at the rise of Adolf Hitler and his National Socialist German Workers' Party – the 'Nazis', or

'Narzis' as Churchill pronounced it – and the rapid build-up of the German military machine. In 1935 he wrote in an article in *Strand Magazine*, 'When Hitler began, Germany lay prostrate at the feet of the Allies. He may yet see the day when what is left of Europe will be prostrate at the feet of Germany.'[3]

At first his dire predictions fell on mostly deaf ears. The majority of people in Britain didn't want to believe that another war in Europe was inevitable, barely twenty years after the conclusion of the 'War to end all Wars'. In his book *The Gathering Storm*, the first volume of his history of the Second World War, Churchill wrote: 'I strove my utmost to galvanise the Government into vehemence and extraordinary preparation, even at the cost of world alarm. In these endeavours no doubt I painted the picture even darker than it was.'[4] Eventually Hitler's increasingly aggressive policies became impossible to ignore. To their credit, a growing number of people in positions of authority accepted the danger even before Munich, and preparations began in earnest so that Britain would not be caught flat-footed should there indeed be an outbreak of hostilities.

In the First World War the Germans had used poison gas, particularly mustard gas, on the British forces mired in the trenches of northern France, with devastating consequences. Among those whose lungs had been severely and permanently damaged by the noxious fumes was Roger's father, the Reverend Edwin 'Ted' Miles, serving as a chaplain to the troops. The aerial bombing of civilians in the Spanish Civil War, particularly at Guernica in April 1937, raised the spectre of gas bombs being used in a possible future conflict, and so in 1938 the British government ordered the mass production of gas masks, or 'respirators'. A booklet distributed by the Home Office that same year gave householders detailed instructions on how to protect their homes and their families in the event of air raids: 'We all hope and work to prevent war but, while there is a risk of it, we cannot afford to neglect the duty of preparing ourselves and the country for such an emergency.'[5]

Doris returned to England as events in Europe spiralled out of control. On 23 August 1939, Hitler signed a secret non-aggression pact with Josef Stalin, leader of the Soviet Union. Having guaranteed that there would be no attack on his eastern flank, Hitler turned his attention towards Poland, a large country where he could expand the Nazi policy of *Lebensraum* ('living space').

By early 1939 the British Government had finally faced up to the realisation that Hitler was not playing by the same rules, and on 31 March Britain and France had pledged to come to Poland's aid in the event of an attack. When German armies invaded Poland on 1 September 1939, Britain had no choice but to issue an ultimatum demanding that they withdraw. No response was received and two days later Prime Minister Chamberlain gravely announced that Britain and Germany were now at war. It was Doris's twenty-third birthday, 3 September 1939.

Chamberlain had been proven wrong and Winston Churchill was vindicated. He was at once invited back into the War Cabinet as First Lord of the Admiralty, a post he had held in the Great War but had resigned in the aftermath of the disastrous Allied landings at Gallipoli. A signal quickly passed through the Fleet: 'Winston is back.'

Nobody knew what might come next, but people did what they could to prepare for an imminent invasion by the Germans. The stockpiling of food and other commodities immediately began. On 10 September Doris's mother May Clayton Greene wrote from her home in Jersey to her son George: 'I'm storing as much food as I can without being piggish – pickling eggs etc. We've never had such a wonderful crop of vegetables in the garden as this year.' Blackout curtains were hastily stitched and stretched across every window so that not a single glimmer of light could escape to aid Germans planes passing overhead. Curbs along the road were painted white to make it easier to get about in the dark. Every person in the country was issued with a gas mask in a cardboard box, which they were obliged to carry with them at all times. There were special children's masks of pinkish-red or blue with 'Mickey Mouse' ears at the side to encourage youngsters to use them. As it turned out, the Luftwaffe never did drop gas bombs on Britain, so fortunately the efficacy of the masks was never put to the test.

Troops of the British Expeditionary Force (BEF) were dispatched to France and moved towards the Belgian border, where they dug in and waited for something to happen. Immediately after war had been declared, the Royal Air Force began dropping millions of leaflets on Germany in a futile propaganda offensive, but apart from some minor skirmishes, there was little movement on the Western Front in the early months of the war; most of the action was at sea.

In the North Atlantic, British military and civilian shipping was harassed by German U-boats and by the Luftwaffe. In April 1940 the Germans invaded Denmark and the strategically important but technically neutral country of Norway. The Allied response was muddled and ineffective. Among those who saw action in the abortive Norwegian campaign was Doris's brother, Lieutenant George Clayton Greene, in the battle-cruiser *Renown*.

In a tense debate in the House of Commons on 8 May, Chamberlain realised that he had lost the confidence of Parliament. He confided to Churchill that he believed there had to be a Government in which all the parties would serve, but that he was not the one to lead it as he did not have the support of the opposition Labour Party. Only two members of the Cabinet had the stature and experience to work with the other political parties and lead a coalition National Government, Winston Churchill and Lord Halifax, the Foreign Secretary. Churchill's 'long years of largely unheeded warnings about the rise of Nazism had given him an unassailable moral right to the premiership,'[6] writes Andrew Roberts in *The Storm of War*. Halifax withdrew himself from consideration on the grounds that he could not effectively lead the government from the House of Lords. On 10 May Neville Chamberlain went to Buckingham Palace to submit his resignation to the King, who then sent for Winston Churchill. As well as leading the British National Government as Prime Minister, Churchill also took for himself the portfolio of Minister of Defence. 'His assumption of this additional function and title', explained Lord Normanbrook, a member of the Cabinet Secretariat, 'had the result that, for the first time, responsibility for the strategic conduct of the war was vested in the Minister holding the supreme political power. He showed from the start that he intended to take personal charge of all matters affecting the strategic direction of the war.'[7]

The next six years would prove this to be a most fortuitous outcome, for Winston Churchill was uniquely suited to this particular task at this particular time. He was sixty-five years old, an age at which most men of his age were expected to retire and collect their pension for the next eleven years, but as Andrew Roberts points out, Churchill was 'still at the height of his very considerable intellectual and oratorical powers'.[8] In his own *History of the Second World War* Churchill wrote: 'At last I had the authority to give directions over the whole scene. I felt as if I were walking with destiny, and that all my past life had been but a preparation for this hour and for this trial.'[9] Few would disagree.

At dawn on the very day that Winston Churchill took over the reins of government, Friday, 10 May 1940, a massive force of German infantry and Panzer divisions smashed through the Ardennes Forest into Belgium and the Netherlands, trampling the complacency of the defenders. It was the Lightning War – *Blitzkreig*! A second wave of German troops encircled the British forces from the south, through France. Gradually the BEF was pushed back towards the English Channel. It seemed that they must all be killed or captured, but over the course of nine remarkable days, an impromptu flotilla of some 850 British vessels, ranging from naval destroyers to small pleasure craft, rescued in excess of 338,000 British, French and Belgian soldiers from the beaches of Dunkirk in one of the most improbable evacuations in military history.

Now there was nothing but the sea between the German armies and Britain. The so-called Phoney War was over. All across the country church bells fell silent, for it was decreed they would be rung only to warn the population in the event of an invasion.

Many in the Cabinet believed that a German victory was inevitable and pushed for a negotiated settlement with Hitler. But Churchill was having none of their defeatism. By the sheer force of his will and his personality he persuaded the doubters that Britain must resist the Nazis at any cost. In a speech on 4 June 1940 Prime Minister Churchill sounded a note of defiance that resonated with the British people:

> We shall fight in France, we shall fight on the seas and oceans, we shall fight with growing confidence and growing strength in the air, we shall defend our island, whatever the cost may be. We shall fight on the beaches, we shall fight on the landing grounds, we shall fight in the fields and in the streets, we shall fight in the hills, we shall never surrender.[10]

Legend has it that after the speech Churchill muttered in an aside, '... and we will hit them over the heads with beer bottles, which is about all we have got to work with.'[11] Although apocryphal, the remark has a ring of Churchillian authenticity.

The new Prime Minister was sixty-five years old, corpulent, and a notoriously hard drinker. Knowing how important Churchill was to the war effort, the Cabinet decided that a professional was needed to keep an eye on his health. At the behest of Churchill's close friend Lord Beaverbrook, Sir Charles Wilson, a prominent London physician and Dean of St Mary's Hospital, was appointed as his personal doctor, a position which both men approached at first with some reluctance. Ultimately, however, Sir Charles remained with Winston for the rest of his patient's long life.

This was the second time in the twentieth century that Britain and Germany had battled for supremacy in Europe. Doris's marriage was another echo of the past. Her mother, May Guy, had also been a nurse, and her father William Henry 'Harry' Clayton Greene had been a senior surgeon and lecturer at St Mary's Hospital and Medical School.

Harry was born in Wallasey, Cheshire in November 1874, the same month that Winston Churchill was born at Blenheim Palace, the ancestral home which had been given by a grateful nation in the early eighteenth century to the victorious general John Churchill, first Duke of Marlborough. Harry earned his degree at Corpus Christi College, Cambridge, and having passed the Primary Fellowship examination he entered St Mary's in 1898, obtaining his Fellowship of the Royal College of Surgeons (FRCS) in December 1901. He was a keen cricketer and played on the hospital's team. Harry served as Dean of the Medical School from 1907 until 1910. Zachary Cope, who knew him well, describes him as

> a tall, dark and handsome man ... a wonderful teacher and a brilliant operator who impressed the students by his forceful personality and his remarkably clear exposition of surgical principles ... he left a great impression on the students whom he taught, and greatly helped to raise the standard of surgery at St Mary's. He was very forthright in his speech and spoke as he thought, but it was well said of him that to those who knew him intimately he revealed a charming personality and a loyalty nothing could shake.[12]

One of the school's students at the time was an up-and-coming young doctor called Charles Wilson. Wilson's biographer Richard Lovell writes: 'Charles's surgical outpatient appointment as a student was under William Henry Clayton Greene ... Then aged 30, he also was to play a part in Charles's later career. Clayton Greene ... came to be regarded as the outstanding surgical figure at the hospital during the first quarter of the century.'[13] Wilson himself thought highly of his mentor, writing to his mother: 'Clayton Greene, our Dean and one of the junior surgeons whom I think is about best man on gastroenterostomy, has asked me to dinner on Friday.'[14]

Harry was appointed Full Surgeon and Lecturer in Surgery in 1911. During the war he received a royal appointment as surgeon to the King George V Hospital and to the King Edward VII Hospital for Officers. He also served on the hospital ship *Liberty*. On 4 November 1915, as the Allied offensive stalled in the mud of northern France, with massive casualties on all sides, Harry and May were married at St Marylebone Parish Church.

May had had an unconventional upbringing by the standards of the late Victorian world into which she was born. Her father, William Hannaford Guy RNR, was a captain in the Merchant Marine, and his wife Polly (baptised as Mary, as was her daughter, though neither woman was ever known by that name) frequently accompanied him on his voyages. May was born in Rio Grande do Sol, Brazil, on 15 October 1892. For much of her girlhood she lived in Brooklyn in New York City. Here May learned the humorous songs of the American music-hall and the minstrels, as well as the poems of Henry Wadsworth Longfellow, which she later taught to her children and grandchildren.

Thomas and Polly's elder son Julius died in America at the age of nineteen, and in 1910 they returned to England with May and her younger brother Lester. The family settled in Lynton in North Devon, and after she finished school May trained to be a nurse. She was twenty-two years old when Harry Clayton Greene took off his top hat, went down on his knees on the floor of the taxicab in which they were travelling and asked her to marry him. Harry was eighteen years her senior, a respected and successful surgeon; May recalled years later, 'I was afraid to say no!'

Nonetheless, and despite the difference in their ages, it was a happy marriage. Doris was born on 3 September 1916. She never liked her name; she told us that her father had seen a playbill featuring the beautiful American actress Doris Keane and decided that it would be a suitable name for his daughter (May was not consulted). Her brother George was born on 4 February 1918.

Doris and George had a carefree childhood in their parents' comfortable home at Number 9, Wimpole Street. They were well cared for but not pampered. It was a comparatively modest household for its time, with a nanny, a footman, a cook and a kitchen maid, and a housemaid called Edith who Doris described as 'barmy'. The two children walked to their open-air primary school in nearby Regents Park, and on the way they would wave to the firemen at the local fire station and to the coal-man delivering coal in his horse-drawn wagon. Doris was a high-spirited little girl who was close to her good-natured little brother and the two of them enjoyed playing childish pranks together. On one occasion, Doris later recalled, the two of them got onto the house telephone and called through to their father's consulting room, pretending to be a patient. Of course their breathless giggles quickly gave them away, but they thought they were being frightfully daring! When she and George were not invited to an end-of-term party at the school, the pair of them marched onto the lawn and danced around calling the other children 'stuck-up paste pots', the worst insult they could think of.

Doris was a voracious reader, and always had her nose stuck in a book. She loved going to the pictures with her grandmother Polly or with 'Auntie Gussie', Harry's sister Annie Augusta. When she was about six Doris had had rickets, a vitamin D deficiency, common in those days, that caused children's bones to soften, and she was made to wear tight laced-up boots to support her ankles. She hated wearing them, but they were apparently effective, for she grew up with long, straight, shapely legs of which she was always a little vain (even in her 80s, at a regular exercise class with friends, she claimed that she could still kick her legs higher than anyone else). Summer holidays were spent by the seaside in Hunstanton in Norfolk, at the home of Polly's cousin 'Uncle Herbert', sometimes accompanied by Harry's glamorous younger sister Alice, an aspiring playwright and author. Alice's novel *His Grace* was published in 1922, although to modern tastes it appears dated and almost unreadable.

Harry Clayton Greene was at the top of his profession as a surgeon and lecturer. In 1919 he was awarded the CBE, and he received the French *Légion d'Honneur* for his work at the French

Hospital in London with which he had been associated since 1903. However, in 1924 his health was undermined by a severe septic infection followed by diphtheria, and he retired with his young family to the Channel Islands. In those days there were no antibiotics to treat such infections, although in the Research Department of St Mary's Hospital a Scottish doctor named Alexander Fleming was conducting research into antibacterial agents. (Fleming's breakthrough discovery, in 1928, of what he called 'penicillin' would save innumerable lives in years to come.)

But there was no magic bullet for Harry. He died in Guernsey in 1926. May was only thirty-three. She never remarried.

After Harry's death, May moved with her two children to the island of Jersey. Doris attended a primary boarding school in Seaton in Devon, then completed her secondary education at Godolphin School in Salisbury, where her favourite activities were reading, tennis, netball and lacrosse. Doris was very happy at school. She was in the running to be Head Girl, but was seen talking to two friends who had been confined to the 'San'. This was strictly *verboten*, and so she missed the opportunity. 'I didn't mind,' she later said – she never aspired to be in a position of authority. Going home to Jersey for holidays she travelled in a small plane which landed on the hard-packed sand of the beach, to her intense delight and the consternation of the beach-goers.

Doris loved living in Arden Lodge, their comfortable home near St Helier. She played tennis and golf, went sailing and swimming, took skiing holidays in Switzerland with May and George – all sports which she continued to enjoy well into her sixties. Later she had fun driving her sports car around the island's relatively traffic-free roads without such petty restrictions as driving licences and speed limits.

May, still beautiful and chic, had many suitors, but none of them met her exacting (and sometimes capricious) standards. One was rejected on the grounds that he had 'sweaty hands', and another because he wore yellow shoes. 'Can't be doing with that,' she told Doris. She was well aware that her own mother Polly had remarried soon after William Guy's death because she had few other options and it was expected of her, although (according to May) Polly never liked her second husband. Fortunately May had the means to remain single and independent by choice.

George entered the Royal Naval College at Dartmouth in South Devon as a cadet in 1931 a few weeks after his thirteenth birthday, followed by a stint at the RN Engineering College in Plymouth. Upon graduation he joined the Navy as an engineering officer, and was posted to *Renown* in August 1939.

Doris had hoped to train as a medical student but failed her first Medical Board (MB) examination, a necessary preliminary. At that time there was little encouragement for women to become doctors and, ironically, had she passed the exam she would not have been able to train at St Mary's Hospital Medical School. During the First World War female students had gradually infiltrated the school and had proved themselves to be extremely able, as well as bringing in much-needed fees. But the men returning from the war resented the competition from the women and began agitating for their exclusion. Using the flimsiest of excuses, these short-sighted young men were supported by many of the older consultants, particularly the misogynistic Sir Almroth Wright, and from 1924 until 1947 there would be no female students at St Mary's. (Seventy years later, women made up about 60% of the medical school entrants.)

So Doris followed her mother into the nursing profession and, in October 1937, she began her training at her father's alma mater. Her starting pay was £2 a week plus room and board, and her hours were from 8 am to 6 or 7 pm. Among the other trainee nurses starting that same day was Jill Hippisley from Wells in Somerset. Jill was fun-loving and ebullient; she made Doris laugh, and the two women became lifelong friends.

St Mary's is one of London's major teaching hospitals, situated on Praed Street in Paddington, a few minutes' walk from the mainline train station. Across the street the conveniently located Fountains pub has been a favourite drinking hole for students, patients and staff since 1823. Alexander Fleming was a regular, and the story goes that the spores he used to make penicillin came from this ale house.

The hospital and associated medical school were founded in 1851, financed by donations from the wealthy bourgeoisie who lived south of the Paddington canal to provide medical care for the poor who lived to the north. Their philanthropy was leavened with a healthy dose of enlightened self-interest, for most of their servants came from the northern area and they were anxious to keep at bay the diseases born from poverty and squalor. Praed Street itself was a notorious haunt of prostitutes, but when the Bishop of London donated a parcel of land just across the Paddington Canal Basin from St Mary's Church, this was the location selected for the new building. The founding governors were determined that the hospital would take a modern scientific approach to medicine. In 1878 a young surgeon called Walter Pye was appointed as Lecturer in Physiology. His book, *Pye's Surgical Handicraft*, first published in 1884, became the standard text on surgical methodology for the next century. In 1919 Harry Clayton Greene edited and largely rewrote the eighth edition, to include much new material and the experiences of his own ward teaching; the twenty-second edition was published in 1991. Other distinguished St Mary's consultants such as Zachary Cope (knighted in 1953), Aleck Bourne, R. M. Handfield-Jones and Arthur Porritt (knighted in 1950), wrote standard textbooks that went through many editions.

The physiology department and its laboratory brought prestige to the hospital, and another step forward in scientific medicine was taken in 1902 with the appointment of Almroth Wright, already an acclaimed pathologist and bacteriologist who had developed an effective typhoid vaccine. Harry, who had won the Kerslake Scholarship in Pathology and Bacteriology the previous year, was Surgical Registrar at the time. Despite his occasional wrong turns and his antediluvian view of women, Wright (who was knighted in 1906) put the St Mary's Immunology Department on the map. By the end of the First World War, Wright and his team, which included the diffident Alexander Fleming, were in the forefront of antibiotic research. In her comprehensive history of the hospital, Elsbeth Heaman notes that 'the complaint was made that science was becoming more popular than rugby at St Mary's'[15]– strong words indeed, for their prowess on the field was a source of great pride.

In 1920 Charles Wilson, who had served with distinction in the Royal Army Medical Corps during the war, was appointed Dean of the Medical School. Zachary Cope calls him 'the Great Dean'. 'Wilson combined in himself several great qualities seldom seen together,' writes Cope. 'He saw clearly both the near and the distant view; he was a remarkable though critical judge of character; he had a facility for putting his views into excellent and telling words, and he possessed the power of quick and determined action.'[16] He radically overhauled the organisation, setting up two clinical units with Harry Clayton Greene as director on the surgical side and Dr Wilfred Harris on the medical side, and took major steps to improve the hospital's ailing finances.

One of his more controversial innovations was a change in the way students were selected and scholarships awarded, moving from a system based on competitive examinations to one based on his personal choice of men of character. The criteria were akin to those required of a Rhodes Scholar, including a 'fondness for, and success in manly outdoor sports such as cricket, football and the like'.[17] Since Wilson was a passionate supporter of rugby football, critics suggested that he was using the scholarships to lure rugby players so that St Mary's would win the Hospitals Cup. Actually, rugby was not incompatible with professional excellence; top players such as Tom Kemp, Carmichael ('Ca') Young and Arthur Porritt also became outstanding doctors. In *Doctors at War* Craig and Fraser state: 'He looked for men of character and courage, capable of working in a team and gentlemanly in behaviour,'[18] – 'intellectual athletes', suggested Kevin Brown, St Mary's Hospital Archivist, in our conversation. Lovell writes: 'By the end of the 1930s [Wilson] was presiding over a student body largely of his own choosing, characterised by great *esprit-de-corps* and reflecting remarkably wide interests.'[19]

The combination of medical students and rugby players at St Mary's meant, inevitably, a plethora of bawdy songs and off-colour jokes, which Doris called 'lowies'. However, as the 30s drew on, Wilson, who was knighted in 1938, grew somewhat remote from the medical school, and even from the rugby players: 'his passion for Rugby football did not extend to joining in the boisterous evenings that many players enjoyed. Neither the beer drinking, nor renderings of *The Virgin Sturgeon* were to his taste.'[20] To Doris, he was always 'The Dean', and it was he who was responsible for bringing her future husband to St Mary's.

Roger was born in Liverpool, just a few miles from Harry Clayton Greene's birthplace in Wallasey, on 1 May 1915, six months before Harry and May's wedding. His Welsh mother, Annie née Jones, a banker's daughter from Bala, had been one of the first women to graduate from the University of Aberystwyth. At university she had met an athletic theology student, Edwin Griffith Miles from the mining town of Aberdare in Glamorgan, South Wales. He was 'Ted' to his friends and family, and has been described as 'a vibrant, vital personality ... [with] strong rugged features and a radiant smile'.[21] Annie and Ted were married on 12 August 1908, one month before Winston Churchill wed Clementine Hozier. (The entry in Ted's diary on his wedding day reads simply, 'At last'; Winston recorded that he married and lived happily ever after.[22]) Annie was a gifted linguist and had been a secondary school French teacher after leaving university, but she gave up her career without question after her wedding, as was expected of women of her class and generation. The couple had four children, Marian, Margaret, Roger and Richard.

Ted had been advised that sea air would be beneficial to his health, and in 1919 he became the minister at St George's Presbyterian Church in Felixstowe on the Suffolk coast, where Roger spent his happy childhood years and where he developed his lifelong love of sailing and the sea. In 1928 the family moved to Cheam in Surrey, where Ted was the first minister of the new St Andrew's Reform Church. Roger was an enthusiastic, though not exceptional, sportsman; he enjoyed horse-back riding, cricket, and playing tennis and golf with his siblings.

Roger attended Bradfield College in Berkshire where he was a classical scholar. He had not thought of going into medicine until Charles Wilson saw his riveting performance (in Greek) as Clytemnestra in *Agamemnon*, one of Bradfield's renowned productions of Greek tragedy, in June 1934. His bravura portrayal of a woman scorned was evidently convincing; 'Clytemnestra's passion', said reviewer Ivor Brown, was 'splendidly declaimed by Miss Miles'. Wilson declared that Roger would make a fine addition to St Mary's Medical School (which was known for the quality of its dramatic productions as well as the quality of its doctors). Judging by the enthusiasm with which Clytemnestra wielded her knife, and by the review in the *Bradfield College Chronicle* which noted, 'he [Roger]was much helped by the possession of beautiful and expressive hands'[23], he was obviously cut out to be a surgeon! The Dean recognised the young man's potential and decided that he met the criteria for admittance, which Cope lists as, 'high intelligence, outstanding character and considerable skill at games'.[24] In his future career Roger amply fulfilled Sir Charles' expectations.

Roger gave up his classical studies. He passed his first MB in July 1934 and was awarded a scholarship. In October he entered St Mary's Hospital Medical School and during the next five-and-a-half years of his training he specialised in surgery, completing his core studies and becoming a Member of the Royal College of Surgeons (MRCS) and Licentiate, Royal College of Physicians (LRCP) in January 1940. In August 1940 he was appointed Casualty House Surgeon, just before the beginning of the Blitz.

Even before the surrender of France on 21 June 1940, it seemed inevitable that Hitler's next target would be Britain itself. Just a few miles off the coast of north-western France lay the Channel Islands, an anachronistic remnant of Britain's medieval French holdings. Despite Churchill's 'fight to the end' rhetoric, the War Cabinet decided on 19 June that they were indefensible and of no strategic value. All military personnel were quickly pulled out, abandoning the islands to the enemy. They were strategically unimportant to the Germans as well, but Hitler knew there was propaganda value for the Third Reich in occupying even this insignificant British outpost.

There was little planning by the authorities for an orderly evacuation of the civilian population, and there was much confusion as about a third of the islands' total population of 90,000 fled. Thousands more stayed put, determined to tough it out, including the indomitable Sybil Hathaway, Dame of Sark.

George had a few days leave from his ship and went to Jersey to help his mother. Local farmers who were staying on agreed to occupy May's house, Arden Lodge, to prevent the Germans from doing so, and to look after her dog Hector. Before they left the island, George dug a hole in the raspberry patch in the vegetable garden behind the house and buried a large leather trunk containing the family silver. George rejoined his ship while May went to Stamford in Lincolnshire to see her solicitor, Conyers Lowe.

One of the more distressing preliminaries to the evacuation was the slaughter of several thousand dogs and cats, whose owners were unable to take them when they left and were reluctant to turn them loose to fend for themselves. May was not going to let Hector suffer the same fate. She returned by herself to Jersey to put the house in order and to rescue her dog.

But she had left it too late. The last boat back to England sailed without her and German troops occupied the island on 1 July. May was trapped. The story of her subsequent escape has long been part of our family lore, and is well documented at the Underground Hospital Museum in Jersey.

In September 1939, May had written to George:

Just give those Huns one for me. So absurd sending our airmen to drop leaflets on Berlin – risking their lives. Why not do the thing properly! Give them a few bombs! I can't see any German dropping leaflets! I'm afraid I'm in it whole-heartedly – no parley with me. 'Shoot to kill' is my motto! We've seen enough of the Germans – at least I have – one cannot trust them! Not an inch! Be on your guard, whatever you do, when you come up against them. You are so large hearted and straight – but darling, you cannot deal with devils with your character. So do not trust any of them – they are evil! I wish I were a man and younger, so I could help to subdue them.

My darling, forgive me for going on this way, but I hate them. I was through the last war you know, and they showed no mercy – neither would I, if I had anything to do with them. So, please if you get into a corner with them, keep your eyes and brains skinned! You can't trust them.

There was no way that May was going to stay in Jersey under German occupation. She was determined to escape, and the only way to do that was by boat. Although the Germans had announced that anyone trying to escape would be shot on sight, May reasoned that it would take them a little while to arrange sentries at all the places where boats were moored. She drove to the main port of St Helier, parked in a quiet corner of the quay and went down to the yacht harbour. There she met the skipper of a Dutch merchant ship whose crew had sailed off while he took his sick cook to hospital. He had found a boat, abandoned by its owner, in which to make an escape. He agreed to take May and Hector with him on the next suitable tide.

At 3 o'clock on the morning of 3 July, a small boat bearing six people and a dog slipped out of St Helier Harbour in the darkness under the very noses of the German guards. Accompanying May, the skipper and the cook were Henry Kite and two young men from the Le Riche grocery store, Pip Cotillard and Arthur Marret, who had brought with them a large box of groceries. The Channel Islands have particularly strong tides, and leaving on the ebb they were able to paddle and drift out of the harbour without being seen or heard. Hector was as quiet as a mouse. They were well out to sea when they started the motor and headed towards England. They were making good progress when the engine stalled from lack of oil. Undeterred, the boys produced three pounds of best Jersey butter from the grocery box, which they melted against the exhaust pipe and then poured over the sump. That did the trick. That night they were within twelve miles of the south coast of England when the engine seized up for good.

They hove-to until dawn when they could see the shoreline. May knew at once where they were. She recognised the lighthouse on the promontory called Start Point and informed her shipmates that, more by luck than judgement, they had ended up close to the mouth of the River Dart where her son had been to school at the Royal Naval College. Lookouts ashore had spotted the little vessel and the coastguard sent a lifeboat to tow them into Dartmouth. May later recalled that the Dutch captain had kept hold of the boat's tiller the whole time, and that Hector had behaved very well. Their escape was not only one of the first, it was one of the few to make the much longer journey to England rather than to France, and certainly the only one that featured a middle-aged English woman and a Chow.

May settled in London and became a volunteer driver for the St John Ambulance Service during the terrible nights when German bombs rained down on the city in what came to be known as The Blitz.

Doris was the night nurse in charge of the operating theatre at St Mary's that September as she and her colleagues awaited casualties from the anticipated bombing. She later told us how kidney dishes, swabs, bottles of disinfectant and other equipment had been neatly laid out in readiness. As the first of the wounded were brought in, Doris was horrified to see that brick dust from the disintegrating buildings had been ground into the wounds and the skin of the victims. It quickly became apparent that swabs and disinfectant were woefully inadequate for the task, and the staff ended up sluicing the patients down with buckets of water to clean the wounds before surgery.

Working beside Doris as they calmly and efficiently treated those caught in the nightly air-raids was the handsome young Casualty Officer, Roger Miles. Roger was affable, cultivated and charming, with a droll sense of humour. Doris was at the same time pragmatic and romantic, a little bit untidy, and by her own admission 'shockingly lazy'. She was highly competitive; in later life she always won the Mothers' Race at her children's Sports Day, and the Sailing Club Ladies' Race. Even into her 90s she was a mean bridge player and always liked to win at Scrabble. Roger didn't care so much about winning, for him just playing the game was what mattered. He was unassuming and uncomplaining, with a tolerant and generous nature. He was slow to anger, although when really pushed he could sometimes show a flash of temper. Colleagues and students later remembered him as kind, patient and empathetic.

Roger and Doris fell in love and stayed in love for fifty years.

Act Two

Doris had proved to be an outstanding student nurse, consistently receiving excellent marks in her subject examinations. Her final report described her as 'personable, capable, helpful and professional'.[1] On 27 June 1941 she officially completed her training and was certified as a State Registered Nurse. In November 1941 she was the winner of the coveted and prestigious Gold Medal for Excellence in Nursing, awarded each year to just one person based on performance in the Hospital final exams and overall progress during training.

Shortly after their wedding, Roger completed his medical residency. He joined the Royal Naval Volunteer Reserve as a Surgeon Lieutenant and spent most of the next four years at sea. Doris remained at St Mary's. They corresponded copiously during Roger's long absences, and Doris's letters offer a fascinating window into a bygone world, unfiltered by the lens of history. They also tell a love story, of two young people separated by the very war that brought them together. Their mutual devotion lasted all their lives, and it shines through in her letters.

Paper was in short supply in 1942, and Doris wrote on whatever came to hand, preferably the medium-sized blue Basildon Bond writing paper that she favoured all her life, but sometimes on plain white paper or sheets of flimsy, on the hospital's letterhead, on tiny pieces of note paper, or on lined foolscap if that was all that was available. Occasionally she would splurge and send an air letter – shockingly expensive at sixpence when an ordinary letter cost just a penny-and-a-half. (Like her mother May, Doris was a careful money manager; her brother George was not so thrifty). It's not known if the air letters arrived more quickly to justify the additional expense. She wrote in her own inimitable style and, apart from some minor 'tidying up', I have transcribed her letters unchanged.

Doris lived for Roger's letters. 'You can't imagine how marvellous it is when letters come, because that's all we exist for really,'[2] she told him. Presumably hers were equally important to her husband, and it says a great deal about his character and his love for his wife that Roger carried so many of Doris's letters through the vicissitudes of his wartime naval service. Unfortunately, we don't have any of his replies. Years later I asked my mother what had happened to the letters she had received from my dad. She couldn't remember when they had disappeared; with obvious regret she thought they must have been cleared out during one of the family's several post-war moves. Perhaps, after all, it was Roger who was the more romantic one.

July 1942

By the summer of 1942, Britain had struggled through nearly three long, dark years since hostilities were declared on September 3, 1939. The daring of the Royal Air Force fliers, the fabled 'Few', in the 1940 Battle of Britain had prevented the Luftwaffe from gaining control of the skies and had thwarted Hitler's invasion plan; ultimately the Germans were able to control only the Channel Islands, a short distance off the coast of Northern France. But people were well aware that this was at best a temporary reprieve.

Two years earlier the country's new Prime Minister, Winston Churchill, had promised 'blood, toil, tears and sweat,'[1] and those were just about the only commodities in abundance. Food, clothing, petrol, even soap – almost everything was rationed. Urban children were uprooted from their families as they were evacuated to the comparative safety of the countryside. Housewives worked in armament factories, on the buses, railways and canals to keep the transportation systems going, and in hospitals, offices and power plants, wherever they were needed. Debutantes and East End shop girls alike volunteered for the hard and unfamiliar life of a Land Girl. For many women this was their first taste of independence from husbands, parents or domestic service, a forerunner of what we might now call 'female empowerment'. Their involvement wasn't always voluntary, though; since December 1941 women could be conscripted into work, and they never received the same pay as their male counterparts. Tens of thousands of servicemen had been taken prisoner, killed, or were missing in action. Close to three million more were on active service. Allied shipping losses in June 1942 were the worst of the entire war. Scarcely a family was untouched by the conflict.

But the British people were not easily subdued and they rose to the occasion. Everyone was anxious to do their bit. School children collected newspapers and scrap metal for recycling. Grandfathers joined the Home Guard, drilling with the very weapons they had used in the previous European conflict, the Great War of 1914–1918. Popular songs such as *Hitler has Only Got one Ball*, to the music of the *Colonel Bogey* march, and *We're Going to Hang out the Washing on the Siegfried Line* lampooned the enemy. The BBC radio programme *Music While You Work* beamed light-hearted, sing-along music into factories and offices to boost morale and increase productivity. And a line from a song by Britain's sweetheart Vera Lynn encapsulated the zeitgeist: 'I know we'll meet again some sunny day'.

The entry of the United States into the war after the Japanese attack on Pearl Harbour in December 1941 brought renewed optimism to the beleaguered British. However, a series of crushing victories by the Japanese in the Pacific in the early months of 1942, the loss of Hong Kong and Singapore, and the recapture by the Germans of the Libyan port of Tobruk in June, dispelled any hopes that the war would end soon. Still, there were glimpses of light in the prevailing gloom. The US naval victory at Midway put the Japanese on the defensive for the first time. Massive British bombing raids were wreaking havoc in Germany. And the strategically important little island of Malta thumbed its nose, David-like, at the Goliath of the Third Reich.

For two years Winston Churchill had cajoled, encouraged and inspired his fellow countrymen. He had developed a close relationship with US President Franklin D. Roosevelt, and had worked doggedly to secure Roosevelt's support for the British war effort. He seemed indefatigable, but the Prime Minister was then sixty-seven years old, overweight and under constant stress. His diet was indulgent, he drank alcohol to excess, smoked cigars, slept erratically and took little exercise – a lifestyle that would be roundly condemned by today's medical profession. So it was not surprising that in December 1941, while visiting the White House, he experienced chest pains and shortness of breath.

Churchill's personal physician since 1940 was Sir Charles Wilson, Dean of St Mary's Hospital, the same man who had encouraged Roger to enter medicine and who had become a mentor to the young surgeon. Sir Charles suspected that his patient had suffered a mild heart attack and faced a difficult dilemma. He was fearful of the ramifications should such information become common knowledge, but if he did nothing and Churchill's condition worsened, he would be blamed. In Washington he had seen at first hand the concealment of personal infirmity in the interest of the greater good. Polio had left President Franklin Roosevelt unable to stand or walk unaided, but with the help of his closest associates the extent of his disability was hidden from the public. In the end Sir Charles decided to tell no one of his diagnosis.

Roger had completed his medical residency in early 1942 and joined the Royal Naval Volunteer Reserve as a Surgeon-Lieutenant. (The RNVR was popularly known as the 'Wavy Navy', after the 3/8-inch wavy sleeve 'rings' that RNVR officers wore to differentiate them from career Royal Navy officers, such as Doris's brother George.) Roger's first posting in March 1942 was to the light cruiser HMS *Trinidad*, accompanying the Russian convoys through the gauntlet of German U-boats to the Arctic port of Murmansk. *Trinidad* was torpedoed and bombed; irreparably damaged, she was scuttled and sank on 15 May. Roger fortunately escaped serious injury, though for the rest of his life he carried a small scar across his nose caused by a superficial head wound.

In June, Doris and Roger enjoyed a short leave together before he was reassigned to the destroyer HMS *Tartar*. His ship was posted to the Mediterranean Sea in support of the Allied campaign in North Africa, but for security reasons Roger was not allowed to tell his wife his whereabouts.

Formerly, a St Mary's nurse who married was required to resign. The exigencies of war, however, meant that the hospital needed to retain all of its qualified staff, and under the more enlightened and sympathetic administration of Matron Mary Milne, who was appointed in December 1940, the rule was relaxed and Doris was allowed to stay after her wedding in January 1942.

Jill Hippisley had joined the Queen Alexandra's Royal Naval Nursing Service (QARNNS) in June and was working at the RN Hospital in Gosport, near Portsmouth. In her absence Doris's closest friend at the hospital was Dorothy Pugh, née Cooper, three years younger than she. Like Doris, Dorothy had wanted to be a doctor but had settled instead for nursing. She was newly wed to a doctor, also named Roger, who was serving as a medical officer with the Royal Air Force and had recently been posted to the Middle East. Doris and Dorothy lived in at the hospital, but were moved away from their unmarried colleagues to separate quarters on the top floor, which they dubbed 'Married Alley'. There the two young women eked out their rations as they shared their loneliness and some laughs over many cups of tea.

May Clayton Greene, Doris's mother, had a flat close by in Hinde Street, with her canary and her Chow dog Hector. Having survived his epic escape from Nazi-occupied Jersey, Hector was content with his status as a DP (Displaced Pet). May had obtained a job in the lingerie department of D. H. Evans department store, which she and Doris laughingly referred to as 'The Corsets'. Roger's parents, the Reverend Ted and Mrs Annie Miles, were not far away at The Manse in Cheam, just south of London. Doris would often spend the night at May's flat, or with her parents-in-law, or with her sister-in-law Marian in Surbiton.

Doris worked in the hospital's prestigious new Lindo Wing, which had been opened in 1937 and named after its wealthy benefactor. She got on well with the senior doctors, many of whom had worked with or trained under her father Harry Clayton Greene, including Frank Juler, Zachary Cope, and the redoubtable Arthur Dickson Wright, who she refers to as 'Dickson' or 'ADW'. The magnificently-named Ranald Montague Handfield-Jones (H-J, as he was known to everyone) was in charge of the emergency medical serives at St Mary's. He had been Harry's house surgeon and close friend, and had a paternal affection for the daughter of his mentor, having acted *in loco parentis* by giving her away at her wedding. She was particularly fond of the ophthalmologist Dr Frederick Williamson-Noble, 'Willie', who had told her that she ought to be a surgeon, although for some reason she had developed an aversion for dealing with what she called his 'eye cases'. The senior cardiologist Dr Alfred Hope-Gosse was also a specialist in diseases of the lungs. At this time he was treating Roger's father, who suffered from dangerously high blood pressure and whose lungs had been weakened by a gas attack in the First World War. Dr Hope-Gosse was a genial Australian, well-liked by the medical staff and popularly nicknamed 'the Goose'.

That July Doris's favoured doctor was ~~her good friend Douglas~~ 'Duggie' Macleod. Duggie was a charming and modest man, a first-rate gynaecologist with an impeccable lineage – his father, grandfather and great-grandfather had all been surgeons. Doris was eagerly awaiting the imminent return from Scotland of her brother George. She had exciting news to share: she was pregnant with her first child, affectionately known as 'little Horace'.

St Mary's Hospital, London W2

Saturday, 18th July

My darling,

The end of another week, and I've been here for a fortnight. It seems so much longer, and this place is so gloomy. Everybody seems to be leaving or to have left, it's very dull! But I'm not really moaning, everywhere is dull without you, and at least one gets a laugh occasionally here. I think it's the weather that's depressing me, it's really miserable today, cold and wet, and you know how cold weather affects me, my poor nose even is beginning to turn blue!

Reports have come in that your mess bill is the largest in the Navy! Is this true? The report came to me from an outside source, but I said I was sure there was nothing in it as you were a most moderate drinker, in fact you had almost given up imbibing altogether.

Ma arrived home from Stamford the other day with two bottles of whiskey in her bag, one of which is being put away to celebrate George's long-awaited return.

I've had another letter from Mr Tweddle today about the insurance, and things seem to have become complicated. I wish you were here to cope, but I think I did manage to get it fixed. The thing is, darling, that if we do have Horace we really should get some form of home organised for him, if only to have somewhere to leave him when we didn't want him all the time, and it's only fair on him – but the trouble is where and how and when. Any suggestions? I think if you agree and Ma agrees and Horace agrees, Ma and I might get together somewhere, possibly in or near Cheam, because I couldn't stay on at Ma's flat indefinitely, in fact I'd hate to stay there at all – and when you come I know you'd like to be near your home. Write and tell me what you think.

Also dear, could you write to Duggie, so that your letter reaches him around Monday or Tuesday the 27th? I'd like you to write before I go and see him, which I intend to do, all being well, about next Wednesday or Thursday week. I shan't know what to say!! I'll be like those dames that come into Casualty – 'Please doctor am I going to have a baby?' But I'd rather go to Duggie than anyone else, and I'm certainly not going to the Medical Super first!

By the way, can you lift any more travel vouchers? Or did I ask you about that before?

No letter today or yesterday. I wonder if that means you are cracking off somewhere, or have just missed the post! I miss hearing from you, but please don't make an effort of getting them off. I can always re-read the handsome bunch I have collected – I wonder if you have read my old ones yet. I'm afraid they were somewhat gushy as far as I can remember, so don't leave them lying about for the Sick Bay Attendant to read – but I forgot, he can't read can he?

Sunday

The Goose was in today and asking how you were, and if your father was getting less pain now he's taking the tabloids. I had to admit that I wasn't aware that he was taking any tabloids, and old Goose looked at me as though I was a bit nuts and whipped away. Willie Noble was also in, and I asked him about my eyes, because I've had some more of that stupid flickering lately. He says it's migraine, which is quite possible as Papa used to get it badly, and George is 'a martyr to it' (as they say). However as I get no headaches with it I imagine a good dose of salts in the morning will do the trick. Willie N. was just back from a holiday in Cornwall – 'If ever you and Roger want a nice little place to go to, excellent golf course – charming little hotel, very cheap, pound a day stuff'. Thanks very much, I thought, you can keep it, I'd rather go to our hut in Wales. Still he meant well. He thinks you will be able to get well ahead with your Primary, like he did, but I pointed out that you seemed to spend most of your life cyphering, and he said, 'Oh but they do that in three watches – I did'. So I told him you weren't so lucky. Any sign of the Bishop yet? I hope you won't have to turn out of your cabin for him. And darling not too much of this gun-warming, or I'll write and tell the BMA! I do want a whole husband back.

Willie Noble told me a funny story about cyphering. If I can remember it properly it went something like this:

Apparently there are two kinds of cyphers, fleet orders and Admirals cypher, and until you have begun you don't know which one you are doing – well, a cypher came through from the Admiral to the Commanding Officer, and was decoded as 'abstain from this licentiousness'. When they had got as far as that they decided it was the other cypher. I didn't think it was so very funny, but I had to laugh for the little man. We get on very well Willie and I. He told me I ought to be a surgeon, he was sure you would be awfully pleased. I said I was sure you would be, and it was an idea!! But how I hate having his eye cases in.

You don't forget to write to Miss Earle will you dear? And also Duggie – and don't be worrying about me, because I'm doing fine. I get a huge thrill out of Horace, I go round looking at people, and thinking, 'you poor selfish things, you don't know what it is to have organised a Horace, or to have someone to think of and live for that means more to you than yourself.' I think we did feel some of that 'First, fine careless rapture' don't you? Just us in the whole world and nothing else mattered. And now it will be us and Horace. I hope he's a nice Horace, and doesn't inherit all our bad qualities – of which I've many you haven't yet had time to discover. Darling come home soon so that we can talk about him!

Packets of love to you sweetheart, and my loving thanks for everything

God Bless –

X X X Doris X X X

St Mary's Hospital, Paddington

Thursday, July 30th

My darling,

I hope before this letter arrives you will have had my telegram with the good news. We are pronounced definitely 'preggers', and (I calculated wrong) the DDE is March 12th next. I confess I was all of a twit this afternoon, and set out for Harley Street hours before I needed to – consequently I had to pass the time walking up and down Wigmore Street looking with great interest in the shop windows which all appear to be either chemists or spectacle makers. As I was going up Harley Street I found a bird paying a call on my hand, which if you were superstitious you would recognize as one of the luckiest things that can happen to you!

Duggie was charming, he took my blood pressure etc and pronounced me perfectly normal and fit. He eventually did a pelvic exam, and said although it was so early there was no doubt about it. He said there was no reason why I shouldn't stay on here as long as I felt like it, provided I didn't do any lifting. Take glucose and calcium and eat hearty and all would be well. He was very sweet, and said I made a very good patient.

I then broke the news to Ma. I expected her to be terribly pleased, but at first she was very upset and kept talking about bombs and 'waiting till things were settled' – but I made her see the other side of it, and she came round in the end and is really very thrilled. I think she is a bit worried about me, because she apparently had such an awful time with me and George. But I pointed out how Duggie would have it delivered in no time at all, and everything would be easy.

She thinks a small house somewhere in the Sutton area would be an excellent idea, and she could run it for us when we weren't there, and look after Horace if we had to leave him.

We seem to be starting on the air-raids again – nothing serious at all, the guns pop off nearly every night now for an hour or two, and it's just a bit unsettling. I think if we organise some kind of hovel in the next few months it will be a good thing.

In case you do get a chance to phone next week, here are my movements as far as I can tell:

Monday evening at flat

Tuesday afternoon at flat, evening at Mary's

Wed evening at flat, afternoon at Mary's

Thurs afternoon at flat, evening at Mary's

Friday afternoon and evening at Mary's

Saturday at Jane's wedding

Sunday probably at Marian's

You could always make a personal call to the Wing, both the porters are in league with me, and the evenings I'm on I'm there till 9. Darling, do try and get through again even though it does cost 3/- a go. If you phone the flat we can always reverse the charges and have another 3 mins. I'm so longing to hear your voice again.

Unless you are really keen to tell the family about Horace I think we might wait until they return from Wales and I can tell them myself, I'd very much like to – I know they will be very pleased.

Another Thursday, and as far as I can make out Horace is six weeks old today – sort of BC 6 weeks dating! Darling Roger, come home soon and tell me you love me and are proud of me – I'm thinking marvellous good thoughts so that he shall be born with a nice mind and no hair lips or other oddities!

Goodnight my darling one,

All my fondest love to you,

Doris

(No letter today, perhaps there will be two tomorrow)

August 1942

Winston Churchill travelled extensively throughout his tenure as Prime Minister, to see for himself conditions on the ground, to meet the troops, to discuss strategy and tactics with his military commanders, and to confer with other world leaders. He logged enough air miles to earn elite status in any of today's frequent-flyer schemes, sometimes in the comparative comfort of a Skymaster flying boat, but often in uncomfortable, unheated military aircraft.

The Soviet Union was engaged in a desperate struggle with German forces, and Stalin was pressing for the opening of a Second Front in Europe. Churchill, however, was well aware that the Allies did not yet have sufficient strength for a full frontal assault. American public opinion, and that of many US politicians, was that the war in Europe was not much of their concern and that American efforts should be concentrated on fighting the Japanese in the Pacific. Churchill strongly disagreed, and his arguments convinced President Roosevelt. In July 1942, Roosevelt had written in his instructions to his representatives who were travelling to England for talks:

> American concentration against Japan this year or in 1943 increases the chance of complete German domination of Europe and Africa. On the other hand, it is obvious that defeat of Germany or the holding of Germany in 1942 or in 1943 means probable eventual defeat of Germany in the European and African theatre and in the Near East. Defeat of Germany means the defeat of Japan, probably without firing a shot or losing a life.[1]

Agreement was reached for an Allied invasion of western North Africa, codenamed 'Torch', no later than 30 October, to defeat General Rommel's Afrika Korps and perhaps enable an invasion of Southern Europe the following year.

Tunisia and Libya were the only places where British forces were directly engaged with the Germans, but the North African campaign was not going well. German forces had captured the port city of Tobruk and were pushing east towards the Egyptian border. Churchill had serious doubts about the High Command in the Middle East, and on 2 August he set off for Cairo via Gibraltar to sort things out. His personal physician went with him, as some members of the Cabinet were concerned about the Prime Minister's health and the dangers of his travels. It was a wearisome, dangerous journey, for there were many hostile aircraft patrolling the Mediterranean.

'The bomber was at this time unheated', Churchill later wrote, 'and razor-edged draughts cut in through many chinks. There were no beds, but two shelves in the after cabin enabled me and Sir Charles Wilson, my doctor, to lie down'.[2] In his entry for August 3 Wilson records: 'Two mattresses had been dumped in the after-cabin, and I passed the night in comfort. The PM was less happy; he dislikes draughts – and after all it is rather a feckless way of sending him over the world when he is approaching his seventieth year. However, he soon forgot his discomforts in sound sleep, and when we got to Gibraltar this morning he was ready for anything.'[3] After reviewing the situation in Cairo, Churchill made a number of significant changes to the command structure, including giving the command of the 8th Army to General Bernard Montgomery.

The island of Malta, strategically situated on the shipping lanes between Axis-controlled Sicily and the North African coast, was a crucial base to support the British forces in Libya and Tunisia. For close to two years, it had been under siege by German and Italian planes and submarines. The island had been supplied with food, fuel and other necessities by Allied convoys and protected by the fighters of the RAF, but at a heavy cost in lives and materiel. Despite brutal bombing and severe shortages the people of Malta held out with great determination, earning the highest civilian award for valour, the George Cross, in April 1942. But by July the island was desperately short of all essential commodities and the population was faced with the threat of starvation. It seemed as if an Axis invasion was only a matter of time.

On 15 August the miracle for which the embattled people of Malta had been praying finally happened. The tanker SS *Ohio*, fatally damaged and lashed between the destroyers HMS *Penn* and *Ledbury* for support and with a minesweeper guarding the stern, limped into Valletta harbour with her precious cargo of oil intact. As the last of the fuel was unloaded, the crippled tanker sank to the bottom. The supplies brought by the convoy of Operation Pedestal enabled Malta to survive for a few more months until the siege was lifted in October following Allied military successes in North Africa.

In Britain, the newsreel footage of *Ohio's* arrival that was shown in British cinemas was a shot in the arm for the demoralised public. Although Doris could not be officially told where her husband was serving, she had correctly guessed that his ship *Tartar* was accompanying the Malta convoy, and she cheered along with her fellow countrymen.

In an essay published in the *St Mary's Hospital Gazette*, Roger described the life of a naval doctor:

> To many of us this war time experience is our first launching out from the confines of wards and out-patients into the world where people are normally healthy and where if a man is unwell there are no labels stuck on or near him with the Latin name of a disease on it, and perhaps above this the name of an eminent consultant whom one knows has got to take the responsibility in the end. Here are no convenient X-Ray or Physiotherapy departments, no Dispensary with plenty of exciting alternatives should one medicine become monotonous, and no bright nurses to answer and cope with those distressing practical questions of bowels and diets and dressings ... I am in many ways a better doctor. I have lived among other people and performed many other tasks hardly included in the medical curriculum.
>
> ... no one in a seagoing appointment is going to pretend that medicine pure and simple takes up more than 20 per cent of his working day. The doctor, besides the routine chores allotted to him which most of us take on willingly, can make himself extremely useful and busy in his capacity of being an officer ... He is in contact with the troops and should feel himself responsible for doing all he can for their mental as well as their physical health.

A Naval doctor stands or falls by his Sick Berth Attendant (it is he who is called 'The Doctor' on the lower deck; we are just 'The Quacks'), for Naval medicine is a pleasant combination of history, tradition and an unbounded faith in the efficacies of the doings of Nelson's time ... A well trained SBA (Sick Berth Attendant) does know these things, and if he is an expert you will do well not to question his words or actions ...

... The treatment of casualties is, needless to say, the main reason for having a doctor in a small ship, but so far, luckily, I have had none in my own ship's company. On various occasions, however, casualties and survivors from other ships come under one's care and, in addition to numerous honest-to-God sailors, I have coped with two Russian dock workers (one, I think, was a female), several German and Italian prisoners, six nurses (who got very wet, but were luckily no worse off), one Arab, whose toe I removed, and a dog who, a few hours after being torpedoed, gave birth rather stormily to a litter of four.[4]

On 10 August Churchill left Cairo and, with a brief overnight stop in Teheran, flew to Moscow, reaching the city on the evening of 12 August. He was not looking forward to his meeting with Josef Stalin, the leader of 'this sullen, sinister Bolshevik State'.[5] Churchill was a devout anti-communist, but he recognised that, for now at least, he and Stalin were on the same side and he felt honour-bound to discuss the realities of the situation personally, particularly the fact that there would be no Allied landing in Europe that year. Stalin understood the strategic advantages of 'Torch', although he was highly critical of the decision not to open a Second Front in 1942. In the end the two leaders parted on cordial terms. Churchill recalled Stalin saying, '"Why should we not go to my house and have some drinks?" I said that I was in principle always in favour of such a policy'.[6]

From Moscow Churchill returned to Cairo for another visit to the Desert Front. He also met Lord Gort, the valiant Governor of Malta, who Lord Moran reported as 'hardly recognisable – stones lighter ... with sunken cheeks and tired eyes,'[7] for the Governor had conscientiously shared the starvation rations of the civil population, at severe detriment to his health. The Prime Minister stayed there for a week, arriving back in England on 24 August.

The British people were already suffering emotional fatigue from the mostly bad war news. They were far more stirred by the death in a military plane crash of the King's younger brother the Duke of York in late August than they were by the massive German assault on the Russian city of Stalingrad, and more interested in listening to his funeral service on the radio than they were in hearing about what Winston Churchill had discussed with Josef Stalin.

There had been more bad news just a few days earlier. On 19 August 6,000 Allied troops, mainly Canadians, landed at the German-occupied Channel port of Dieppe in northern France in what was supposed to be a 'trial run' for the real invasion. However, the operation was badly planned and executed and achieved few of its objectives. The landing was quickly repulsed and the commandos withdrew, but not without massive casualties. Although deploring the heavy loss of life, Churchill rationalised the failed operation by claiming that it had provided invaluable information for launching a full-scale invasion and that it had turned Hitler's attention towards his western defences, thus relieving some of the pressure on the Russians. He was probably right, but to most people, the Dieppe Raid looked like just another fiasco.

The operating theatres on the upper floors of St Mary's had been closed in the early months of the war for fear that they were more vulnerable to falling bombs. The artist Anna Zinkeisen, who was a St John volunteer at the hospital, was allowed to use one of the empty rooms as a studio because the light was excellent for her painting. She became friendly with Doris and painted her portrait in 1942; it is still in the possession of Doris's family. Anna became a celebrated portrait painter whose subjects included HRH Prince Philip, Lord Beaverbrook, Sir Arthur 'Bomber' Harris, and Sir Alexander Fleming; her self-portrait hangs in the National Portrait Gallery. The hospital itself never actually sustained a direct hit, although Doris later told her grandson how she remembered looking out of her upstairs window and watching a bomb falling, 'turning end over end', into a neighbouring street.

Although the so-called 'Battle of Britain' in the autumn of 1940 had established British air superiority, the Luftwaffe continued to harass towns and cities the length and breadth of the country. The south-coast city of Portsmouth, with its large naval dockyard, was a frequent target. Doris's best friend Jill Hippisley, who was stationed in nearby Gosport, wrote to her about the concentrated bombing attack they suffered in August.

Doris's happiness regarding 'little Horace' was short-lived, for on 17 August she suffered a miscarriage and was confined to the hospital as a patient under the care of Duggie MacLeod. She was devastated by the loss and missed her husband, but she had a great deal of support from the hospital community, which was like an extended family to her. Doris and Roger had many friends there, and they were especially close to two couples with whom they remained lifelong friends: Duncan and Audrey Gregg, and Jack Suchet and his soon-to-be-wife Joan. Duncan was the Medical Superintendent at St Mary's, in charge of the junior doctors. He was a genial and warm-hearted man with just the sense of humour that appealed to Doris. Jack Suchet had emigrated from South Africa and entered St Mary's on one of Charles Wilson's 'Rugby Scholarships'; he would go on to become an eminent gynaecologist. Jack was an enthusiastic bridge player and a connoisseur of fine wine. Doris enjoyed the company of Dorothy Pugh, and Jill's letters from Portsmouth cheered her up.

Doris and her brother George had few close relatives, and none of their own generation. Roger, on the other hand, had many Welsh uncles, aunts and cousins from Annie's large extended family, and was one of four siblings. Marian, born in 1909, was the eldest. In September 1941 she married John Gilbert, a scientist and inventor who was a pioneer in the fields of radar and television broadcasting. They lived in Surbiton, a pleasant suburban area of south-west London close to the River Thames and just a few miles from Cheam. Marian was kind to her new sister-in-law and Doris became very fond of her.

Margaret was four years older than Roger. A graduate of Bedford College, London, she was a teacher at Badminton School in Bristol. The girls-only boarding school, whose graduates included Indira Ghandi and Iris Murdoch (she and Margaret remained lifelong friends), had been evacuated to the North Devon town of Lynmouth when Bristol became a target of the Luftwaffe's bombs. Margaret was a die-hard socialist and a woman of strong opinions and formidable intellect. Doris initially found her rather intimidating until she got to know her better and discovered the engaging person underneath the no-nonsense exterior.

Richard, the youngest, born in 1917, was as charming and easy-going as his brother Roger. In 1936 he won a history scholarship to Exeter College, Oxford (a later alumnus was Roger Bannister, the first man to break the four-minute mile, who trained at St Mary's and became a distinguished neurologist). The sub-rector's report describes Richard as 'a capital fellow ... good socially'.[8] He was a founder member of the University Liberal Club and showed a keen interest in international politics. He was a valued member of the College rowing team, and like his brother Roger he enjoyed sailing, cycling and golf; the two young men once bicycled from Cheam to Aberystwyth, a feat that took about a week. After gaining his BA degree in Philosophy, Politics and Economics (*PPE*) in 1939, Richard enlisted in the Royal Navy and served with the Arctic convoys before being promoted to Sub-Lieutenant in July 1941. A hearing defect due to a congenital deformity of his right ear precluded further active service, and he was posted to the Navy's shore establishment at Malvern in Gloucestershire.

In the summer of 1942 Richard was selected as the Royal Navy's representative at the International Youth Assembly in Washington DC. One of the organisers had been Richard's tutor at Oxford, who decided that his former pupil was just the chap for the job. Representing the Royal Air Force was 22-year-old Wing-Commander Francis David Scott-Malden DFC, recently decorated for his part in the Dieppe Raid, and for the Army, Captain John Cochrane.

Richard was given some leave in order to spend some time with his family before the three young men flew to Washington via the neutral city of Lisbon on 30 August. (To travel in, Richard wore a grey suit belonging to Roger that he had 'borowed' from his brother's wardrope in their family home in Cheam.) Doris was very pleased to see Richard before he left for the United States, for she was fond of her brother-in-law. After ten days in hospital recovering from her miscarriage she was given a month's leave, and spent much of this time relaxing in Cheam or with her sister-in-law Marian in Surbiton – somewhat bittersweet for Doris, since Marian was expecting her own first child in January. But Doris was a down-to-earth woman not prone to melancholia or self-pity, and despite her loss, it didn't take long for her natural optimism to reassert itself.

St Mary's Hospital, Paddington

Wednesday, August 19th

Roger my darling,

A very bitter disappointment for you, I'm afraid we've lost Horace. I don't know yet why it should have happened, but there was nothing we could do about it. Duggie and Duncan both coped magnificently and whipped me straight into Victoria Ward, and did everything possible. I'm <u>perfectly alright</u> so don't do any worrying about me. Just write and console me as I'm feeling very miserable.

Will write more later, hope you are alright – longing to hear from you again.

All my love, sweetheart,
Doris

Victoria Ward,
SMH, Paddington

Friday Aug 21st

Sweetheart –

I'm going to start a nice long rambling epistle that will probably go on for some days. Yesterday I dispatched rather a morose and sketchy letter to you by Air Mail, which I hope won't take too long to reach you. It's so miserable not being able to get in touch with you quickly, and knowing that you probably won't get this letter for about 3 weeks.

I hope you weren't too dreadfully disappointed about Horace – it was just the baddest of bad luck, but Duggie says it very often happens and we mustn't worry about it. So you won't will you? Promise? I'm perfectly all right, and hope to be out of here pretty soon, and then you'll be home again before I know it.

I saw Peter Baly's ship mentioned in the paper, so I know where you've all got to. Take care of yourself, darling, won't you, and wear your tin hat and everything, I need you so much to come back to me whole and not in bits.

I'll tell you the details of the last few days when you come home, because they are not exactly cheerful matter for a letter. I was admitted on Monday afternoon and it was all over by 9 o'clock on Tuesday night, and now I've settled down to a delightful week of bedpans, swabbings and stewed plum! Dorothy is grand and comes in every day and we have a good giggle. Her Roger wrote me a very sweet letter today which I thought was charming of him. She made me laugh tonight. She said that years ago when she was off sick in Mitchell Bird Ward she so hated having to have bedpans that she never drank anything all day, and waited until the middle of the night to have one. I feel rather like that now. Sister was very upstage the first few days and wouldn't let me have any visitors at all, fairly shooed them away from the door, she even told Jack Suchet I was asleep, at a time when I quite obviously wasn't, which was pretty mean of her. I poured out my troubles to Duncan the other night, and he agreed that she was simply a bitch, pronounced as spelt. However she's just one of those things I suppose. If trials and troubles are meant to sweeten your character I should be turning into a lump of sugar at any moment now!

Aren't bowels an awful trial when you're in bed? They never seem able to strike the happy medium with aperients. Very bad management somewhere I feel.

I've begun to be a bit obstreperous at last (really I have) and demand aperients and salts and lights to read by, and clean sheets – a real neurotic type – but I do object to being in semi-darkness from eight o'clock onwards, and this morning I got black-currant jam all over my sheet – very messy.

Darling I wonder if you are thinking about me now. I've been looking at your picture for five minutes, and I swear it moved. I wonder how and where you are and what you are doing. I can at least picture you in your bunk. Do you sleep in your clothes? You might buy me some pyjamas at your next port of call.

Your two letters yesterday were so lovely to have, specially arranged to arrive on Thursday 8/ 12! They made me feel a new woman, ready to face the world and Sister Victoria! I hope there will be some more tomorrow. I quite agree, it's stupid to go on saying how much we miss each other – as you said we are to each other everything that matters most in the world – (9 o'clock, lights out – DAMN this woman. Aha, I can see in the dark! That's fooled her!) Oh my darling how can I not say that I miss you when every minute I long to have you back, when every day is empty if there isn't a letter from you, and nothing matters any more except that you should come back to me. I don't want to make it harder for you by writing like this, and you know that I get along fine, but you do mean so very much in my life darling, so very much more than I ever dreamed possible (now they've put all the lights out and I really can't see, so goodnight for today my love. More tomorrow. I'm thinking of you.

X X X X X X X X X X X not bad for total blackness?

Victoria Ward,
St Mary's Hospital, Paddington

Thursday, August 27th

My darling,

Thursday again, and a marvellous batch of letters from you to celebrate. It was good to hear again, and to know that there will be a more regular news service for a while.

Your last letter was written on the 24th, and you had not heard from me – but I expect by now you will have had quite a bagful of mail and will know the worst. Don't be too disappointed darling – I think you felt that something like this might happen didn't you? Your letters were so sweet. I'm glad my back numbers came in useful.

Of course I don't mind a bit about the beard, I'm sure it's a very handsome one and that it makes you look most distinguished. It's your face after all. Keep it until you come back, and if I dislike it intensely I'll tell you.

I'm so thankful you got no other injuries than the jellyfish bite. I'm longing to hear all about the trip. I gathered of course where you had been to, although not until the party was over. Was it very hair-raising? I wish I could disguise myself as an SBA. Actually the cable's arrival didn't worry me at all. I knew it was from you, it came with the letters, and I opened it quite calmly. I was very glad to have it. So glad you managed to see Michael Walker, I will write to Mig at once, I'm afraid I've been rather lazy about correspondence lately.

I heard from Jill this morning. She's on night duty on the emergency wards, 30 DCs – she says 'utterly continuous oxygen and coramine, the air raid casualties at Mary's being merely district visiting compared to this' – so you can imagine what she is coping with, and being bombed as well, and spending most of the day in the cellar. She wrote a very cheering letter, and I hope to see her soon. I might even take a trip to

Pompey for one of her half-days. Also had a very sweet note from Tilly Turner which I thought was very pleasant of her. Everyone has been very kind and sympathetic, and I really feel that I haven't done a great deal to deserve it.

No more sign of Richard, I expect he was very busy, I think today is the day he is due to leave. He has to go in civvies and take his uniform, as they land at Lisbon on the way, so I don't suppose he would have much room in his bag for bringing home any extras.

I'm meant to be leaving here today. But Duggie hasn't been yet, so I may not escape until tomorrow. I shall anyway be at Marian's over the weekend and the beginning of next week, so if you get a chance to use the wires do try, even if it is unsettling. Yesterday I took a stroll round the block, and feel surprisingly well after my 10 days in bed. Mentally I still feel rather low – it's only natural I suppose, I had been planning so much. I'd even got as far as naming it, subject to your approval of course.

Poor Dorothy is also very depressed. Roger went to Halton yesterday to do a ten days tropical medicine course and in 3–10 weeks he is going East so perhaps you did pick the best job after all. She is going to try and find a hovel of some sort near his present station in Essex, so that she can be with him until he goes. If she and I both manage to get another Horace organised we might do worse than set up house together. However that's being a bit previous. She's been very good while I've been here, in spite of the Devil-Sister who wouldn't let her in to see me for days. Old Sister Hyde is still here, in the corner opposite. She has at last taken to her bed, and there sits in state surrounded by screens, and receives weekly visits from Sir Almroth Wright who brings her in little bunches of flowers.

I'm afraid I haven't been able to send you anything exciting to welcome you back. The socks have been finished for some time, but they want marking. I did dispatch a soap box some time ago, I hope it's arrived. The portrait still isn't finished – Anna has gone away for a holiday – but I think she only wants one more session, or two at the most. Has she written to you yet? I think she ought to cut her price for the delay.

I'll consider the subject of more photographs. What is the size of the frame you have got? At the moment I'm looking frightful, with unwashed hair and a spotty face from being in bed. Up till last week I really think I was looking rather nice, and being a bit plumper was most becoming (so I was told) – how vain I am! But I like to look nice for you dear, and I've always had rather an inferiority complex about my looks, so I always feel very set up when you say nice things about them.

Anything more you want in the way of comforts? I've managed to squeeze another 12 oz. of wool out of the WVS, but I thought if you really didn't need anything further I would make George something for once. Darling I've forgotten to thank you for the hair grips – where did you manage to pick them up? A most surprising and welcome gift, you're a very thoughtful and marvellous man.

Duncan rather shook the Sister-hag this morning by asking me where your photo was. You know she won't let me put it out during the day. She actually had the grace to blush. I'm getting into her bad books now because I'm feeling well enough to be obstreperous. There's a movement on among the girls to put your picture up on the centre ward table as I can't have it on the locker. Good idea!

That's about all for now darling – I must sit up and take my nourishment (boiled chicken and plums again). Ma has just been in – says Richard hopes to look in at the flat after all, so I hope to see him.

I feel so much happier now for having your letters. You're not the only one you know who benefits from being married – I feel just the same as you do in all and every particular. It's a marvellous feeling of having somebody all the time who thinks and feels as you do about things, and I'll always be grateful to Sister Brownlow for putting me on the Theatre when she did.

All my love my darling – Keep well and God bless you,
Always yours, Doris

St Mary's Hospital,
Paddington, W2

Thurs Aug 27th – Friday, Aug 28th

Darling love,

I had to write again tonight, just to tell you I love you, and am so glad you are in the comparatively near neighbourhood again. I saw Richard today, and he seemed hopeful of your getting some leave, perhaps a 48 hrs or something, but I'm not hoping too much. He was in terrific form – he doesn't leave for another day or two, and is coming up tomorrow to see a Paymaster Captain in the Wing who is just back from eighteen months in Washington.

I'm still not out of this place, Duggie not having put in an appearance – but I'm going out tomorrow anyway, and I'll come back and see him some time – I just couldn't stay in this place another day. It's a pity though, because I would like to get to the bottom of this miscarriage and make sure it doesn't happen again.

Richard came to tea at the flat this afternoon (I had been let out until 5) and very chivalrously brought me back in a taxi. Outside the hospital we ran into H-J, who embraced me lovingly in the middle of the road outside the Medical School to the intense delight of rows of students. He said he had been meaning to come in and bring me some grapes. Very kind thought. He looks thinner, but still very full of joie de vivre, chucking his keys about in the old style.

I feel happier tonight than I have done since I came in here. I wonder if you have had my letters by now – I expect you have. I'm afraid they were rather incoherent, but it was so hard to write about. I don't think I've ever felt so utterly miserable before as I did when I realised that I wasn't going to be able to keep Horace. But we will try again won't we? I'll have an intensive rest course and get very fit.

Goodnight my precious love, you are so close to me tonight – All my love and millions of kisses – Yours always my darling

X X X X X X X X Doris X X X X

Friday

Saw Duggie this morning. He says my insides are perfectly OK, anteverted uterus, no sign of any retroversion, and that it was just one of those things. In three months' time we can have another shot, but not before then. Seems a long time, but I suppose he knows. Anyway I don't suppose there is much chance of your being home before that is there?

I'm going to take a month off, and then I think I shall come back here again, it really seems the most sensible thing to do. I'm feeling very well, so no worrying.

Lots of love darling,

Doris

September and October 1942

Richard and his companions arrived in Washington at the end of August, and on 2 September the President's wife Mrs Eleanor Roosevelt wrote in her syndicated newspaper column *My Day*: 'Since my arrival, I have had the pleasure of meeting four young British delegates to the International Student Service Assembly. One of them, Wing-Commander Scott-Malden, was decorated for his part in the Dieppe raid. Another, a very young Scotchman [sic], Captain Cochrane, has returned recently from Libya. There is a young naval officer, Lieut. Richard Miles, and a young minister, the Reverend Alan Booth. They were an interesting group to talk with'.[1] This was the start of a warm friendship between Richard and Mrs Roosevelt which would last for the next twenty years.

In the Soviet delegation to the Student Assembly was a young Ukranian woman, Lieutenant Ludmila Pavlichenko. With 309 confirmed kills she was the Red Army's deadliest sniper (by contrast, the celebrated American Chris Kyle had 160 confirmed kills). Ludmila is among the top five most lethal sharpshooters in history and still the most successful female sniper. American isolationism and apathy towards the war in Europe was still of major concern to Roosevelt, Churchill and Stalin, and when the Assembly was over Ludmila joined Richard and the other Brits for a PR tour of the United States, sponsored by Eleanor Roosevelt, to raise public awareness and boost support for their cause. For the rest of September and most of October they criss-crossed the country, making appearances in cities such as New York, Boston, Minneapolis, Chicago, Denver, Seattle, Portland, and even Hollywood. Ludmila was a popular draw, though she bristled at being viewed as some kind of exotic, alien creature. 'Hands which had clutched the smooth stock of a sniper's deadly rifle were glamorized with red fingernail polish and held a black cigarette holder', was the lead-in to an article in the *Seattle Post-Intelligencer*. 'Ludmila stepped off the train in leather boots, the tops of which were hidden by her calf-high olive skirt. Amply proportioned, she wore the medal of Russia's highest order, the Order of Lenin, on her bosom. She had short, dark hair stuffed under a magenta-trimmed cap. She wore no lipstick'.[2] No wonder Ludmila got so exasperated. Reporters had been warned that she did not want to discuss 'romance or frivolity', and she resented some of the more stupid questions put to her. When asked if she wanted to get married and have a family when the war was over, the newspaper reported that Ludmila said (in Russian) something that sounded like, 'Mind your own business!'[3] (Ludmila had, in fact, been briefly married to a fellow soldier who had been killed just a few months earlier; she never talked about it.)

Britain desperately needed more help from America, for in October things were still looking grim. William Manchester sums up the situation: '[In Russia] All that remained for Hitler to secure his victory was for [General] Paulus to reach the banks of the Volga and hold his ground. The possibility of Stalin negotiating a separate peace with Germany once again dominated Churchill's thoughts. Montgomery, meanwhile, was not yet ready to attack in the desert ... In the Atlantic, the U-boats were still sending more tonnage to the bottom than the Allies could replace.'[4] In Malta, the supplies that had been delivered at such cost in August were dwindling fast and the island again faced starvation.

At the end of August Rommel had tried to goad Montgomery into a battle in western Egypt, but Monty had refused to rise to the bait; he would join battle only when he was good and ready. For some weeks there was a stalemate as the two opposing sides faced each other across a line running south from El Alamein to the vast Qattara Depression, during which time Montgomery built up his forces and equipment. Rommel was short of men, machines and petrol; the supplies that Hitler had promised him had never materialised. By 23 October Montgomery was ready, and the 8th Army pushed forward on a broad front. For a week the battle wavered to and fro. The Germans fought courageously but, out-manned and outgunned and desperately short of fuel, they had little chance. Hitler ordered

Rommel to stand fast, but after a token halt of a few hours, he turned and headed to Libya with his few remaining tanks as fast as he could. Montgomery had defeated the Desert Fox, Egypt was safe, and North Africa was ready to be lit up by Operation Torch.

Following the successful conclusion of Operation Pedestal and the delivery of the supplies to Malta, Roger's ship HMS *Tartar* had sailed back to Scapa Flow before joining the escort of two Arctic convoys heading to the Russian port of Archangel. This was familiar territory for Roger, for he had sailed these waters in the spring of 1942 while on his first posting, HMS *Trinidad*. That outing had not ended well, for *Trinidad* had been irreparably damaged and scuttled. *Tartar* was more fortunate; she had been in many tight corners over the course of her eventful service and was nicknamed 'Lucky *Tartar*' due to her seemingly miraculous ability to escape from trouble and danger.

The harassment of the trans-Atlantic convoys by German U-boats severely disrupted imports to Britain from North America and the Empire, and of course no food could come in to the country from the Continent. A system of rationing for food and petrol was deemed the only way to ensure that what was available was equitably distributed, and a Ministry of Food had been established to implement the scheme. Allowances were made for people with special needs and those in certain occupations, but in theory a duchess could get no more butter, sugar or tea than her housemaid. Every civilian, even the King and Queen, was issued with a ration book containing coupons, and obliged to register with their local shops where they would collect their supplies in exchange for the appropriate coupons. When something special arrived, people would queue; bananas and oranges were a rare treat.

It was a bureaucratic nightmare for the small shopkeepers who had to ensure that their customers got no more than their fair share as well as to complete all the additional paperwork that the government required. Grocer Kathleen Hey wrote in her diary:

> Once down to the Food Office yesterday and twice today before I could get the Points Vouchers which are supposed to be handed over on demand. Their excuse was that they were busy. Apparently shopkeepers are never busy or only run their businesses as a sideline to their main preoccupation of keeping up with the Food Office instructions. It grows worse every week – the forms to fill in and pamphlets to read. And every little mistake

is the cause of a card which demands our presence at the Office immediately. How one-man businesses carry on is a mystery unless they have a permanent messenger to run back and forth to the Food Office. It would really be better and a great savings of stamps all round if instead of sending round these inspectors to 'snoop' they would send them to help the shopkeeper to fill his forms in, or over any difficulty he may have over the many rationing regulations, and point out any errors he may be making or small points of the law which he might be unwittingly breaking ... What the powers-that-be don't realise is that a grocer cannot spend all his time getting the answers right – he must serve his customers in and between whiles.[5]

Nonetheless the system worked reasonably well in achieving its objective, which was to ensure that everyone got their fair share and that everyone received a variety of food. Indeed, many people enjoyed a healthier diet during the war than they had previously. The much-maligned 'National Loaf', made from a coarse wholemeal flour with added vitamins, was in fact a good source of fibre-rich nutrition. Dried eggs brought in from America were a poor substitute for the real thing but they did provide much-needed protein. People consumed less meat, fats and sugar, and they were encouraged to grow and eat more vegetables. The Ministry of Food put out posters and propaganda promoting healthy eating, with cartoon characters such as 'Dr Carrot'.

In June 1941 clothing was added to the list of rationed commodities, and in early 1942, soap and shampoo, because of the shortage of fats and oils. Sugar rationing began in the summer of 1942. It was to be twelve years before all the restrictions were finally lifted.

Of course there were some unscrupulous people who tried to game the system and who circumvented the restrictions in whatever ways they could – using the ration book of a dead relative was a favourite ploy. There were a number of black marketeers and many petty infringements. However, the vast majority of people obeyed the rules and made do with less. They came up with imaginative substitutions for missing ingredients; in one of May's cookbooks was a recipe for 'flourless, eggless, butterless, sugarless cake' (there was no mention of its edibility!). Every scrap of left-over food was used in some way or fed to the animals.

Fresh vegetables and fruit were not rationed but imports were in short supply, so people were encouraged to 'Dig for Victory' by creating 'Victory Gardens' to grow vegetables in their backyards, in vacant lots and on any available waste ground. In the countryside game was sometimes available, and people raised rabbits for the pot. Foraging for wild food, now trendy among today's health-conscious foodies, was a free way to supplement the diet with mushrooms, berries, rose hips, hazelnuts, chestnuts and samphire. Even the lowly and abundant nettle could be cooked to provide a nutritious green vegetable. When faced with family scepticism about this latter addition to the menu, Annie's friend Maudie Hamer, sister of British film producer Robert Hamer (*Kind Hearts and Coronets*) declared: 'But nettles are <u>heaven</u>!' She was known ever after to friends and family as 'Nettles' Hamer.

Alcohol and tobacco products were not officially rationed either, but were expensive and difficult to obtain, although there seemed to be plenty available at the St Mary's parties. Coal, which almost everyone used for heating their homes and their hot water, was sometimes scarce, and everyone was encouraged to conserve. People were asked to draw a line five inches up in their bath and fill the tub no higher than that with hot water. Even the baths in Buckingham Palace had this line drawn on them. (It would not, however, have suited Winston Churchill, who liked to soak in two baths every day.)

Very little was thrown away. School children collected scrap paper, and a call from the Ministry of Aircraft Production for pots and pans to be melted down to make aeroplanes resulted in a veritable mountain of scrap metal as the people responded to the appeal. 'Make Do and Mend' was the order of the day. A 1940s housewife would be unimpressed by what passes for recycling today. Everything that could be was mended or reworked into some other useful item. Doris wrote about wearing her stockings until they literally fell apart, and her friends renovating their shirts to make them last longer. Young women going to meet their fiancé's relatives were advised to wear stockings with a neat but noticeable darn, so that the prospective mother-in-law would be impressed with the girl's thrift and her skill with a needle. Food coupons had to be used within a short time limit, but people could save up their clothing coupons in order to buy a more expensive item, or give them as gifts to family and friends. Doris used her coupons wisely, and with their innate fashion sense she and Jill always managed to look smart and stylish. Wool to make a scarf, a jumper or a pair of baby's booties required half the number of coupons as the finished item in a shop so, like millions of other British women, Doris took up her needles and started knitting.

As the war progressed the amount of the ration was reduced. Of all the restrictions it was the paucity of her butter ration, down to just to two ounces per person per week by the middle of 1942, that Doris found most irksome. Andrew Roberts neatly sums up the impact of rationing: 'For those of a naturally economical – even miserly – nature, the Second World War was a godsend; for those who enjoyed life's indulgences, such as cosmetics and silk stockings, it was a series of tribulations.'[6]

In 1940 community kitchens were established by the government, initially to provide hot meals for people who had been bombed out of their homes. They were at first called 'Communal Feeding Centres', but Churchill decided that this sounded too Soviet-like and decreed that 'British Restaurants' had a more patriotic ring. 'Everybody associates the word "restaurant" with a good meal,' he told the Minister of Food, 'and they may as well have the name if they cannot get anything else.'[7] The food was basic, filling and cheap; a three-course meal cost one shilling (a little over £2 in today's money). Prior to decimilisation in 1971, there were twelve pennies (*d*) to the shilling (*s*) and twenty shillings to the pound. The restaurants provided 'useful extras' such as corned beef hash and Spam in addition to the basic rations. Anyone could eat there. Even such a simple meal was a welcome bit of luxury for many people who could not afford to eat out often; the British Restaurants proved wildly popular and proliferated rapidly.

In the first years of the war rich people were able to circumvent austerity by eating out at posh restaurants, which could obtain plentiful supplies of expensive unrationed food such as lobster, fish, rabbit and game. There was a great deal of public resentment about this subterfuge, and in the summer of 1942 the government decreed that no establishment could charge more than five shillings (25p) for a three-course meal, equivalent to about £12 today, as well as setting some restrictions on what could be served. Now besides *filet de sole bonne femme*, a fancy menu might feature the more mundane *kipper sur toast.* The new rules meant that it was not just the wealthy who could afford to enjoy a good meal out. Then, as now, The Ivy in Covent Garden was a popular and highly rated restaurant. Thanks to the government's price cap, it was within the means of Doris and her friends, and it was one of their favourite venues.

Just because there was a war on did not mean people stopped enjoying their favourite pastimes, as far as they could. They went to dances, to the pub, to the theatre and to the pictures. Ever since she was a little girl and had been taken to the cinema by her grandmother Polly (who had died in 1936) and her Aunt Gussie, Doris had always loved 'going to the pictures'. Her enthusiasm was shared by many, including the Prime Minister himself. Churchill had frequent private screenings at Downing Street and Chequers, often late at night, which his guests were expected to watch with him.

The propaganda value of cinema had long been recognised by Adolf Hitler and his Minister of Propaganda Josef Goebels, and brilliantly executed by Leni Reifenstahl in her malignant masterpiece *Triumph of the Will*. British film makers were slower to capitalise on the power of the medium, but, with the backing of the Ministry of Information under the leadership of Churchill's close friend and confidant Brendan Bracken, did eventually produce a number of successful, morale-boosting films. Some were blood-free movies with handsome, wholesome leading men, intended to demonstrate the nobility of war in a righteous cause, with none of the attendant horrors; they showed no guts but much glory. Others were of outstanding quality. A recent film *Their Finest* (2017) is an affectionate chronicling of how the wartime producers, writers and directors wove the required elements – a heroic story, indomitable women and grace under pressure (and a dog) – into a picture that could be successful in both Britain and America.

The First of the Few depicts the work of R. J. Mitchell (played by Leslie Howard) who designed the iconic Spitfire fighter aircraft but died before he could see his planes save the country in the 1940 Battle of Britain. The heroic actions of the RAF pilots were lauded in the immortal words of Prime Minister Winston Churchill, from which the film derived its title: 'Never in the field of human conflict was so much owed by so many to so few'. Tragically, Leslie Howard himself died shortly before the film's American premier when his civilian plane was shot down in 1943. Under the leadership of Michael Balcon, Ealing Studios turned out several well-received productions, including *Convoy* and *Ships with Wings* (both starring H-J's friend, the popular theatre actor John Clements). *In Which we Serve*, one of the finest films made during the war, was based on the naval exploits of Lord Louis Mountbatten aboard HMS *Kelly*. It was written and produced by Noel Coward, who also composed the music, starred as the ship's captain, and co-directed (with David Lean). The film was nominated for an Academy Award, losing to *Casablanca*, but Noel Coward was awarded an Honorary Oscar for outstanding production achievement.

Films now had to appeal to an audience made up largely of younger women. Productions such as *Went the Day Well?* and *Millions Like Us* were set in the homeland and featured strong female leads. Although it was a Hollywood production, 1942's *Mrs Miniver*, the uplifting saga of the eponymous English housewife who shepherded her family through the first year of the war with her spirits, her hair and her make-up unruffled, undoubtedly raised the spirits of the embattled British people and did much to win over American public opinion to the Allied cause. The film won an Academy Award for Best Picture and a Best Actress award for its star, the luminous Greer Garson. Two years later, Laurence Olivier's imaginative telling of Shakespeare's *Henry V* pressed England's greatest playwright into the service of his country nearly 350 years after he wrote his play. The stirring tale of how brave King Harry and his gallant little English 'band of brothers' defeated the numerically far superior French forces at the Battle of Agincourt in 1415 was a popular as well as a critical success, and won a Special Achievement Oscar for actor/producer/director Olivier.

Paper for civilian use had been in short supply since 1940. Newspapers were half their pre-war size, envelopes were reused (sometimes to the consternation of the postman), and photographs of ordinary people and everyday events were rare. Official standards governing the printing of books resulted in thinner, smaller volumes with condensed type, less white space and inferior paper and bindings. The demand for books was on the increase, however, and the popularity of subscription lending libraries such as the Times Book Club, to which Doris and Roger belonged, soared. They both loved to read. Doris had catholic tastes and was as happy to curl up with a thriller as with a classic. She had enjoyed the racy and controversial best-seller *No Orchids for Miss Blandish*, which had been adapted as a successful play in 1942 and after the war would be made into a film starring Walter Crisham, another of H-J's friends.

Jill Hippisley had been reassigned to the WRNS Sick Quarters in Oxford where she was having a grand time juggling boyfriends and 'painting the town red' with a number of charming American officers stationed nearby. Romance was in the air, despite the war – or maybe because of it. Cynthia Helms, who joined the WRNS in 1941 when she was just eighteen years old and worked for Doris's brother-in-law Richard at Malvern Naval Establishment, poignantly describes the effect of the war on teenagers forced into maturity too soon, trying to come to terms with the sudden shocking disappearance of friends and lovers: 'Young people typically share a sense of immortality, but war changed that for us. We all had an acute sense of our own mortality, and the old Latin phrase *carpe diem* (seize the day) ruled the day... Marriage represented stability in the midst of chaos. It seemed everyone was rushing off and getting married.'[8] It certainly seemed that way at St Mary's in the autumn and winter of 1942/1943. Doris writes about a number of friends and colleagues who are getting married, and the weddings that she herself attended. In early August she and Jill had been guests at the marriage of their friend and fellow nurse Jane Griffiths Hughes, and there were many more to come. A wedding was a chance to celebrate, to enjoy life and to assert hope for the future.

Following her discharge as a patient from the hospital in late August, Doris was given time off to recuperate from her miscarriage. Her brother George was on leave from the battle-cruiser HMS *Renown*, before he was moved to the Mediterranean to support the landings of Operation Torch. Doris and George had always been close and she was delighted to have his company while she was staying at May's flat. She divided her time between London with May, Surbiton with Marian, and the comfortable house of her parents-in-law in Cheam, a large suburban village on the Surrey border south of London, about an hour by train from Paddington. Nowadays Cheam is within the bounds of Greater London, but in 1942 it was still surrounded by countryside, on the edge of the beautiful North Downs, where Doris would take the dog Timo for long rambling walks. Ted and Annie lived in the

Manse (as the residence for a Presbyterian minister was called), an imposing Edwardian house with large, elegant rooms. Their neighbours were Mr David Tweddle, an elder of the church and the family's insurance agent, and his wife. The Manse had a sizeable garden (backing onto a golf course), where Doris enjoyed relaxing with a book or writing a letter to Roger.

I have only one of her letters from September and none from October. In early October Roger had four days' leave while *Tartar* had her boilers cleaned, and Doris joined him in at the North British Hotel in Edinburgh (now the elegant Balmoral Hotel, where the Queen Mother Elizabeth was a regular visitor for lunch). Although there is no follow-up correspondence, they had not seen each other for several months and it is not hard to imagine the joy of their brief reunion.

The Manse, Cheam

Saturday Sept 19th

My darling,

Another week, and I'm afraid I've only written you one letter since last week-end. I've spent the week coming and going between here and the flat. Margaret and I were here for two nights and it was very pleasant, although, quite illogically, I'm still rather afraid of her. She set off for Lynmouth on Friday armed with a rucksack and a packet of cheese sandwiches.

We went up to Town on Thursday and saw the Leslie Howard film *The First of the Few*, very good I thought, and emerged as usual with a red nose and damp handkerchief. Things seem to upset me these days much more than they ought to. Tonight I found myself crying while listening to a man talking on the wireless, and *Land of Hope and Glory* and *So Deep is the Night* invariably make me weep. This I feel is a bad thing and must be conquered. I've always wept very easily and it's been a source of great humiliation and annoyance to me. Perhaps you could put a plug in my lachrymal ducts for me?!

Ma is down with me for the week-end. She's completely laid out after a week spent coping with George's clothes – you can't imagine the filthy state they were in, oil over everything and moth-holes the size of London. We got him off to Edinburgh this morning. He had an evening out with the boys last night, and returned somewhat whistled but very quietly at 3 a.m. this morning. Needless to say he went to Edinburgh with something of a head, although I dosed him up with APCs. Actually he's been very good this leave, stayed at home with us, and been really pleasant, and last night was his only break out. I'm very sad he's gone, but I expect we shall see him fairly frequently during the year.

Another wedding on the list – Eric Norman and Nurse Hirst. There's a positive rush to get wed – and Mrs Robbie Willson is popping off with her first quite soon. Marian's doctor has assured her that she's not going to have twins, so she's not doubling the output of vests and whatnots – she's very well, we're going over there tomorrow for lunch. John has been having a holiday and has taken the car engine apart. I'm still enjoying being the lady of the Manse, and still answering strange questions on the telephone to the best of my ability. The latest query was from an undertaker who wanted to know the fees of the organ, I was afraid I couldn't help him!

Saw a very good flick at the small place in Baker St last night, Leslie Howard in *Pimpernel Smith*. The only trouble with films nowadays is that all the people in them seem to have more or less the same parts (and same people) in every film. There's one man, Francis Sullivan, who has been the head of the Gestapo for years.

I expect you are having colder weather now – sure you're well equipped? Dig into Aunty May's comfort store and see what you can find. I'm very busy just now knitting patches into George's many moth-eaten jerseys, but hope to find time to knit some things for Marian and also some warm winter vesties for myself – I'm beginning to feel chilly already and it's only September. If I had a fuel target I'm afraid I should exceed it before Christmas.

Future movements are still slightly unsettled. I aim at going back to the Wing quite soon (as the founder and original member of 'Married Alley' I feel I should be there to keep an eye on the new girls) – probably at the end of the week or the beginning of the next. Until then I shall be in the flat trying to get some order into the chaos which is my wardrobe, at present scattered in suitcases all over the place. I'm going to leave spares down here so that I can come without carting sponge-bag and things every time.

I bought some lovely soap the other day. Apple blossom and lime blossom, so what with that and the French fern I shall smell like a blooming garden!

I'm afraid this is rather a dull letter sweetheart, but I'm feeling lonely and I've got a cold – so I think I'll pack it up and have a boiling bath and get into bed. I couldn't manage 'our bed' after all, but perhaps it won't be too long before we're in it together again. Oh my darling I'm just counting the days and they are so slow.

Goodnight my dearest one,

All my love darling,

Doris

November 1942

By the first week of November the battle of El Alamein was over. The outnumbered Afrika Korps was in full retreat westward, abandoning their Italian allies to be taken prisoner by the victorious 8th Army. This was Britain's first decisive military victory and it was a tremendous morale booster both on the battlefield and at home. On 8 November Operation Torch was launched with Allied landings along the North African coast, at Casablanca, Oran and Algiers. The forces of Vichy France in Morocco and Algeria put up minimal resistance and quickly capitulated. British and American troops moved into Tunisia, effectively trapping the German forces in a vice between the Allied armies in the east and west.

Now it was only a matter of time before the Germans could be expelled from North Africa and an invasion of Italy could begin. The siege of Malta was effectively ended; with the protection of Allied planes flying from captured airfields in North Africa, convoys could now reach the island in safety. In Russia, the German offensive had stalled in the Caucasus. At last it seemed that things were going the Allies' way. It was too soon to tell if this apparent turning of the tide was just temporary or a real reversal of fortune, but it certainly heralded a new phase in the progress of the war. On 10 November 1942 the Prime Minister gave a speech at the Lord Mayor's Banquet. 'This is not the end', he asserted. 'It is not even the beginning of the end. But it is, perhaps, the end of the beginning.'[1] That Sunday, 15 November, on Churchill's order, the church bells once again pealed out to celebrate the victory, after lying silent for more than two years.

Since their attack on the US fleet at Pearl Harbour on 7 December 1941, the Japanese had swept across the Pacific, capturing the Philippines, Guam, the Solomon Islands, Java, and other strategically located islands, and taking Hong Kong and Singapore. After the invasion of Burma, neighbouring Thailand quickly capitulated, and the Japanese began building the notorious 'Death Railway' across that country to threaten British India. For months they had seemed unstoppable. In August American forces had recaptured the island of Guadalcanal, but the Japanese fought back fiercely and a bloody and protracted battle ensued. Finally, between 12 and 17 November, in the Second Battle of Guadalcanal, the Americans decisively pushed back the Japanese. Just as the Battle of El Alamein had been the turning point of the war in the European and North African theatre, this would prove to be the turning point of the war in the Pacific.

George Clayton Greene was stationed in Scotland with the home fleet. He had been engaged to a young lady called Pamela, but the engagement had recently been broken off. (Regrettably, I know nothing about Pamela or their relationship; George never spoke of it to his family in later years.) Heartbroken and yearning for active duty, he volunteered for service in the Pacific. There were no Royal Naval vessels there at that time and so he requested and was approved for a transfer to the Royal New Zealand Navy.

On the other side of the Atlantic Richard Miles had returned to Washington following his cross-country PR tour. He had been promoted to Lieutenant and offered the job of White House Liaison officer attached to the British Embassy. The Ambassador at that time was that same Lord Halifax who had been Winston Churchill's rival for the premiership in 1940. Richard was lodged in the home of Marion and William Wasserman, a leading investment banker who was the chief of the United States lend-lease mission to Australia. Marion Wasserman was a close friend of Mrs Eleanor Roosevelt, who the Wasserman's daughter Marie, a teenager at the time, told me 'was always interesting and charming'. To this day Marie remembers Richard as a very nice, kind gentleman who introduced her to sailing on Chesapeake Bay.

Life in London wasn't easy under the wartime restrictions – the shortage of food and basic necessities, the increased work and responsibility that most women had to shoulder, the gloom of the nightly blackouts. To the usual difficulties faced by young women travelling around the city on their own were added the hazards of trying to navigate around in the dark. The danger of errant bombs was ever present, even though the Luftwaffe had reduced the constant air raids on the capital once the possibility of invasion was lost and had turned their attention to cities of no strategic value, such as Exeter, Bath, Norwich and York, in an effort to terrorise the civilian population and as retaliation for similar British air strikes against Germany. And always there was the nagging fear for husbands and fathers, sons and brothers on active duty, particularly when their exact whereabouts or activities were unknown. With their characteristic resilience, however, the British people carried on with their daily lives and soon adapted to the 'new normal'.

Everyone had their own way of dealing with air raids. One member of Ted's congregation at St Andrew's noted in his diary, 'Over the first prayer, air-raid warning sounded. Mr Miles went straight on with Lord's Prayer and Benediction – shortest service on record!'[2] With her usual unflappability, Doris regarded the raids as a minor nuisance. 'We always thought we would win, and when the bombs dropped you just got under the patient's bed and then got up again,' she told her granddaughter, who remembers taking Doris to the doctor when she was ninety-six, shortly after she had been diagnosed with atrial fibrilation. 'Have you been under any stress lately, Mrs Miles?' asked the doctor. 'Stressed?' Doris retorted, 'I've never been stressed in my life!'

Not everyone endured the aerial bombardments with such equanimity. Doris and Roger's future son-in-law Peter Stevens was five years old when a bomb fell into the back garden of his grandparents' house in Essex, where he had been evacuated from his home in London. With his little sister he crouched under the 'Morrison shelter', a heavy steel table designed to protect people from falling debris, until the two children were pulled out by a young Air Raid Warden and carried into a nearby public shelter. Seeing a sheet of flame engulf the back wall of the house, Peter let out a primal scream. 'I've never been so scared in all my life!' he told me. In the pitch-black of the shelter the frightened little boy called out to the friendly warden for reassurance: 'Are you there, mister? Are you there?'

Doris was well aware that whatever civilians on the home front had to put up with, these problems were trivial compared to the dangers and difficulties that those serving on the front lines faced every day. Their friend Tony Oddie was back from active service with a badly broken arm, and she writes about the sailors on the Arctic convoys suffering from 'anxiety neurosis'. (In the First World War the condition was called 'shell shock'; nowadays we call it Post Traumatic Stress Disorder.) At the time of the Dunkirk evacuation, Dorothy had worked at Park Prewett, the military psychiatric hospital, where she said that 'a lot of the men were in an awful state.'[3] Doris had been very dejected after her miscarriage and she didn't want Roger to worry about her. So she tried to maintain a positive tone in her correspondence and made light of the inconveniences. She wrote about socialising and shopping, the comings and goings of family and friends, of colleagues and the routine activities of the hospital.

In the middle of the 19th century, nursing had been considered a demeaning occupation suitable only for family members of the afflicted person or for unskilled slatterns; the character of the drunken Mrs Sarah Gamp in Charles Dickens' 1843 novel *Martin Chuzzlewit* is probably the best known stereotype of these Victorian nurses. Traditionally, nursing care had been provided for centuries by nuns and these dedicated women were not included in society's general disapproval of their task, but it was widely believed that a hospital ward was no place for a respectable young lady. Things began to change after Florence Nightingale's pioneering work among the wounded of the Crimean War in 1855. 'The Lady with the Lamp' became a popular icon and was largely responsible for a paradigm shift in the public's attitude. In 1860 Florence Nightingale opened Britain's first nurses' training school at St Thomas's Hospital in London. In the 1870s it became standard practice for hospitals to appoint a matron, herself a trained nurse, to organise and oversee all the nursing staff. In 1887 the British Nurses' Association was formed and the first register of trained nurses in what was now a recognised profession was established.

By the time of the First World War nursing had become thoroughly respectable. Large numbers of gentlewomen came to St Mary's as nurses, including Queen Victoria's great-granddaughter Princess Alexandra of Connaught. 'I grew very fond of the old Hospital', the

Princess is quoted in Elsbeth Heaman's history of St Mary's. 'It was a home from home to me, and I used often to wonder how I was going to settle down to a different kind of life when the war was over.'[4] In 1919 Parliament passed the Nurses Registration Act which allowed formal State Nurse registrations. By the time Doris entered St Mary's in 1937, hospitals had a well-defined hierarchy, from the probationers at the bottom, registered or staff nurses, sisters (the name reflecting the conventual history of nursing), with 'Matron' firmly at the top. The Matron was responsible for the education and welfare of the nurses and for the nursing care of the patients.

In 1942 this position at St Mary's was held by the admired and respected Miss Mary Milne. Unlike some of her predecessors, Matron Milne was no martinet and, having lost her own fiancé in the previous war, she took a sympathetic attitude towards the love lives of the young women in her charge. She was not at all cowed by the paternalistic attitude that permeated the male-dominated hospital. In 1941 two brothers suggested forming a musical society of nurses and medical students. Ms Milne swept aside the usual chauvinistic objections of the fossils: 'The nurses work with the men, so why shouldn't they play with the men?'[5]

Nurses' uniforms had changed little since the turn of the century, except for shorter skirts. Dorothy Pugh's photograph might have been taken in 1907 or 1917 instead of 1937. In the picture of Doris accepting her Gold Medal she is wearing a simple long-sleeved blue dress with a wide belt and stiffly starched white collar and cuffs (both removable), and on her head an equally stiffly starched white cap tied under her chin – what she called 'the starched appurtenances'. Over this she wore a crisp white apron that she refers to as 'the armour'. The outfit was completed with black stockings, sensible shoes and a watch pinned to the front for timing a patient's pulse. It was uncomfortable, impractical and utterly traditional, very different from the utilitarian 'scrubs' so often worn today. Looking on is Matron Milne in an even more elaborate white cap, reminiscent of the wimple worn by the original nursing nuns. The amount of laundry that must have been done at St Mary's to keep all this stuff pristine boggles the imagination!

After completing their Medical School courses, junior doctors were required to undergo further training as residents, or 'house doctors'. These young men were in the charge of the Medical Superintendent, Doris and Roger's good friend Dr Duncan Gregg. Next in rank were the registrars, and at the top of this parallel medical hierarchy was the formidable senior surgeon, Arthur Dickson Wright. Imagine James Robertson Justice as Sir Lancelot Spratt in the film *Doctor in the House* progressing through the wards like a battleship with a flotilla of anxious medical students and house doctors scurrying along in his wake, and you will have a picture of 'Dickson' doing his rounds. In a continuation of St Mary's tradition, Dickson Wright had been house surgeon to Doris's father, and Roger in turn had been Dickson's house surgeon – he was one of the few who could stand up to the great man, and he delighted his friends with his excellent and irreverent impersonation. Many found Dickson Wright intimidating; Elsbeth Heaman calls him 'the master of the pithy put-down',[6] and says he 'loved to infuriate the nurses by ducking around the back staircases so he could burst in and surprise them.'[7] But despite his bombast, and despite frequently wanting to shake him, Doris liked and respected her father's former protégé.

It was not just at St Mary's but in society as a whole that women were still treated somewhat as second-class citizens in the years between the two world wars. It was 1928 before they were all granted the right to vote. Middle-class women were not expected to aspire to having their own career; a husband and children was supposed to be the zenith of their ambition. Systematic family planning was in its infancy, and what birth control services existed were usually available only to married women (their unwed sisters were assumed to be chaste). In 1918 scientist Marie Stopes, a renowned paleobotanist, published a controversial but popular book called *Married Love,* which brought her to national prominence and enabled her to open London's first birth control clinic in 1921. Marie Stopes was opposed to abortion, believing that women only needed to prevent conception. Over the next few years she opened several other clinics across the country, which she and her husband funded. It is probable that her motivation was not entirely altruistic – she believed in eugenics, the selective improvement of the genetic quality of a population, and she was anxious to slow the birth rate among what she deemed 'the worst end of our community'. Nonetheless, she was an important pioneer in the expansion of women's reproductive rights.

Abortion was illegal except in cases where the mother's life was in jeopardy. Aleck Bourne was a senior gynaecologist at St Mary's and had qualified there while Doris's ~~father Harry Clayton Greene~~ was Dean of the Medical School. By all accounts he was a kind, compassionate and principled doctor of considerable moral courage. In 1938 he performed an abortion at St Mary's on a 14-year-old girl who had been assaulted and gang-raped by a group of off-duty soldiers. Bourne was aware that the patient's life was not immediately threatened by her pregnancy, but he believed that termination was justified because of the risk to the girl's physical and mental health. He deliberately called the police, in order to set up a test case in the court. The judge agreed that he had been justified in carrying out the procedure and Dr Bourne was acquitted. For thirty years the ruling freed gynaecologists from the fear of prosecution should they terminate a pregnancy for medical reasons, until the law was liberalised in 1967. Despite playing an important role in the move towards such relaxation, Aleck Bourne was very much against abortion for merely social reasons and he later campaigned strongly against the 1967 Act.

Many of the hospital's illustrious doctors, as well as nurses and staff, attended the big party at the end of November when Doris and her friends celebrated the wedding of Dr Tom Kemp to Ruth Keat. Like Doris, Ruth was a nurse who had trained at St Mary's. Tom was one of those 'intellectual athletes' beloved by the Dean, an exceptional rugby player who captained the England team in 1940 while still a medical student. Among the guests was H-J with his fiancée Lilian Tudor-Jones, who had the delightful nickname of Sunbeam. He was a first-class teacher and an excellent cricketer, suave, charming and sociable; H-J's parties were always the highlight of the festive season. Doris was delighted when her brother George turned up just in time to escort her to the wedding, where a very good time was had by all.

Lindo Wing, St Mary's Hospital

Tuesday, Nov 3rd

Darling,

Two letters this morning, also your last Will and Testament which I will lodge in the bank for safe keeping. It doesn't look like a Will without any red seals and things, but I'm sure it will fill the bill. Thank you darling for doing it.

A letter from Jane today sending me some snaps of the wedding, I'm afraid I look rather depressed. Also a long rambling screed from Jill, who is painting Oxford red according to her, and is bringing Elmer up to Town soon. I'm afraid I get a bit confused among the many chaps she talks of. Apparently she kept Elmer waiting for an hour and a quarter the other day, and got thoroughly told off for doing so, which delighted her!

I've been spending <u>lots</u> of mun today, £45 to be exact – with which I bought some 60 savings certificates. I've told the Bank in future to buy 15 for me out of your allotment every month. That means that some of the £20 is left in the account for any hotel bills and such like! I was going to tell them to put the whole £20 in every month, but I think it's better to have some cash in hand for the various things that may crop up. Anyway 15 a month will soon mount up, and when I reach the 500 limit, we can start again in your name. At that rate we will have a nice substantial sum tucked away.

Today's Funny – Title of week's best-seller –

No (morchids) for Miss Blandish, by Dr Marie Stopes

More kids

It took me some little while to grasp it, so I've written it out to explain!

I had Anna's portrait over in the Wing today, and showed it to Willie Noble – he was most impressed and is sending up his 'artist friend' to see it – whoever that may be, Willie has some very queer pals.

Darling I'm afraid my letters are getting duller and duller – it's you now who writes far better letters than I do – I promise you a better one tomorrow. I'm feeling a bit tired tonight, and I think I'm going to have a cold, so I'll do a quick turn into bed wrapped in all my woolly bed-wear. Dear sweetheart how I wish you were here to make me laugh, you're the only one who can, apart from Jill who only makes me giggle – I'm turning into a glum old hag! Goodnight my dear love,

Always your own, Doris X X X X X X X X X

St Mary's Hospital

Monday, 16th November

Darling,

An awful thing nearly happened today! The Acting-Sister of the First floor – your good and hard-working wife – nearly got caught by the Matron guzzling hot buttered toast! Luckily the eating stage of the proceedings had not been reached but I was hard put to explain away a pile of nice thick slices of bread sitting cut on the table. She (Matron) very rarely comes to the Wing at all, and today she marched straight into the kitchen and began asking questions about everything there – very awkward!

Apart from that incident life goes on quietly in the Wing. All the patients are listening eagerly for any mention of your ship on the wireless. They are quite a nice crowd now – very varied, with one imminent death and several quite heavy routine surgicals (no prostates thank God!). And not one of Willie Noble's blessed eyes which is a break. He tried to push another detached retina onto us, but we weren't having it. Our prize case, the Thrombo Angietus I told you about, is not doing so well now. His other leg and back have gone completely in an unbelievably short time, and he's now on Luminal gr6 and Hyoscine 100 p.r.u. – so you can imagine what he's like. He's taken to plucking at the blankets and pawing you if you go near him – I've never seen quite such a terribly tragic case.

At the other end of the line we have a land girl who keeps her window wide open and sits up in the most cracking draughts and seems to thrive on it. In the middle an aged female gall bladder of Zachy's, and the rest is made up of a haemorrhoids of Dickson, a Ca-Cervix of Bourne, hernia of H-J and a hypertensive menorhagic nurse who ranges between Nellan and Duggie. We only need a cerebral tumour and a prostate to complete the party!

Actually although I like being Acting Sister I find it rather a strain, and I shall be very glad when Margaret Williams comes back. I'm no good at beating up folk and seeing that they do their work properly – and although I'm interested in the patients and their progress, I get pretty browned off sometimes.

Here is rather a lengthy anecdote, which you may have heard before –

Father was explaining to small son that Giants do not exist in the world. They walked past a shoe shop, and in the window was an enormous pair of shoes displayed.

Little boy – 'Look daddy, Giants' shoes?'

Daddy – 'No, little boy. There are no such things as giants'.

Later they passed an oculists, and in the window was a large pair of spectacles made of neon lighting –

'Look daddy, giants' spectacles?'

'No, you must realise there are no such things as giants'.

And then they came to a pawnbrokers –

'Daddy!'

'No son, there's still no such thing as giants'

Duncan had Leslie Henson in again to see him yesterday, and secured a couple more seats for a show – very useful. He said he invited him to the wedding, but he couldn't come.

Must crawl into bed now – it's awfully cold tonight, I'm afraid you would find my feet a couple of icebergs (if ever I were to need an ice bag in a hurry, one of my feet would do fine.)

So lonely for you darling, keep well and safe, and God bless,

All my love sweetheart,

Doris

SMH

Wednesday 18th Nov

Darling,

Great news today which I expect you have already heard from the family. Richard is staying on in Washington as some kind of liaison officer – I think it's just magnificent for him, and will do him all the good in the world. Won't it sound marvellously snooty talking about 'my brother-in-law at the Embassy in Washington'?! Also I'm told he is getting a Lieut Commander's pay! Before we know what's what he'll be wedded to the daughter of a millionaire, and be settled over there for life – and then we can go and visit him on our vacations – if we get any. Marian told me all about it over the phone this evening, and said the family are terribly thrilled, although details are all very vague. I didn't go down to see her last week-end, as George was here, but hope to go on the 28th after Tom's wedding.

We (you and me) are invited to a party on Dec 14th, by H-J – 'details later old thing'. I said that your presence could not be guaranteed but that I'd do my best to see you were there. I believe drink is being laid in for it in vast quantities. Darling I do want to go to a party with you again – so's I can walk into the room and see people saying to themselves, 'what a charming husband she has got.'

Remember H-J's Christmas party two years ago? I came awfully late, and you didn't know I was coming, and you decided to take me out to dinner in spite of having a rehearsal at nine? You were so sweet, and stood beside me all the time. I believe it was only about the second or third time you had seen me out of uniform, and the reason I was so late for the party was I took so long to dress – (vain thing).

Very little news about all the naval battles they say are going on, except that 'considering the size of the undertaking our losses are light'. I know what that means. Sometimes I get awful moments when I feel quite certain I'm never going to see you again, and at others I look forward to your being home very soon. My love, I'm missing you more dreadfully than ever this time, but it will only make it more wonderful when you do come home.

Forgive this melancholy, darling, and remember I love you with all my heart and soul, for ever and ever

Doris

Lindo Wing,
St Mary's Hospital, W2

Saturday, Nov 21st

My darling,

Three days since I wrote I'm afraid. I'm getting very poor! Not that I haven't had the time, because I have, but nothing much seems to have happened here, and I've no letters from you to answer. Actually I have been pretty busy, because the floor is full of extremely heavy cases, six of them Dickson's, and what brown hair I have is rapidly turning grey. Everything that could go wrong in the last few days has! Awful things like patients being sent to the theatre unshaved, or prepped in the wrong places – nurses putting gum elastic catheters cheerfully into boiling water and, worst of all, not being able to answer Dickson's questions! However I'll survive, but you'll probably come home to find me old before my time, and grey-haired to match you.

Dorothy Pugh is back from Edinburgh, I saw her for a brief moment today, and she is returning to Married Alley tomorrow – so it will be my turn to do the comforting. She's looking terribly well – it's really amazing what a few days with a husband does to us girls. Her Roger is about to embark at any moment now, but they've managed to have a good deal of time together during the last month. Graham Jones was down yesterday, and he and Duncan took me into the MO's room for a gin after lunch, which I didn't really want, but I couldn't very well say I'd prefer a brandy. At last I've been measured for my new uniform, which the Hospital apparently is going to give me as a Christmas present – so if you chance to walk in after about Dec 14th you'll find me very smart indeed in my saxe blue gown!

Latest 'Lowie' – The Navy's supply of serge was running short so the following order was put out:– 'Wren's skirts are to be held up until the Navy is satisfied'.

Ma thinks that's awfully rude, and thinks this one is much better: Why did the bee break his leg? Because he fell off his honey. (Myself I don't think it's so hot.)

Today a very odd thing occurred. I was looking out of my window into Praed Street at lunch time, and a Lancaster bomber (yes it was) flew over, very low, and <u>not one</u> person in the street that I could see looked up.

Ma's job is progressing well. The other day she was summoned to a meeting in the directors' room and found herself with all the heads of the place being given a lecture on business methods and rationing etc. She says she will think about aiming higher, and become a big business woman. She does the accounts like six now, and throws her weight around the department. Very odd. I think I'll try it. 10 till 4 at £3/15 shillings, not bad.

More tomorrow, I must go and have my bath before all the hot water is pinched.

'night darling X X

<u>Sunday</u>

Uneventful day, very cold, my nose is beginning to assume its winter hue. My turret is all right in the summer, but it's definitely not so hot now, very chilly in fact, but I still derive a good deal of pleasure from watching the activities of Praed Street. Do you like me new writing paper? I've acquired half a ream, so if you run short I'll send you some. I'm so longing to get some letters from you, nearly three weeks since the last which was the one you sent enclosing your Will. Perhaps tomorrow there really will be some, although I've given up rushing for the post.

Your mother rang up today while I was at the flat, and told us all the news they had had of Richard. Not very much, except that he had made a great success of the tour and had got a very marvellous job with the naval attaché in Washington. Wouldn't it be great if you managed to land in that direction?! Don't forget size 9½ in stockings!!

Darling I'm just longing to hear from you again, this waiting without any news is so miserable, although I know you are all right, and hate to think of me worrying about you, but I just can't help doing that. It's going to be so wonderful to see you again.

Sweetheart, forgive these rather disjointed letters I'm writing lately, I can't seem to get properly organized to write to you. I'll just send you my love, all my love, and lots of kisses,

Always and ever yours,
Doris

Lindo Wing,
St Mary's Hospital, W2

Wednesday, Nov 25th

My darling,

I was so glad to get your cable yesterday, and I'm looking forward to the promised bunch of mail. The papers have been most unhelpful lately, so I've had no idea at all of your whereabouts, and I was beginning to get the teeniest bit panicky. I don't know whether my letters will reach you any quicker by Air Mail, but I'll try one or two. Your cable has set me up more than a little, it's been so horrid not having any news of you.

Duncan was up this morning – he's very jubilant because he's on the list for January, and can go when they get someone to replace him here – I don't think Audrey entirely approves, but I expect she will be as proud of him as I am of you. I had tea with Mrs Gregg (Dunc's mother) yesterday, and she always talks at great length about Audrey and Duncan, and how she wishes that Audrey was a nurse, I don't quite gather why. Ma came in too, and we came back to St Mary's together, and I brought her in to have a look at the portrait, by which she was duly impressed. Dr Gregg (Duncan's father) has just been made a member of the General Medical Council, and this has called forth many cracks.

John Hill was in yesterday, in very smart uniform with chauffeur-type cap pulled well down. He has been appointed to one of the American four-funnel type destroyers, which has been having such fun and games on the Russian convoys that all the officers and half the crew are at Chatham being treated for 'anxiety neurosis'. Poor John I believe is a bit shaken at the thought of what lies ahead.

Dorothy Pugh is back, and thinks that Roger has definitely gone this time, but they managed to have three weeks together in Edinburgh, which was good. It's nice to have someone in Married Alley again to talk to. I was getting a bit fed up with my own company every evening, and now we have a pleasant cup of tea and a gossip before going to bed.

We've got a very delightful naval lieutenant in, who's had a piece of shell fragment removed from his antrum, which had been in his face since Dunkirk. When he came in I asked him which side it was, and he said 'starboard', without realising. I hope you won't be all nautical darling, and talk about the 'deck' and want to call the house HMS *Something*, or anything awful like that. I think I'd like to forget all about ships and the sea for several years, until we have saved enough to buy a nice cabin cruiser, and a sailing dinghy for the children, only I shall be terrified all the time that they will fall in the water and drown.

I've got the pictures done for your frame – not terribly good, but a little better than Percy Beer's effort – I'll send them to you for Christmas. I had intended buying you a pipe but had great difficulty in finding one, so I gave it up.

I've been along to ask Dorothy if she knew a good 'lowie' I could send to you, but she wasn't very forthcoming, apparently the RAF repertoire is pretty smutty. Her Roger gave a turn at a smoking concert at which he told all the stories he knew, and earned the title of 'dirty old doc!' I shouldn't have believed it of him.

I'm going to Marian's this coming week-end, and hope to get over to Cheam on Sunday. I'm going to try and wangle an extra half day – on the strength of being an 'Acting Sister' – and extend the week-end to Monday. Travelling around in the blackout these nights is no joke, and waiting for a bus is awful – I usually walk back from the flat at terrific speed, brandishing my umbrella!

Tomorrow is pay-day, and I'm awfully tempted to buy a new hat – may I?! I'll keep it till you come on leave, but I feel I want to do something to celebrate your cable, and I think a nice tooty headpiece would be just the thing.

I hope it won't be too many months before you get this letter – just mention pyjamas if there is any hope of your coming back to your original starting point. You should find a nice parcel of clean clothes waiting for you too. I hope you've had enough to last you all this time, I hate to think of the colour your shirts must be! Send 'em all back anyway. Goodbye for now darling, so lonely for you, and I'm thinking of you all the time.

With all my love my darling, and millions of kisses,

always yours, Doris X X X X

Friday, Nov 27th – very late

Darling, I meant to write you a fine long letter tonight, but old Holliday came back from her second honeymoon today, and the Grass Widders of Married Ally (your spelling) have been having a long session over cups of tea, which has only just broken up. We discussed everything from wedding days to new hats and new relations (not to mention husbands). Funny there was one Air Force GW, one Army, and one Navy (me). And I now know quite a lot about messes, and what goes on in them and it seems to me you've chosen the best spot. As far as I can gather the RAF and Army spend most of their time telling dirty stories and talking about women – I was proud to tell them that yours (as far as I knew) was occupied in washing your socks and playing chess. Here's one of the stories – What did the stomach say to the wind? If you go quietly I'll let you out the back way.

I have read through your letters again, and they are so good to have. Darling this separation is maybe something of a blessing in disguise, because I think if there had been no war, and if we had been an ordinary married couple, settling down to family life and earning our bread and butter, we would have missed a lot of this rather lovely romantic and sentimental period. Because it is romantic to have a husband at sea fighting the war, although it's so miserable too, and I admit I'm quite unashamedly sentimental, and it's been a very great joy to me to know that you are too. We would never have had these letters, which tell us so much about each other that would have taken a long time for us to find out. I've been so happy because you can write to me just what you are thinking. Of course I don't mind not hearing what you are doing from day to day, and darling if you only told me one thing in your letters, that you loved me, that would be enough. I'm going to write lots more tomorrow, but now I must get the old swede down to look my best for the wedding tomorrow (Tom Kemp's). Detailed report in our evening edition. Very happy tonight my darling, and thinking about you so much.

God bless dear Roger X X X

Saturday night, Nov 28th, at Marian's

My Darling,

Marvellous day today, magnificent wedding, and the day began well with an air mail letter from you of Nov 21. I hope by this time you will have had some of my letters and will know that I've neither divorced you nor had twins – I'm very well and boxing on.

So I guessed right after all as to your whereabouts. Duncan told me today that he knew where you were and that you were all right. When I said well why on earth didn't you tell me that before, he said, you didn't ask me. Foolish fellow! He also told me that Tony Oddie had been a casualty with a broken arm, and that Jock Morrison's boat had been sunk. He didn't say where he got his information though.

Well about this wedding. At 9:30 I was called to the telephone, and it was George, in town again for what will probably be his last leave before they send him off to New Zealand. He had arrived with his friend Scruffy, and hadn't even changed out of his working rig before he left Glasgow! So we arranged that he should call for me at Mary's and we should go the wedding together. He arrived ten minutes late, and informed me that he had been in Shepherds' since 11:30, so you can imagine!

In church (St Michael's, Star Street) we sat behind Audrey, Min and Graham Jones. George, on seeing Graham, was overcome with alcoholic giggles, which continued throughout the service much to Audrey's disgust The church was very full, all the types, nurses, maids, a sprinkling of honoraries – Bourne, Pickering, Smale, Willie Noble – and a gaggle of handsome ushers headed by Duncan, who has just about got the art of 'ushing' taped, and who conducts all the younger and better looking dolls to their seats with his hand under the elbow. The Mary's choir was there, and George demanded loudly, 'who are the dolls in the choir?' Ruth looked very pretty in white with all the trimmings, and there was a lot of very pleasant Tchaikovsky music.

After the church we went back to Mary's for George to spend a necessary penny (in spite of my careful directions he landed in X-ray), and from there we went on to the reception with Graham Jones, Bill Young and Brierley in the Daimler which had taken Tom and Ruth. I'm not quite sure how we managed that, but we did, and Graham and George enlivened the ride by singing hymns as loudly as they could.

The reception was at Holme House in Regent's Park, it's an RAF officers' mess of some kind and there were lots of WAAFs and flight sergeants handing round sticky buns and cocktails. We went in as 'Mrs Miles and Mr Miles' but nobody seemed to notice, and for the next two hours a good time was had by all. There seemed to be a vast supply of beer, and George procured some whiskey from somewhere. H-J of course was well to the fore with Sunbeam (wearing a rather scrumptious sapphire ring on the third finger L. hand) – one of his cracks was, 'Well, old boy, I always say, if you want to go to bed with a telephone, marry a doctor'. Tom was in great form, I rather suspect the slightest bit tiddly, and made an excellent speech, starting off 'my wife and I' which was cheered.

I had a long chat with Tiffy Moore, who is now at the Admiralty doing boards and very bored (sorry) – every other day off, and nothing to do. So he's coming to the Wing for a cup of tea, and I hope will be around for some of the Christmas festivities. What a nice thing he is – he cheered me no end by saying that after a year such as you have had, you will be perfectly justified in putting in for a shore job. He was most interested in the beard and is keen to see it. Can't you have a photo taken?

I came down to Marian's with Graham Jones, whose fiancée lives in Malden, and we had a very pleasant chat. He's being married next Saturday.

Many stories were told, but the only one I can remember at the moment is this one of Duncan's: No drawers, no flaps, no leaf – what is it? (answer later!)

The family have had a cable from Richard and also a parcel of Christmas gifties including a fountain pen for you, which your mother is keeping, as we thought it was a bit of a risk sending it to you just now. Talking of Americans, this is Min's story – 'Utility knickers, one yank and they're on – two Yanks and they're off!'

It's Sunday now, and I'm writing this surrounded by animals, two cats and Sue the dog. Marian and I are just about to take a short sharp walk before lunch, it's a beautiful day, but very cold. My nose has taken on its winter hue, but otherwise I feel fine. Marian is very well, about seven more weeks to go, and is quite frankly enormous. Lots of fluid the doctor told her, but it's sitting round the right way and everything is going well. Lots of little garments being rapidly completed, and cots and pots and things around. Makes me envious, but there it is. As you say it would be so much nicer to get one organised when you were home, although I should think you would be pretty bored having a wife like a barrel and not able to do much or go anywhere.

Later

The walk did not materialise, it's turned much colder, so we just ate a large lunch to the accompaniment of Tommy Handley, 'After you, Woad – No, after you, Fossil'. I'm whipping back to Town after tea, as George leaves tonight and I'd like to see him off.

Answer to Duncan's story – 'Utility Table'.

Monday

I must finish this now or it will never be posted.

All my very best love my darling, very large lumps of it –

Always and ever yours, X X X Doris

December 1942

Following the British victory at El Alamein and the Allied landings in Morocco and Algeria, General Erwin Rommel, 'the Desert Fox', had advised Hitler that continuing the fight there would be futile and recommended that all Axis forces be withdrawn from North Africa. Hitler furiously rejected his advice and instead poured tens of thousands of German and Italian troops into Tunisia, stalling the Allies' eastward advance. Meanwhile, in Russia, the Germans had captured the city of Stalingrad on the banks of the Volga River, but in late November they had been encircled by the Red Army and both sides settled in for a debilitating siege. With little interesting news coming from the battlefields, other, more dramatic events seized the public's attention in early December. Britons were appalled to read of the terrible loss of life when fire swept through the Cocoanut Grove nightclub in Boston. It is still the worst nightclub fire in history; 492 revellers died in the overcrowded fire-trap and thousands more were injured.

And everyone was talking about the Beveridge Report. Officially entitled *Social Insurance and Allied Services*, the report had been drafted by economist William Beveridge under the auspices of an interdepartmental committee. The report contained sweeping and innovative proposals to tackle the worst social problems, the Dickensian-sounding 'five giants', as Beveridge called them: Want, Disease, Ignorance, Squalor and Idleness. It was a massive compendium that spelled out a system of social insurance, covering every citizen regardless of income, a comprehensive policy of social progress offering a cradle-to-grave welfare state. It was issued as a Government White Paper on 2 December.

The report caused quite a buzz. Everybody had an opinion, and it was the main topic of discussion at dinner tables across the country. Most Britons were in favour of Beveridges's proposals. People could see that Government services had improved their lives, and they wanted more. Ironically perhaps, social welfare services had increased substantially during the war years, class inequality had been somewhat reduced and upward mobility was in reach of millions. Despite the grumbling, the Government's rationing scheme had ensured that even the poorest had enough to eat. Families appreciated the low-cost milk and school meals they had been provided with since 1940. The Beveridge Report also called for a substantial increase in the old age pension (first introduced in 1908 under the Liberal Government, which had included the young Winston Churchill, as a benefit for the elderly poor).

Churchill and his Conservative colleagues were sceptical of the new proposals, mainly because of the huge and unknown cost of implementing such an ambitious scheme. Although Churchill had been a champion of welfare reform as President of the Board of Trade and Home Secretary before the First World War, now he saw this as a distraction from the Government's most important job, which was to win this war. Although many Labour MPs believed that the proposals contained in the report should be acted upon at the earliest opportunity, the Government ultimately voted to wait until the war was over and the effect on the Treasury's depleted resources could be calculated.

In the conclusion of his report, *Planning for Peace in War*, Beveridge had outlined three facts: 'that the purpose of victory is to live in a better world than the old world; that each individual citizen is more likely to concentrate upon his war effort if he feels that his Government will be ready in time with plans for that better world; that, if these plans are to be ready in time, they must be made now.'[1] The British people's hope for that 'better world' would contribute to the Labour Party's election victory in 1945, and the Beveridge Report formed the basis for the post-war Welfare State introduced by Clement Attlee's Labour Government.

The British people enjoyed the escapism of 'going to the pictures', and newsreels kept them abreast of what was going on in the world, but in those pre-television days the majority of people got both their news and entertainment from the radio. Almost every household had a 'wireless' on which they could tune in to the latest news broadcast, listen to a concert, a play or a comedy show, follow the commentary of a cricket match, or hear the Prime Minister cajole, encourage and inspire them with one of his speeches.

One of Doris's favourite programmes was *It's That Man Again* (*ITMA*) featuring the comedian Tommy Handley and a host of wacky characters, including the much loved Mrs Mop the charlady. The show gave the country many popular catchphrases, one of which, 'After you, Claude – no, after you Cecil', was said to be shouted by RAF pilots going in to attack. Another very popular programme was *The Brains Trust,* in which a panel of experts answered questions put to them by the audience. The programme had been started in January 1941 under the original name of *Any Questions?* to encourage members of the forces to ask questions and get answers. It was unscripted, unrehearsed and broadcast live. The participants did not know beforehand what they would be asked and they had to give spontaneous answers. The questions ranged from the most serious moral conundrums to the utterly frivolous, and listeners loved the witty and intellectual verbal sparring among the members of the panel. From time to time guest experts would be invited onto the programme, as in the one that Doris writes about that featured three of St Mary's senior consultants: Arthur Dickson Wright, Aleck Bourne and pathologist Professor Wilfred D. Newcomb.

Roger's letter in the November issue of the *St Mary's Hospital Gazette* confirmed that he was still in the Mediterranean in the company of friends: 'We feel it worthy of mention that during the passage of the most recent convoy to Malta, there were amongst the ships taking part no less than six St Mary's men ... Although the team were not able to effect a complete rendezvous in Gib[raltar] (which was perhaps just as well for that rocky outpost) many of us did meet at different times, and the event was celebrated needless to say in the traditional manner.'[2]

Richard's touring companion Ludmila Pavlichenko had gone to England in November, where once again she caught the public's attention as she embarked on a successful fundraiser for the Red Army. Richard, meanwhile, was enjoying his posting in Washington DC: 'I love it', he said in a letter to Roger, ' and while I well may have scruples at being so far away, I know I couldn't be in a boat, and if you've got to be in an office what could be better? The work is of course most interesting and keeps one busy, and out of hours just to be alive here is an education.' Mrs Eleanor Roosevelt had taken a liking to the young naval officer and invited him to spend Christmas at the White House. He wrote to his sister Marian at the beginning of January: 'I had a wonderful Christmas and New Year with dear Mrs R, who has been so kind to me all the way through. It was wonderful to meet the President off duty and I felt very nervous but very proud. The more I go into the matter, the more I think he is the most remarkable man in the world.' Richard had not yet met Winston Churchill!

There were more weddings to come. Their close friend Jack Suchet announced his engagement to Joan Jarché, daughter of prominent Fleet Street photographer Jimmy Jarché. And 'H-J's done it again!' H-J was fifty years old in December 1942, had been married twice before and had two children. Now the newspaper declared that he was about to marry for the third time, to the considerably younger Sunbeam.

Smoking was commonplace in those days before the dangers were widely recognised. More than one brand of cigarettes even touted its health benefits: 'For your throat's sake, smoke Craven A.' Roger remembered the medical students smoking in anatomy class to cover up the awful smell and taste of formalin. Winston Churchill was frequently seen with a fat cigar in his hand; it was an important part of what nowadays would be called his 'image'. However, as Doris was soon to observe, the cigar was not always alight and he rarely smoked more than the first inch or so. Newsreel footage and photographs of President Roosevelt showed him using a long cigarette holder clenched between his teeth. Doris never smoked cigarettes, although her mother May did. Roger had one from time to time, switching later to little cigarillos before quitting altogether. People kept cigarettes in handsome wood or silver boxes to offer to guests. Large table lighters, often of fanciful design, like the one that Doris bought for H-J and Sunbeam, were popular gifts. The Dunhill lighter made of brass and wood and shaped like an old-fashioned flintlock pistol that was a wedding present from Anna Zinkeisen, graced the table in Doris and Roger's sitting room for many years after the war.

Today's texting teens are hardly the first to use initials and acronyms to indicate commonly used phrases in their messages. Because of the need to be brief in letters and telegrams, Second World War lovers came up with a plethora of codes; probably the most well-known is SWALK ('Sealed With A Loving Kiss'). Many used the initial letters of place names. These apparently caused headaches for German intelligence agents who intercepted the messages. A reference to 'ITALY' would cause them to scan in vain for hidden strategic information, little realising that the writer was telling the recipient 'I Trust And Love You'. Doris sometimes included BOLTOP ('Better On Lips Than On Paper') in her letters to Roger; she may have written other coded endearments on the envelopes.

Doris loved the outdoors, and would have been happy to settle after the war in North Wales, where the Miles family had a holiday home near the little seaside town of Aberdovey, not far from Annie's home town of Bala. *Tan-y-Craig*, 'the House under the Rock', was not so much a house as a simple wooden chalet, tucked under a rocky outcropping and surrounded by woods and fields. Doris referred to it as their 'hut'. There was no electricity or indoor plumbing; oil lamps supplied light and cooking was done on a coal-fired range. Water had to be fetched in buckets from a nearby stream. Just up the hill was the *ty-bach*, a tiny wooden hut in which there was a chemical toilet. The amenities may have been basic, but Roger and Doris enjoyed staying at *Tan-y*, as it was always known to the family. The house was located in the glorious Welsh countryside in the southern part of what is now Snowdonia National Park. Just a few minutes drive away was Aberdovey's expansive sandy beach, where they could sail on the sheltered waters of Cardigan Bay or enjoy a round of golf on the links course which undulated through the dunes.

Roger's friends and contemporaries Tony Oddie, Peter Baly, Ca Young, Alec Mathison, John Hill, Jock Morrison, Richard Lovell, Ivan Jacklin and Michael Walker had already finished their medical training and had joined the armed forces. Roger was pleased to find that Peter Baly was also serving in the

Mediterranean in *Tartar's* sister ship *Ashanti*. Others, like Duncan Gregg, Brian Brierley, Graham Jones, Bill Young and Eric Norman were eager to sign up as soon as they had completed the required stages of their hospital residency and arrangements had been made to cover their positions for the duration. Happily, there were still plenty of reliable young men to escort Doris and the other nurses. George's departure to New Zealand had been postponed until the New Year, so he was able to spend the holidays with his mother and sister and to accompany Doris to several social events, letting their hair down and getting up to harmless mischief together as they had done as children.

As the holidays approached, people brought down from their attics boxes of pre-war decorations, augmenting them with chains made of brightly coloured paper stuck together with flour-and-water paste. Customers bought whatever they could find in the shops to give as presents. Christmas cakes and puddings were made with sugar and dried fruit that had been carefully hoarded from the rations. Despite wartime austerity there seemed to be an abundance of drink available at the hospital. 'Bugger the Boche!' Everyone was determined to make the best of what they had and enjoy themselves this Christmas, and to hell with Hitler!

Lindo Wing, St Mary's Hospital, W2

Wed, Dec 2nd

> **MR. R. M. HANDFIELD-JONES AND MISS L. D. TUDOR-JONES**
> A marriage has been arranged, and will take place shortly, between Ranald Montagu Handfield-Jones, M.C., M.S., F.R.C.S., and Lilian, younger daughter of Mr. and Mrs. Tudor-Jones, of 9, Hurlingham Gardens, S.W.

Darling,

Well, H-J's done it again, and of course the hospital's comment is 'third time lucky'. I offered my sincere congratulations this morning, and said I hoped they would be very happy; he answered with something of a twinkle '– after my rather chequered career'. He has asked me to a party on Dec 14th, so I imagine if that's not the actual wedding day, it's some form of celebration of it. What about a wedding present? We must give them something, but it's rather difficult to know what. Could you bring back some tasty bit of North African art? Or perhaps a portrait of you in beard would be welcome. (Don't forget I want one of those.) I wonder if the wedding will be very quiet, or if he's going to ask half the hospital. Will it have to be in a registry office? I suppose so, pity.

More awards for the big Russian Convoy published in the *Times* today. I'm sure you ought to have got something, you really deserve it, and I've always wanted to go to Buckingham Palace. I had a letter from Denys (the Lieut) yesterday. He is still in hospital in Malta and they are threatening to whip out his gall bladder, so if you ever get to Malta it's the 90th General Hosp and the name is Richardson. He seems to be pretty fed up with being stuck there, and anxious to get back to England and to his newly acquired fiancée (horrid word I agree). This time last year we were right in the middle of the 'fiancé' business. I think it was rather a nice time, although not be to prolonged more than about four months. You were very considerate about not producing rows of relations to view me, there's a lot to be said for large families with flocks of aunts and cousins, but there's even more to be said against them.

I posted off on Monday a very expensive Air Mail letter, and I shall be interested to know how soon it reaches you. If you are likely to remain in Southern waters until after Christmas will you in your next letter put 'Answer to your question of Dec 2 Yes or No' (as case may be). It's rather horrid not knowing when you may be coming back, because although your home base is such miles away, at least it seems nearer.

The hospital is preparing for Christmas festivities, the girls are practising the old carols, and no doubt I shall take my stand in the hall on Christmas morning, and sing with the rest. What I should like to do though would be to go to St Peter's – I went last year. Darling do you know, apart from the wedding, we've never been to a C of E church together? And much as I admire your father's church, I'm not a Presbyterian, yet! I've always had a secret delight in High Church services, although I've been very bad in the last few years about going. Anyway Mr MacDonald is enough to make anyone turn agnostic or Parsee (lovely thought! Don't they worship the sun? Do you remember

Kipling's story about the Parsee who sat on top of a palm tree eating plum cake?)

Rather a pleasant picture of Tom and Ruth, isn't it?

By the way Mr MacD asked me to remember him to you when next I wrote. I told him you had grown a beard so that you could look fierce and the sailors would respect you, also to frighten your wife – he was awfully impressed.

FORMER ENGLAND RUGGER CAPTAIN, Dr. T. A. Kemp, and Miss Ruth Keat, who used to be a nurse at St. Mary's Hospital, Paddington, married in Paddington. Miss Keat's father is the wing-commander in charge of A.T.C. training.

I did like the growth dear – honest. And anyway even if I had disliked it I shouldn't have said. It's your face and your growth, and you must do what you like with it. Never do what other people say, it's a very very bad thing, and I'm always trying to stop myself from depending on other people and not being able to make up my own mind. All of which is a lot of bulsh, and if you told me to do anything I'd do it. (But then I did promise to obey you, and I'm glad we had what Dorothy Sayers calls the 'old vulgar Prayer book form', it's much more romantic than the new version.)

Latest report from the desert (quite true). Ca Young was ill (no one knows what with) and was in hospital. One day the doctor looking after him told him they had decided to call in a specialist. All set for the specialist, and can you guess who it was? Right first go – Uncle

Tom in the flesh. I suspect there was some small celebration between the patient and specialist.

George rang up last night to say he's been transferred to the Royal New Zealand Navy from today and will be off at any moment. I gathered from his brief account that he will be Senior in a cruiser out there – I don't know the name. Ma is very upset, but after all it's his life, and if he thinks he'll do a better job out there then who are we to stop him. It's a horrid thought all the same. I don't suppose we shall see him for years, and I expect mails will be very bad. But then we haven't seen a great deal of him since the war began, and it will be marvellous for him to go there. We have got some vague cousins in Auckland, perhaps he'll marry one, and settle down after the war on a sheep farm. We'll have very cosmopolitan relations then, with Richard and his probable millionairess bride in America, and now George in NZ I think we'll have to settle in South Africa, and then we will be half way.

I wonder what you are doing tonight sweetheart? Playing chess, or perhaps writing to me. I imagine you so often in your little cabin. Is it warm? Dorothy and I were having a little gossip tonight and cheering each other up by saying again how we are glad that both our Rogers are doing what they can to win the war, and that we are proud to have you there. We get on famously because she talks at length about her Roger, and I talk at length about mine, and we neither of us take much notice of what the other is saying, and both are happy.

I wonder if you have got the pictures by now – they are not good. I should have gone to a better place, but Mike was so enthusiastic about the joint that I thought it must produce something worthwhile. However I'm hoping to get the portrait photographed at any moment now, which should be really good.

Nearly midnight, so I must pack this up. It's been lovely talking to you, and I hope this won't take too long to reach you.

Nearly two months since you left. I suppose the old boiler is still horribly clean, or else you've managed to scrape it on your wanderings. But I'm counting the days till the next one, and if you should be in a position to send a gram beforehand, and the place is the same as last time, wire 'Same again' and I'll be at the North

British when you arrive. What a day that will be. Every time you come home is more exciting and wonderful than the last, and when you do eventually come home for good, it will take me several months before I'm convinced you're not going away again. We'll have so much time to make up, and we'll have to work hard.

Good night now my darling love.

Always and ever your very loving wife X X

Lindo Wing,
St Mary's Hospital, W2

Saturday, Dec 5th

Dear love,

In the words of a now popular dance tune, 'There's nothing new to tell you, I've said it all before' – nothing of importance anyway. The world-shaking events that are taking place make very little impression here – we read the papers every day, and shake our heads gloomily and say, things don't look so good in Tunisia – but the daily round continues, and a laddered stocking is a greater disaster than the sinking of four troopships. The nightclub fire in Boston has caused much more concern lately than anything else.

The family (your wife's family) is immediately concerned with the impending departure of George for NZ. We went today to see the Chief Clerk at New Zealand House, he was perfectly charming, and explained that, owing to your party, shipping had been somewhat held up, but that they should be able to provide a passage by the end of the month – in the meanwhile if George wanted any advances of pay or anything he was to go to him. Charming! Apparently George gets extra pay now he's been three years a Lieut, and extra again for being lent to the Royal New Zealand Navy, and also no income tax to pay, as they don't have it out there! Charming again! Also they give him a fortnight's notice of sailing, so he will be here over Christmas, which will be super, although I doubt if I shall see a great deal of him. He came down from Glasgow last night, and after going to NZ House, we spent the rest of the morning in Shepherds consuming large quantities of ale – at that time of the day it doesn't agree with me, and I arrived on duty at 1 P.M. feeling a bit whistled, and hoping ADW wouldn't arrive and notice my beery breath (he didn't).

My Christmas present to myself arrived today. Very tasty. You will no doubt be able to guess what it is – quite right, new clothes – to be kept for the next leave. George brought our presents down with him, and thinking that he would be off at any minute gave me mine this morning. A very handsome nightdress case in the MacLeod tartan – (the woman in the shop told him it was that, he thought it was 'just a pattern'). It's rather nice, being all yellow and black, but I don't think it would look very appropriate on my virginal turret bed, which is becoming more of a problem as the days go by. The shelf from N to S has become so marked that I can only sleep on half of the mattress, and I daren't turn it in case the other side should be much worse.

Heard a funny today. Quite good:

A woman went into a chemist's shop –

Woman: 'I want a corvette, please.'

Chemist: 'A <u>corvette</u>, madam?'

W: 'That's what I said.'

C: 'But madam, do you know what a corvette is? It's a baby destroyer.'

W: 'Yes, that's what I want.'

Getting very near January 8th – our first anniversary. Is there any possible chance of your being back for it? George was very pessimistic and says that your ship can have a complete refit out there without coming back home, so you will probably be away for ages! Miserable body that he is. Anyway I'll find some means of celebrating, even if I have to do it alone. Duncan was asking me the other day when it was, and said he would see to it that the day was duly noted.

I was looking through the November *Gazette* today, and saw the letter you and Peter Baly wrote. Darling it gave me the same old thrill as your notes in the Lodge used to give me, and the old heart did a Port 180° (very nautical!). I wonder if you have had the same lot with you this time. Shame about Tony's ship – I've been to many a fine party in her wardroom. Duncan told me he'd had a broken arm.

Talking of casualties, remember the friend of Emma's we once met at the Savoy? Mary Clarke or MacBreen, I think. Well she went on a binge the other night, came home and felt pretty ill – phoned up

Emma who went round straight away – 1 a.m. – and by 6 a.m. she was dead from a cerebral haemorrhage. Moral – don't drink gin.

<u>Sunday</u>

I've been on a small toot today. Went with George to the officers' Sunday Club at Grosvenor House this P.M. but we seemed to be sitting at the wrong table, having taken our seats with someone called Nancy (she's a 'young hostess'), and after one or two rather sticky moments with the Lady Somebody, who was head girl of the table, I departed. However I enjoyed seeing the show. Very highly organised, with Lady This and That, and lots of debs all calling each other 'dear', a sort of Mayfair way of picking up a man as far as I could make out, all highly respectable and proper. I apparently had crashed into a table for lonely men and young hostesses, which didn't do at all, as the lonely men were meant for the young H's, and as George left with Nancy I got rather stuck. However, I ate my 3 shillings-worth before taking a honey-sweet farewell of the hostess, who almost pushed me out of the room saying she hoped she wasn't making me go. I told George it would be rather fun to try and break the place up – everyone was so terrifically polite and on their best behaviour. He thought we ought to start a bowling match on the dance floor.

George is going back to Glasgow tonight, but I hope he will be down again in time for H-J's party on the 14th. I feel such a lemon going to parties alone.

My hair is growing to enormous lengths, but I daren't cut it in case I cut all the perm out by mistake! So when you come home it will no doubt be hanging down my back. Very pretty.

Hospital headlines very dull lately. Nurse Burrows was whipped off for an acute appendix and twisted ovarian thing last week – she very conveniently developed the trouble on the day Dickson was operating, so all was well. Lots of people have been getting married at intervals, and one of our misguided members has gone so far as to produce an infant without being married – all very scandalous and hushed up.

I've been dashing round the shops frantically trying to find Christmas presents, very difficult as everyone else in the world seems to have the same idea. All I've succeeded in getting is a pink china pig and two bottles of hair shampoo – which make very acceptable gifts if given to the right people. Wish you were here to come shopping with me, I think we'd have a lot of fun. I spent hours in Goode's the other day, it's a most delightful shop with lovely things in it. Needless to say I have also spent hours in both Bumpers and the Times Book Club, although your chess manual came from Mr Selfridge.

So longing to hear from you again my darling. This separation business is a bad thing, I think it's time it stopped. Take care of yourself won't you, no bathing among the jellyfishes. Dearest I think of you so much. This time of waiting just doesn't mean a thing, and I think I must be the most uninteresting person in the world for the poor folk who have to live and work with me. However, 'Box On' is the motto, so on we box.

Dear I love you, and send you all my love
God bless, my darling,
Always yours, Doris

Lindo Wing,
SMH, Paddington

Dec 11th, Friday

Dearest Roger,

There was something so funny I was going to tell you and now I've forgotten what it was – pity. I remember thinking at the time I must tell Roger about that, and now I've no idea what it was. Nothing very funny happens often these days, except Esmé Rees who always makes me laugh, and Dickson who usually does (when he doesn't make me want to hit him).

There's rather an amusing conversation going on in the kitchen at the moment over the respective merits of marriage and single bliss. Ivy, the woman, is all against marriage (she's married to a communist) and is saying how much better it is to be free, and how deceitful men are. Esmé Rees and another nurse are supporting her, and saying how much better it is to have a lot of men friends and to have a good time. Poor saps. I explained patiently that never having been married they couldn't very well know what it was like. According to them 90% of husbands are unfaithful to their wives and make no secret of it, and they both said nothing would induce them to get married until they were about 30 and had had their share of good times. Funny because it wasn't a question of sour grapes. I suppose they just haven't come across the right type of man. Also, I rather query their idea of 'good times' which seems to consist of going to nightclubs every night and waking up with a thick head in the morning. But I didn't feel like telling them how being married to the right person makes every minute you're together a far better time than you've ever had before, and how good for you it is to have someone to think about besides yourself. How marriage alters your whole life, and how lovely life becomes. She'll find out.

Dorothy and I went up this evening to see Mrs Willson and the baby Christopher John. She had a very bad time, and a bad tear, but is feeling fine now, although somewhat exhausted. The babe is a magnificent specimen with a head simply bulging with brains. I'm so jealous of her!

A shocking short letter darling, I'm going to have a cuppa with Dorothy, her room is warmer than mine owing to her having purchased a small electric fire, and we usually have a warm before going to bed. Terribly lonely, and longing so much for you to come home.

Bless you darling for being my own dear husband.

All my fondest love always,

Doris

Lindo Wing,
St Mary's Hospital, W2

Monday, Dec 14th

My darling,

Once again I takes up my pen to give you all the red-hot piping news from the Home Front. Everything going according to plan, and everybody looking forward to making whoopee over Christmas on a very limited amount of this and that. George arrived down this morning, and looked in here before he started off round the pubs. He informed me that he had a large sum of mun in the bank, and that it was his intention to spend it all before he left! I can see poor Ma will be white-haired by the end of the fortnight. I'm being very good and living on my pay, and I've exactly 6 shillings and sixpence to last me until Thursday (not counting the sixpenny collection though).

Today is H-J's weddin' day. He came in this morning resplendent in striped trousers and morning coat, I expect he daren't bring his top-hat in! I imagine the knot tying is to take place in a registry and the big celebration is tonight as I told you. George and I are starting across the road at 6 and joining Duncan at 6:30, so by the time we get to the Berkeley we should be in pretty good form! I'll give you the low down on it tomorrow. At the moment I'm on duty, and the girls are having a very entertaining discussion on make-up hints. I've gleaned a very good tip on how to make your eyes sparkle, which I intend trying! I shan't tell you what it is – in any case I shan't need to use it when you're home because as you may have noticed, luv makes the old optics twinkle a treat.

I went down to Marian's for the week-end, and yesterday we went over to Cheam for the children's Christmas Service. It was really delightful, and your father looked so well and happy, and quite competently dealing with swarms of children clasping every imaginable toy – inducing the young ones to part with them, and coping with traffic blocks caused by a large toy motor car and an elephant on wheels. We sang carols lustily, and except for one or two disasters of children who lost their parents and started to yell, and frequent exits to spend pennies, the afternoon was a great success. There was a terrific flirtation going on in front of me between a small girl of about 3 and a small boy of about 4. At one point they both left their parents and started walking up the aisle together.

We went back to tea at the Manse, and saw the photographs that had come from America – one very good one of the three boys on a massive balcony with a microphone, and one of Richard and Ludmila sitting side by side on a sofa, both looking extremely fierce, and Ludmila showing two large knees beneath her skirt. No more news of Richard, but Ludmila wrote to your mother saying how sorry she was not to be able to see her, and how much she admired Richard and hoped he would be successful in his diplomatic career (sounds big doesn't it!!). I wonder how long he will be over there.

By the way did I tell you about the present I got for H-J and Sunbeam? I meant to I know, but I think I forgot to put it in my last letter. It's a Dunhill pistol lighter, exactly the same as the one Anna gave us, and cost 56 shillings and threepence. Quite an appropriate choice, don't you think? I had a look round because I thought some old silver in the way of a milk jug would be rather nice – but all I could see was very new-looking and I think cheap silver is terrible, and everything worth getting was so expensive. I saw the lighter quite by accident, and I think it was the last one they had. I hope you think that will be all right. I hate getting things without you, it would be such fun to choose them together. Whatever happens I'm not going to buy any furniture by myself (although by the time we get as far as that all furniture will be utility, and all exactly the same, so we shan't have any choice anyway). We'll probably have to make our own, and eat with wooden spoons off bits of board. Do you ever think of what our life now might have been? It's a bad thing to do I know, but I wonder how near to our dreams our future life will be. I've no doubts about it darling – I know we're going to get on very well, even though we're bound to start arguing sometime. I'm not awfully obstinate anyway, and I can't argue to save my life, so you'll win every time·

Well darling, in the words of Mrs Mop, 'TTFN' or 'Ta-Ta for now' – I'll continue this tomorrow, I'm afraid when I come in tonight I shan't be able to add very much,

X X X

<u>Some very late hour.</u>

A marvellous party – I haven't enjoyed myself as much for many a day. I'll recount it all tomorrow – at the moment I'm just the teeniest bit tight and am making rather unsteady tracks for bed. Darling sweetheart, how I wish you were here.

All my love X X

<u>Tuesday</u>

Being in a more sober state this morning I can proceed to tell you about the party. It was really a most excellent party although composed of widely varying types. George and I had a preliminary noggin across the road at 6 with Duncan and then went on to his flat where we had another while he changed his shirt. There we were joined by Bill Young and Hugh Glanville's young brother. After a further noggin we all piled into a taxi, and arrived at the Berkeley Buttery only fifteen minutes late, and in very good form. The Happy Couple were already there, also Duggie and Mrs Duggie, John Simpson and Sunbeam's sister. We had a couple more there and then walked for miles, round corners and through dining rooms to the restaurant.

I was very pleasantly situated between Duggie and Duncan, both of whom were very attentive. I had a long talk with Duggie about you, and what a fine chap you were. Other subjects of conversation at the table included Russia and politics, baldness, women medical students, John Simpson's broken heart, and the MacLeods' ducks. After dinner we went back to the bar, and many light ales were consumed. The Bride and Bridegroom left at about a quarter to eleven, and we packed up at about 11:30, wandered our way slowly and hilariously to Mary's, and arrived soon after 12. A very excellent evening having been had by all.

Mr and Mrs H-J are giving a cocktail party next week when they get back from Cornwall – which should no doubt be very agreeable and start off the Christmas festivities.

Tiffy came in this morning for some coffee, he thinks his job would suit you down to the ground, 12 to 12, every other day off. You could get quite a lot of work done on the days off (!). I suggested you did a swop and he thought it would be an excellent idea. Tom Eland has departed at last for Freetown, much to Mrs Duggie's disgust as he used to bring her back supplies on his trips to Canada. I don't suppose Freetown has much to sell, although I've heard they get silk stockings from South America, so keep your eyes open if you ever get there.

Duncan had a card from Peter Baly last week saying that he and you, Alan and Alec Mathison expected to spend a white Christmas. I wonder if that means what I think it means. It's so horrid not knowing where you are, but just that you are tearing madly about the ocean surrounded by gangs of submarines and whatnots. By the way, the amazing story I told you of Robert being called in to see Ca Young when he was ill is not true at all, as Ca is in Egypt and Robert in Palestine – but it was a good story all the same.

I think I'll try and get this letter off by Air Mail tomorrow, although I doubt if it will reach you any more quickly that way. So in case it does take weeks, a Merry Christmas to you my darling, and a very happy New Year; and in case it's longer still, and Jan 8th is reached, 'I looks towards you', my own love and very dear husband.

Always and ever yours, Doris

December 19th

Darling Roger,

You would have been amused by *The Brains Trust* on the wireless yesterday. Some of our Mary's chaps – Aleck Bourne, Newcomb, and of course Arthur Dickson Wright – were on. Their question was: 'What is the opinion of the Brains on that part of the Beveridge Report relating to the Medical Profession?'

Bourne – had read every word of it, and recommended every student to read from page this to page that, and to weigh every word – most important step, etc., etc.

Newcomb – hadn't enough money to buy it.

Dickson – thought it was a colossal piece of humbug when the world was in its present state to make plans for social security, and to hand over the control of the practice of medicine to a lot of civil servants. He hated civil servants, he had enough of them for patients, they had pimples, and they all had their bowels on the brain. Plenty of good brains in the Profession, quite able to organise it by themselves. He fairly let fly, you can imagine the delight.

There were lots more questions, the cracks I remember I think all came from Dickson – here are a few.

Re snake charming – I blew a gourd instrument once but the snake just shot back into its basket.

Re spiritualism – Nobody ever converted me. I operated on a medium once, but I didn't see any ectoplasm or pictures of his grandfather popping out of the wound. He didn't get better any quicker than anyone else, and he eventually went to America heavily in debt.

Re the effect of endocrine glands on the course of history – Hitler's not a eunuch. He suffers from hyperthyroidism and has a man named Schwarb to treat him. Schwarb is a Jew, so Hitler had to make him an honorary Aryan.

They don't seem so funny written down, but when Dickson said them they were very good and caused much mirth.

Tonight the choir sang carols in the chapel, and I managed to slip in for the end. I've given up singing in the choir, too lazy, but I like listening. Afterwards I brought Mrs MacLeod up to Married Alley to see the portrait, by which she was much impressed, and being the daughter of an artist could appreciate properly. What a charming person she is.

Dorothy and I are now going to have our evening cuppa, over which we are going to compose an Airgraph New Year greeting to send to Robert. His address in case you haven't got it, or have lost it, is 91st General Hospital, MEF.

It's about time I heard from you again, and I've got all the porters lined up to whip any letters across to me the moment they arrive. What a day that's going to be. Sweetheart you seem so terribly far away when there is no news, but I've got a nice warm feeling in my heart because I know you're thinking of me, and that actual miles and thousands of miles don't really matter.

Goodnight my dearest, joy of my heart, I love you so.
Always and ever,
Doris

Lindo Wing, St Mary's Hospital, W2

Dec 23rd

Dearest Roger,

The festive week has begun very pleasantly, and we are now all set for the 25th. As usual everything is turning out to be much better than was expected. On Monday evening we took Ma to see *Flare Path*, very excellent show, thoroughly enjoyed by all. Yesterday I did a hurried dash out with George to do remaining Christmas shopping and to go to Gieves. Oddly enough we were no sooner out of the flat then we found ourselves in a pub! Very strange! However we did eventually get to Gieves and other places. I found some very nice pillow cases for Marian's pram, and I thought some Marcovitch cigarettes would be all right for John – I had thought of a pair of braces but find the all-elastic ones are almost impossible to get.

We (all of us) are going down to Cheam on Boxing Day, to share in the turkey with your parents, and Duncan has asked George and me to share a duck on Christmas Day, so it looks as if we are going to do well! Last night we took Tiffy Moore to introduce him to Shepherds. He was very impressed by the place, and we had many pints of ale and a very pleasant evening. It was a most wonderful moonlit night, and we walked back from Shepherds across the park, and Tiffy told me all his troubles. It appears that Donald Brooks is responsible for putting him ashore for twelve months, and he is pretty furious about it and thinks that even at the end of the time he may not be allowed to go to sea. It is bad luck for him, he just loathes being in London. He was telling me that Jock had a shore job again, and is settled with wife and brattie at an RN Barracks at Southend! Might be a great deal worse. Darling I wonder where you will get pushed to. Wouldn't a nice spot in Scotland be heavenly? Pity there isn't a shore base near Aberdovey. The time really is whistling by isn't it? I'm sure by next spring you can quite justifiably put in for a rest from the sea. You've been in *Tartar* just about six months now.

Tonight is H-J's cocktail party, when the new Mrs H-J makes her first public appearance. Tomorrow Christmas Eve, we prepare for Christmas

Day, and make paper shades etc. for lights and whatnots, and have a few nogginses no doubt. I have purchased from some very dubious wine shop in Cricklewood a bottle of Cherry Brandy (so called) for the fabulous sum of 35/-, which I shall present to Duncan as my contribution to the Christmas feast. I only hope we shan't all be knocked flat by it! It is absolutely impossible to purchase any type of alc unless you have 'friends' or other influence. A good thing too I think.

The boys on the house are getting into the spirit of the season – when I came in last night I saw the strange spectacle of David Tennant climbing up the stairs outside the railings, and when I got to the top I was met by him and Brierley, both determined to support me into the Nurses' Home on their crossed hands – all very odd! The position was most undignified but luckily no one came along. I meant to write to you last night before I went to bed, but I'm afraid I was rather full of beer, and consequently extremely sleepy.

Robert has sent an airgraph greeting to the Matron and the Nurses for Christmas – very pleasant thought all are agreed. I've been very bad and sent hardly any cards, and of course have received packets, but it's too late now to try and send some in return. I had one from the Andersons which I did manage to return, and I sent one to Blairgowrie and one to Duncan's mother, but that's about all. I haven't even written many letters, somehow I just can't take in any festive spirit.

Jill was up last week with her cousin who lives in Oxford – we had a hilarious tea with much gossip. Next week she is bringing Wink and Ann up for a pantomime, to which we shall probably all go, and the week-end after New Year I'm going down to Oxford to stay with them – at least I may, it's rather a long way to go. One week-end too I've promised to go down to Chichester with Dorothy, her sister Pat has a flat there – it's near Portsmouth. So you see I'm obeying your instructions and getting around, although I wish very much you were here to get around with me.

After H-J's party – After midders.

Well, well, quite a party! The first person I saw was Tony Oddie in battle-dress with shoulder tabs. Compound fractured humerus and fractured metacarpals and severed radial nerve. Looking very well, but says it will be nine months before the Navy will pass him as fit.

Darling I can't write at length tonight – I'll describe it in full tomorrow. We went with H-J to the Ivy and had a terrific meal, marred rather by the fact that my escort (Bill Young) passed out in the middle, rather to Mrs H-J's disgust, but still an excellent party. More tomorrow when I can concentrate!

God bless my darling, and keep safe,

Always all yours, D

Lindo Wing,
SMH, Paddington

Christmas Eve, 1942

DR. J. SUCHET AND MISS J. P. JARCHÉ
The engagement is announced between Dr. Jack Suchet, of St. Mary's Hospital, W.2, eldest son of Mr. and Mrs. I. Suchet, of Capetown, South Africa, and Joan Patricia Jarché, only daughter of Mr. and Mrs. James Jarché, of Edgware, Middlesex.

My darling,

Our first Christmas married – I wonder what you have been doing. I've been decorating the room we are using tomorrow for the celebrations, very smart it is with bits of holly and evergreen stuck round the walls, and in the wardrobe no less than <u>13</u> bottles! We have a patient in who is manageress of the Hammersmith Palais de Danse, and she has presented us with much this and that, four bottles of whiskey, port, gin etc.!

The party opened tonight when Tiffy came up and had a strange drink called 'Whiskey liqueur', which appeared to be extremely potent! I have already popped back several gin and limes and one Dubonnet, and I have a feeling that the sprigs of holly I have just stuck up are all a little bit askew! No matter. I'm going round to the flat now to tuck into half a turkey which Ma managed to obtain by browbeating the wretched butcher. George for once is staying in (he came in from last night's party at 11 this morning) so we shall have a pleasant family party.

Actually I'm a bit tired after last night's 'do', but no doubt I shall feel a lot worse before the week-end is over. Last night's do was very funny. The usual H-J type of cocktail party, with the H-J specials coming round in large white jugs, and seeming to get stronger and stronger as the evening progressed. Sunbeam and H-J very obviously 'just wed' with their arms round each other's necks most of the time. Terrific heat and everybody getting extremely red in the face. Tony Oddie was there as I've told you, and we had a long chat. He seemed totally ignorant of your whereabouts, and said he didn't even know you had been on the same show. There was also a very drunken type called Peter Whitehead, very drunk indeed, who seemed very interested to know I was your wife, and kept coming back to shake my hand. Duggie and I had a moan together about the absence of our spouses and I was introduced to Leslie Bill by H-J as his 'almost adopted daughter'.

After about an hour and a half of the H-J specials I thought it was time I oiled off, so I made my way towards Mrs, and was told firmly that I was going to dine with them, so I didn't argue and had another 'special'. After much to-ing and fro-ing we were organised into two cars (7 of us in H-J's) and wafted down to the Ivy, where we had a sumptuous dinner in the company of John Clements and Walter Crisham. Unfortunately Bill Young passed out and was forced to spend most of the evening in the gents, attended to at intervals by Claude Newham.

However, by the time we got back to Mary's Bill was in very good form again, and no doubt the party was prolonged into the small hours. H-J is funny with a Mrs, although I suppose talking about 'my wife' comes quite naturally to him. There were a great many 'darlings' being flung around, and a good deal of promiscuous embracing. I had a long chat with Claude, beginning on the subject of The Griffin and Reggie Seed, and going on via this and that to the Navy, and the desirability of entering same. He is keen to join the Navy, but his wife is all against it and wants him to go into the Air Force. I told him that speaking as a wife I could recommend the Navy, and I thought it was far better than the Army or RAF, where I'm convinced the messes are sinks of iniquity and whatnot.

12 o'clock, Christmas Eve – Christmas Day

Happy Christmas to you darling, my own dear love.

We've had a very happy evening, Ma, George and I at the flat, and between us we consumed almost half a turkey!! Believe it or not

George, who usually eats very little, ate a whole leg. We had a quiet zizz afterwards, and then they walked back here with me – I was glad they did because it was just on closing time, and the collection of drunks round the district was fantastic. Except for some vague singing noises from Room 3 the hospital is very quiet tonight, the wards all decorated with holly and streamers and red shades. I think when you're alone hospital is a good place to be in for Christmas, but if you were home I think I would prefer the family. What is so good about being married is that however much you enjoy a party you know the best part is when you can discuss it together afterwards, and then forget all about it together.

My darling, I hope it won't be too long before we are together again – I'm so lonely for you.

God bless dear heart, and Good night.

Always yours,

Doris

The Manse, Cheam

Dec 27th

My darling,

We've now got to Sunday, and an after-lunch session at the Manse. Ma, George and I came down yesterday, and I'm staying on until tomorrow. John and Marian came over yesterday morning, and Margaret was here, so we had a very pleasant family party, and made havoc of a vast turkey and plum pudding.

Christmas Day was good, although of course not so good as last year. We started off with breakfast on the Floor (not the deck, but on Floor 1) and polished off bacon, sausage, tomato, mushrooms and fried eggs (reel shell eggs begged from the kitchen), toast, mince pies and tea. Just as we were sitting back and cigarettes were being handed round the Matron arrived to wish us a Merry Christmas and appeared delighted that we were enjoying ourselves. The unfortunate patients received rather scant attention I'm afraid, but they didn't complain, and were very understanding and good when we were slow to answer their bells.

We seemed to have acquired a very large collection of alc, including rum, whiskey, beer, gin and such odd things as cherry brandy, whiskey cocktail, and Dubonnet, lime, ginger ale, etc. The bar opened at 10:30, the first arrivals being Bill Young and Tiffy, with George not far behind. From then onwards it was open all day, with intervals of quiet for recuperation, when the ash was swept under the bed and the window was flung open to let out some of the fumes.

At mid-day we left the Floor to look after itself, and Margaret and I went over to Duncan's noggin session for Matrons, Sisters and the residents. After the Matron left everyone relaxed, and it was no shock to see Bill Young embracing Sister Victoria with much gusto under the mistletoe – to her evident enjoyment.

After lunch I did a bit of work, finding myself alone on the Floor while the rest went over to the Hospital to watch the ward shows (which I'm told were terrible). I made vast plates of sandwiches and threw around the patients' tea trays, and at 4:30 I decided I had done enough work, and went up to the 3rd floor, where Downer and Dorothy were entertaining a vast tea-party, which included H-J's two children, Dr Morris's 2-year old son, Gillian Willcox, Dickson's daughters, and the Mathews, Copes, Julers, H-Js, ADWs, etc. When I arrived, to my great surprise Dickson bore down on me and shook me firmly by the hand and introduced me to a very charming American Sergeant he had with him. After a session up there most of the party came down to the first floor, and we opened up the bar again. Dickson cheerfully accepted a run and lime I gave him and popped it back with no comment. Mrs Dickson was very charming and asked how you were, and when you were coming home.

After that George and Tiffy arrived, and after much coming and going from place to place, and consuming odd nogginses en route, we picked up Duncan and Bill Young and went round to Dunc's flat, where we had quite a party. Ate duck, played sardines and danced, and got just a weeny bit tiddly. I don't think I behaved myself awfully well darling, but then nobody else did either, except Audrey, so it didn't matter perhaps. We broke it up soon after twelve, and found our way back to hospital having pushed Tiffy (who was on duty at the Admiralty and spent most of the evening phoning his SBA) into a vast American Army car with a protesting coloured driver. Dorothy and I had a cuppa before going to bed, and a quiet moan about the absence of our Rogers – but we decided that we had really had a very pleasant time in spite our grass-widowhood.

I was lucky to get away for the rather stale clearing up period. I had a delightful week-end from Friday evening until tomorrow (Monday) at 6. Next week there is the New Year's Eve dance in the medical school on Friday, and George and I are going to take Duncan and Audrey out to a show one evening. It's been lovely having George down and he's been a great success locally! At Duncan's he sang his famous song *With my hand on myself now what have I here*, with very little tune but plenty of vigour.

This morning I walked up the hill with Marjorie Holliday. She says Keith is now a Major, and his field ambulance was the first into Tobruk. She hasn't heard for about a month, but she thinks he is probably in Sirte by now.

Rather a catastrophe this afternoon, because your parents' dog Timo has gone out and hasn't come back. Apparently he is liable to attach himself to anyone and just go off with them – very troublesome.

You've had some nice presents darling, which are being kept for you. Richard has sent a magnificent Waterman pen, and a lovely green leather powder compact for me. Your mother gave me some books including a lovely one with superb pictures of Arctic Regions. Then from me you've a rather prosaic present of three white shirts – but they are Gieves' best, and the last they are making with double cuffs. George bought them but they turned out to be a size too small, so I said I would buy them off him for you. Richard also sent me some silk stockings which was very good of him, and Marian gave me a large box of soap, which is always welcome.

I think I've probably missed the only post here today, so I'll keep this and post it in Town tomorrow. It's been a pleasant Christmas, but I've missed you so awfully much my darling, and thought of you all the time. Keep well my dearest, and come home soon to your very loving Wyf. X X X

St Mary's Hospital, Lindo Wing

Tuesday, Dec 29th

Dear darling,

Your letter no. 57, dated Dec 5th, arrived yesterday, the first for a month and welcome. No sign of any of the Air Mails you talk about, maybe they've got held up over Christmas. It was horrid not hearing from you for Christmas, and lovely to come back to a letter yesterday, even such a shortie. Dorothy heard as well yesterday, the first mail she's had since her Roger left, and she was very set up by it. It's funny how difficult it gets to write when you haven't heard for some time. Do you ever feel that? Everything seems awfully trivial when you know the letter won't reach its destination for weeks. I hope my efforts haven't been very dull, I'm rather afraid they have.

George is in bed with a bad septic throat which I am painting with Mandl's and dosing with aspirin, Ma nearly had a fit when I gave him 3 (5gr tabs) – I hope he will be better for New Year's Eve (selfishly).

Darling heart it was good to see your writing on an envelope again, I'm so looking forward to lots more. It's almost three months since you left, and I'm even lonelier for you than ever.

All my love sweetheart, and God bless,

Always and ever yours,

Doris

Lindo Wing,
SMH, Paddington

Dec 31st, 1942

Dear love,

Just a shortie to say 'Happy New Year' and to wish you lots of luck darling for 1943. I really do feel that things are beginning to look up, and that it won't be too long before the Navy decides it can get along without you. Sweetheart it mustn't be too long, I do so want you back.

Today your Air Mail letter card arrived, sent on Dec 7th. A lovely present for the New Year, I must see if I can't organise some from this end. I sent the family bit to your mother. I nearly sent her the whole thing, and then I didn't, because I don't feel I want anyone else ever to read what you write to me, it's rather like kissing you in public which I always hate.

Sweetheart, I hope you have had some of my letters by now – I know how miserable it is going from day to day without getting anything. I'm afraid they were rather dull efforts, most of them. I'm thrilled by the ciné camera – you <u>must</u> have one taken of yourself, most important, now please do Roger, because I'd love a picture of *la barbe*.

Only eight days to the anniversary. I've just about given up hope of having you back by then, but I'll have a good think about you at 3 P.M. (Actually I'm going with Jill and the children to see *Jack and Jill* in the afternoon, and then to Chichester with Dorothy for the week-end.)

It's 1943 now – I wonder what kind of a year it will be. As long as it brings you home to me I don't really care.

All my love dear sweetheart,

Always and ever yours,

X X X X, Doris B.O.L.T.O.P.

January 1943

In his State of the Union address on January 7 1943, President Roosevelt said to the American people: 'The Axis powers knew that they must win the war in 1942 or eventually lose everything. I do not need to tell you that our enemies did not win the war in 1942.' He summed up the progress of the war during 1942, and then went on:

> I cannot prophesy. I cannot tell you when or where the United Nations [the Allies] are going to strike next in Europe. But we are going to strike – and strike hard. I cannot tell you whether we are going to hit them in Norway, or through the Low Countries, or in France, or through Sardinia or Sicily, or through the Balkans, or through Poland – or at several points simultaneously. But I can tell you that no matter where and when we strike by land, we and the British and the Russians will hit them from the air heavily and relentlessly. Day in and day out we shall heap tons upon tons of high explosives on their war factories and utilities and seaports.
>
> Hitler and Mussolini will understand now the enormity of their miscalculations—that the Nazis would always have the advantage of superior air power as they did when they bombed Warsaw, and Rotterdam, and London and Coventry. That superiority has gone—forever. Yes, the Nazis and the Fascists have asked for it—and they are going to get it.[1]

On 8 January a plan was agreed in London for bombing enemy territory, and on 16 January a major bombing raid was launched on Berlin. The following night the Germans retaliated by bombing London; Dorothy wrote in her diary, 'Air raid warning went at 8:30 pm – real gun fire so quite noisy for about 20 mins.' Then: 'Another warning at 4:40 am. Very heavy barrage.'[2] This time Doris found the raids much more frightening than she had before, as she and Dorothy scrambled out of bed and prepared to take shelter, clutching their most important possessions: marriage certificate, photograph of husband, lipstick.

In Stalingrad the German forces who had occupied the city were now completely surrounded by the Red Army and in the grip of the Russian winter. They were running out of food, ammunition, medicine, fuel and fervour. Hitler refused to let the starving, frost-bitten garrison surrender, expecting them to fight to the last man. Nonetheless they did surrender at the end of January, and 91,000 exhausted German soldiers were taken prisoner. Casualties on both sides had been staggering. It was a devastating loss for the Nazis and a huge psychological victory for the Soviet Union. Stalingrad proved that the once seemingly invincible Wehrmacht could and would be defeated.

Roy Jenkins describes Churchill's travelling in 1943 as 'almost frenetic'.[3] It began on 12 January when Churchill flew to Casablanca to confer with President Roosevelt and the British and American Chiefs of Staff. Sir Charles Wilson, who went with him, reported: 'I found the PM in high spirits, elated to be once more on the move.'[4] His jubilant mood didn't last long. Once again the Prime Minister flew in an unconverted Liberator bomber with minimal accommodation for its illustrious passenger. In *The Hinge of Fate* Churchill describes the journey:

My journey was a little anxious. In order to heat the 'Commodore' they had established a petrol engine inside which generated fumes and raised various heating points to very high temperatures. I was woken up at two in the morning, when we were over the Atlantic 500 miles from anywhere, by one of these heating points burning my toes, and it looked to me as if it might soon get red-hot and light the blankets. I therefore climbed out of my bunk and woke up Peter Portal, who was sitting in the well beneath, asleep in his chair, and drew his attention to this very hot point. We looked around the cabin and found two others, which seemed equally

on the verge of becoming red-hot. We then went down into the
bomb alley ... and found two men industriously keeping alive this
petrol heater. From every point of view I thought this was most
dangerous. The hot points might start a conflagration, and the
atmosphere of petrol would make an explosion imminent. Portal
took the same view. I decided that it was better to freeze than to
burn, and I ordered all heating to be turned off, and we went back
to rest shivering in the ice-cold winter air about eight thousand
feet up, at which we had to fly to be above the clouds. I'm bound
to say this struck me as rather an unpleasant moment.[5]

Josef Stalin had declined to attend the meeting in Casablanca
because he said he needed to be close to the major military action
taking place in Russia. Over the course of ten days the British and
American leaders co-ordinated their strategy for 1943. Churchill
strongly believed that the Allied forces were not yet strong enough
for an assault on France and that the invasion, then under the
codename 'Operation Roundup', should be postponed until 1944.
The successes of 'Torch' and El Alamein bolstered his opinion
that an invasion of Italy via Sicily was the best way of attacking
mainland Europe. The Americans, on the other hand, thought the
emphasis should be on building up their joint forces of men and
materiel in Britain preparatory to launching 'Roundup' in 1943.
Eventually Churchill's view prevailed. Roosevelt and Churchill also
issued a communique stating that the war would end only with
Germany's unconditional surrender; there would be no negotiated
settlement.

Following the Casablanca conference the Prime Minister and the
President spent a couple of days in Marrakesh, enjoying a brief but
relaxing respite from their heavy responsibilities in the pleasure
of each other's company. They had struck up a close and abiding
personal friendship since their very first meeting in August 1941.
At that time Roosevelt told his cousin, 'I like [Winston Churchill]
... he is a tremendously vital person'.[6] Harry Hopkins, Roosevelt's
personal envoy to Great Britain, wrote, 'They established an easy
intimacy, a joking informality and a moratorium on pomposity
and cant.'[7] Although they often disagreed, particularly as the war
dragged on, the two men had great admiration and respect for one
another. Kay Halle, socialite, journalist and long-time friend of

both the Churchill and Roosevelt families, documented Churchill's opinion that 'to encounter Roosevelt, with all his buoyant sparkle, his iridescent personality, and his sublime confidence, was like opening your first bottle of champagne. That physical effect it had on you was like the effect champagne had'.[8]

After Marrakesh Churchill flew to Cairo for four days, and then to meet with Turkish President Inönü in the coastal city of Adana. He was accompanied by Sir Alexander Cadogan, Permanent Under-Secretary at the Foreign Office. Turkey was technically neutral, and Churchill was keen to get President Inönü to enter the war on the side of the Allies. He was unsuccessful in his quest, but was reassured to know that Turkey would remain friendly and would allow the British to build a stockpile of war materiel in the country.

As usual, Sir Charles Wilson had travelled with the Prime Minister to Morocco, though fortunately there was no call on his medical services while they were abroad. He wrote in his memoir: 'I am the only person of the whole party who has nothing to do; I'm here only as insurance.'[9] However, he had reason to be pleased with himself, for he had been named as a peer in the New Year's Honours list, and as 1943 began, St Mary's Hospital was celebrating the success of their Dean. Wilson took the title Baron Moran of Manton in the County of Wiltshire, and on 8 March he would take his seat in the House of Lords.

There was another celebration for Doris and the Miles family on 7 January when Roger's elder sister Marian gave birth to a daughter. She was the first grandchild for Annie and Ted and was christened Sally. Richard wrote to Roger from Washington: 'I forgot to gloat as I meant to over the arrival of our Miss Sally. I felt quite goofy about it, and I hear it has had a wonderful effect on the home life. I am just delighted as could be. Now you buck up and do the same – I'm still not in the running.'

In Roger's absence Doris celebrated their first wedding anniversary on 8 January at the Ivy with her brother George and close friends Duncan and Audrey Gregg, and Jack Suchet and his fiancée Joan. It was a delightful evening, which ended up with Doris slightly the worse for wear. ('Whistled as a coot' is the euphemism she uses, a charmingly whimsical expression that I have come across nowhere else except in her letters.) Later that month, Doris, Duncan and Audrey attended the Suchets' wedding at the Mirabelle, a fashionable restaurant in Mayfair that was one of Winston Churchill's favourite places to dine out. Duncan received his call-up papers shortly afterwards, so there would be no such parties for a while.

On 24 January, following her description of the Suchets' wedding, Doris wrote: 'This time last year we were at Ealing, remember? Very odd place, remember trying to empty the wretched radiator of the car? And the policemen in the bedroom?' This tantalising snippet has puzzled and intrigued me for months, ever since I started compiling this book. It was just a couple of weeks after their wedding, and the car may have been the one lent to them by Roger's brother-in-law John Gilbert.

Here is a possible explanation for their presence in Ealing, a suburb in West London. In 1938, faced with the looming threat of hostilities, a Home Office Committee chaired by Sir Charles Wilson drew up a plan to deal with air-raid casualties in London. The city and the surrounding area was divided into ten sectors with one of the major teaching hospitals at the apex of each. The outlying hospitals would be 'overflow' facilities where patients could be sent, leaving the London beds available for casualties. When war broke out in September 1939 the scheme was immediately implemented, and many medical students and staff were moved to these satellite locations. St Mary's was at the top of Sector 6, which stretched from Amersham to Basingstoke and also encompassed Ealing. So it seems likely that in January 1943 Roger was working in Ealing at the (now defunct) King Edward Memorial Hospital.

However, I can offer no explanation for the policemen in the bedroom! To me this epitomises my regret at not having started this work while my mother was alive and lucid – how I would love to have heard her undoubtedly funny story about this incident.

Doris spent the next weekend visiting Dorothy's sister Pat Reynish, who lived with her architect husband in the West Sussex city of Chichester, not far from Portsmouth. Chichester is a small, historic city founded by the Romans, with beautiful Georgian architecture and a celebrated cathedral dating back to the 11th century. It is the only medieval English cathedral which is visible from the sea (the spire can be seen for many miles and is a landmark for sailors) and the only one to have a free-standing bell tower. The sheltered harbour where Vespasian brought his Second Augusta legion exactly

1,900 years earlier, in 43AD, is close by. It was in this city that Doris and Roger later settled, where they raised their family and where they remained for the rest of their lives. The Crown and Anchor pub in Dell Quay, where Doris and her friends enjoyed a pint on that winter evening, is now a favourite watering hole of their son. Although for Doris and Dorothy the train journey back to London was long, even today it would take close to three hours to travel from Chichester to St Mary's on a Sunday night - and that is without the obvious delays of wartime travel!

The war was never far away and continued to make its presence felt. Jack Suchet's sons John and David remember him telling them of the day some months earlier when a group of young house doctors decided to go to a nightclub, the Café de Paris in Coventry Street. Somebody had to stay behind on duty at St Mary's and Jack drew the short straw. So he was not there that night when the club was destroyed in a bombing raid and thirty-four people were killed, including all of his confrères.

Now Doris was saddened by the news of her friend Surgeon-Lieutenant James MacFarlane, lost at sea on the destroyer *Achates* escorting the Russian convoys. First Lieutenant Loftus Peyton-Jones, who had been a childhood friend of Doris and George in Guernsey and a contemporary of George's at Dartmouth Naval College, survived to write a report about the incident. Peyton-Jones took command of the stricken ship when the captain was killed and continued to provide covering smoke for the convoy until the ship sank, for which he was awarded the Distinguished Service Order (DSO) for gallantry under fire. The unfortunate Lieutenant MacFarlane was posthumously mentioned in dispatches.

It made Doris all the more fearful for Roger's safety, for in September *Achates* had escorted the same convoy as *Tartar*, and both ships had been in the Mediterranean for Operation Torch. She knew that Roger and *Tartar* were still stationed in the warmer waters of the Mediterranean, although that was little consolation. Security concerns precluded him from telling her his exact location, but newspaper reports which mentioned his ship as well as those in which his friends were serving allowed her to make an educated guess as to his whereabouts. She mentions 'Beetle's Wagon', but both the name of his ship and Beetle's identity remain a mystery.

Lindo Wing,
SMH, Paddington

5th Jan, 43

Roger darling,

Scrumptious Christmas cable arrived from you yesterday – undated and no indication of where it was dispatched, but I have my suspicions. Funnily enough Dorothy had two cables yesterday, and when she proudly showed them to me I was able to produce mine, like a conjurer. Tom Kemp told me this morning that you had also dispatched one to the boys, which was much appreciated. The one I had was decorated with festive bits of holly and such, very 'Yulee Tidey' as Jill would say. I gather from the *Daily Mirror* that Alan is steaming about the Med, accompanied no doubt by you and Peter. Tell him from me to keep his hat on tight, and keep yours on too.

Very Great Doctor

SIR CHARLES WILSON, in becoming a peer while President of the Royal College of Physicians, achieves a very rare double honour. Lord Dawson was made a viscount when President, but he had already been a baron for 11 years before he took that high office.

Since the war Sir Charles has become better known to the public, partly as being the doctor of the Prime Minister, whom he accompanied to Washington and Moscow, and partly for his efforts in sending medical supplies to Russia, which he also visited in the autumn of 1941.

All doctors, however, have long known that in Charles Wilson the profession had a physician of great intellectual power. He has made St. Mary's Hospital Medical School, of which he is Dean, into one of the best in the country.

Sorry this enclosure is a bit mucky, I picked it off the kitchen table where it was being used as a tablecloth – Dickson's crack is rather good:–

'I don't know whether to say "My Lord" or "My God".'

Great chitty-chat in the camp over the admission of Mr and Mrs H-J both suffering from boils. His are really pretty bad, and they are both being looked after by Dickson, much complicated treatment, including the use of Penicillin ointment and sub-boil injections of sodium citrate. I went up tonight to say goodnight, and told them about Married Alley and its inmates. They were very amused. Dorothy and I have long evening sessions over cups of tea when we discuss everybody, usually to their discredit, and invariably we come to the conclusion that, miserable as this grass-widowhood is, we'd rather have it this way than have you both sitting back at home and not doing a peanut.

Tomorrow, in honour of our first wedding anniversary, I'm taking Duncan and Audrey, Jack Suchet and Joan, and George to the Ivy for a quiet din, it should be rather fun. I'm afraid it will cost rather a bit, do you mind darling? There's really packets of mun tucked away in the bank, and I'm sure if we were together we'd celebrate in style. Sweetheart I do wish you were going to be here for it – you will be very much there in my heart my darling.

God keep you safe dearest,

All my love to you always,

Doris

Lindo Wing,
St Mary's Hospital, Paddington, W2

Jan 6th

Darling love,

A grand letter from you today – no date, but in it you describe your New Year's Eve celebrations, so I imagine it's quite recent. I haven't had any of the others which you say I should have received by Christmas, so I'm looking forward to packets of mail in the near future. It was grand to hear of your doings, and to know that you are not spending your entire time stoodging around the ocean. You were luckier than we were to have brandy on your pud, but I expect our pud was better than yours was.

Oddly enough Dorothy had a letter from her Roger this morning, and as we've had mail together for the last four times I thought there was probably something for me somewhere. I wonder if you escorted him out. He is allowed to say that he is somewhere in North Africa, but that's as far as it goes. He gave a very amusing description of his duties as chief sanitation officer, and also of his official visit to the local brothel, accompanied by police. A very low and sordid spot I gather. Dorothy is terribly thrilled to be getting letters, but I'm sure he doesn't write as well as you do (shameless flattery, but I bet he doesn't). You can't imagine how marvellous it is when letters come, because that's all we exist for really. In spite of the job, and odd parties and things that crop up, it's not a real life apart from you.

So glad you have seen Alec M. He will no doubt be able to refute the story of the tracheotomy performed by Peter Porter and himself, which I once told you. Please give him my very warmest congratulations on his brattie, and say I'm mighty envious of his wife. Are Peter and Alan still with you? My best regards to them if they are.

The enclosed rather fierce document you must guard with care, <u>not</u> lose, and consult income tax experts on same. It is meant to show my income, and also my modest wages received from Mr Caldwell (who by the way is in Albert suffering from the 'Gastrics'). It may be of some assistance to you when wrestling with the Income Tax form you have no doubt already received. If you have any trouble write to my solicitor, and he will fix things for you. He is C. Conyers-Lowe, Stapleton and Son, Stamford, Lincs, a very obliging man.

We are taking Duncan and Audrey and Jack and Joan to the Ivy tonight, a small celebration of the 8th. I was telling one of our patients about it today, and the nice old thing sent his wife out to buy me an orchid to wear, wasn't it sweet of him? So I shall look very smart.

<u>Midders</u>

Darling, I'm whistled as a <u>coot</u>!! Forgive me sweetheart. We've had a grand evening and Duncan has been a pet. He escorted me to the door and said it was a marvellous anniversary party. Joy and love of my heart I love you, forgive me for being so whistled – Precious husband, X X X X X X

<u>Morning</u>

As a coot last night I'm afraid! Pay no regard. All my love darling – D. X X

St Mary's Hospital, Paddington

My darling,

There's no date to this letter because it's not one of the series, but a special letter written for a special day. I know it won't reach you on that day, but that can't be helped, I'll be thinking of you all the same. I wondered for a long time what kind of letter to write, what you would like best to have, because it's a great occasion, our first anniversary, although we shan't be together to celebrate it.

I'll begin by saying again, 'Thank you darling for marrying me, and for making me so much happier than I ever imagined possible.' I never doubted that we would be happy together, but I never knew quite how happy and wonderful it was going to be. So my grateful thanks, dear Roger, for my married state.

I thought I would tell you some of the big moments of the past year, and see if they were high spots for you too – beginning at 3 pm Thursday, January 8th. That was the first big moment, but not the biggest. My knees shook so! I know that I didn't follow the service very closely because I was concentrating so hard on trying to keep them still. And I can't remember a word of what the old boy said to us, but I can remember your father's prayer.

I know I wanted awfully badly to kiss you, but I felt a bit shy. I can't remember going to the hotel afterwards. All through the reception I kept looking at my ring to make sure it was real, and for once I didn't care if I had a shiny nose or not. When we got back to the flat you told me that I looked radiant, do you remember? I think you were almost as tongue-tied as I was.

I wonder how you felt about that first night. It was like finding a new sense, wasn't it? And sharing a wonderful experience – feeling that there was something I could give you that no one else in the world could, and that by giving it to you I became part of you. You were so dear and gentle, my love, so sweet and kind as I knew you would be.

The honeymoon was fun, wasn't it? I usually get so bored with people on holidays, and end up by wishing I had never come, but I've never been bored with you, that's one of the marvellous things about it, just being together makes everything different and exciting. I liked waking up in the morning and finding you there, and knowing we had a whole day together and another night and another morning. I even liked being alone for a bit, because it was so lovely when you came back.

We didn't know each other awfully well when we got married, did we? I don't think Casualty and the back streets of Paddington taught us a lot about each other, but I always felt I knew you, and that you and I thought about things in the same way. You never asked me if I could cook, or if I had any bad habits, very important points I'm told.

The next spot was a very dim one. It was when I came to Haslar and you had the yellow illness. Darling, how I hated seeing you all yellow in that miserable place, and not being able to do a thing for you. That was a very low day. Basingstoke was a bit better, in spite of the cold, and that Sunday at Bradfield comes very high indeed.

The very lowest moment of all was when you went up to Scapa to join the *Trinidad* – I felt so utterly desolate, and so horribly sorry for myself! That lasted for about a week, but I got over it.

The biggest moment of the year came afterwards, I wonder if you even remember it. It was the day you came down from Glasgow, with a week's growth and a dirty bandage around your head. And I hadn't slept for a minute the night before. But it wasn't meeting you on the station, or the first kiss. I was getting a shirt from the top of the linen cupboard for you, and you put your arms round me, and looked up at me, and darling, you'll never know how near I was to crying all over you.

Wales was fine all the way through, even the rain. And Portsmouth was good too. The next parting wasn't quite so bad, and I was so pleased to have seen the ship so that I could think of you in a definite place, instead of just vague surroundings. The mis-thing was the worst bad patch of the year, but seeing you again made up for it a bit. Edinburgh was in a way even better than Wales, definitely a top line place. But oh, wasn't the time short. Will we ever have long enough together, without that hectic feeling of having to cram so much into every minute? The last three months (it's been three months since you left) have been quite bearable but rather monotonous, and of course the infrequency of mail has been horrid. But I feel that the worst is over, and that if we just go boxing on 'There's gonna be a Great Day'.

Come back soon, my darling, to your always very loving and very proud wife,

Doris

Lindo Wing,
SMH, Paddington

Monday, Jan 11th

My darling,

The stream of mail has ended and letters no longer dribble in, so I suppose there will be another gap of three weeks or a month before I get any more. Actually I've only had three letters you wrote in November, one of Dec 7th, and nothing more until the Dec 15 onwards series, so there may be a few back numbers floating around, unless they have gone to the bottom. There's a horrid feeling of anti-climax after a large bunch of mail – I've re-read the last lot millions of times until I almost know them by heart. Hope there will be some more soon.

Duncan was over this morning. He's had his papers, but now the Medical Committee say they can't release him till March, when I believe Bill Young is taking over, having finished his MB. Anyway Dunc is all set to go, and champing to be off. I was able to give him a few tips, such as keeping testimonials in a safe place, and not placing too much faith in those written by H-J. And I said you would no doubt be writing to give him all the low-down. He is keen to get on to an aircraft carrier, which seems to be the thing to do now. But he is a bit stuck as to what is going to happen to Audrey. I'm certainly very lucky to have such a convenient job for a base, she, poor thing, will be very much at a loose end when he goes.

We've got another potential resident in Married Alley. Esmé Rees has very rapidly become engaged to an RAF pilot, and is being married shortly. She went today to buy the ring, and got it at Perry's – same as mine (but not as nice as mine).

Had a very pleasant week-end with Dorothy Pugh's sister and brother-in-law in Chichester – it's a charming spot, and they are delightful people. He is an architect, and works in Portsmouth, and she is secretary to the Hampshire (or Sussex) Agricultural Committee. They've got a very tasty flat in the main street of the town, quite near the Cathedral, and if ever we get to Pompey again on our travels we are to look them up.

On Saturday evening we walked about two miles to a little pub at Dell Quay, on one of the creeks, and consumed a humble pint in a real old country-style pub. There were two delightful matelots who, with many blushes, sang a song called *My brother Sylveste*, and a Canadian corporal, extremely fat, who, with no blushes at all, sang the Canadian

Army's version of many well-known ditties. So on the way back Dorothy and I gave a few excerpts from the Mary's collection, and we strode home to the tune of *The Virgin Sturgeon* and *The Two Flies*!

Sunday was wet and misty, and we spent most of the morning in bed – two spring mattresses in front of the sitting room fire – very comfy, and in the afternoon we went for a short walk to get up an appetite for a big tea. We caught the 8:44 back, and after much changing, and tubeing from Victoria, we landed up for a cup of tea in the VTR at 12 m.n. It was a good break getting right away, though funny going into that part of the world without you. We had two air raid warnings while we were there, but no 'incidents'.

Did you know that James MacFarlane's ship had been written off? The *Achates*, it was in Saturday's paper, and as far as anybody knows James is missing. Made me feel quite sick. I shall be so terribly thankful when you are safely on dry land again.

I was talking to Jack Suchet this morning about his forthcoming knot-tying. They are going to live at Chiltern Court, and Joan is carrying on with her job. I'm so glad for him, and I'm sure he will make an excellent husband. Not so good as you though. Taking a look round the husbands and husbands-to-be I see around me, I can still give you top marks darling, and that's not because I'm in love with you (I am of course) – but viewing you quite impersonally. You're such good fun, and so intelligent – I can't stand people whose brain works slowly, it's one of my faults.

My congratulations to the Chief on his brass hat. I expect you will be sorry when he goes. You and Henry will be the only old married men left, won't you? I wonder if you will have one of George's pals. Don't let him lead you astray if you do!

I haven't done very much about answering your letters – as you say it's rather dreadful to read nothing but, yes I did so and so, and I'm glad Aunt Fanny's boils are better. Talking of boils, I laughed like anything at your bit about H-J having a boiler-clean – all very pun-like as he's been suffering something cruel with carbuncles and whatnots. However they are better now, and he did a partial gastrectomy on Sunday, on a case which had already had a partial gastrectomy done before, so I should say he had recovered.

George was very amused at the talk of the sailors singing *My Brother Sylveste* – apparently a well known rugger dittie, we sang it coming back from the flat tonight.

Must pack this up now and have a bath, also a manicure and cut my toenails. Are you all right for scissors and nail files, combs etc.? I'll see if there are any instruments made suitable for trimming beards, I should think a pair of theatre dressing sciss would be the thing.

My love to the beard, I'm longing to see it in the full growth, very exciting! Are there still open spaces down the left side?

Goodnight dear sweetheart. I'm loving you all the time, and longing to have you back. Take care of yourself my darling,

Always your most loving wife,

Doris X X X X X B.O.L.T.O.P. O O O O O (hugs)

Lindo Wing,
St Mary's Hospital, Paddington, W2

Saturday, Jan 16th

My dear darling,

Feeling very depressed today – miserable day to begin with, and I always feel depressed on Saturdays when it's my afternoon and week-end on. Also we have a gastric of H-J's, 6th day, vomiting like fun and a suspected paralytic ileus – what a picnic! I must have a quick cup of tea to improve my condition. I'll tell you a story, I think it's rather a pleasant little one:

Small boy had to go to hospital to have his tonsils and adenoids out. While he was in the doctor thought it would be a good opportunity to perform another small operation, namely a circ. All went well, and in a few days small boy went home. Some little time later it was decided that small boy's small sister should have her tonsils and adenoids out. 'Oh it's nothing,' said small boy, 'it doesn't hurt and you stay in bed and have nice nurses to read to you and you get ice cream to eat, but you'll be awfully surprised where your adenoids are!'

Went last night with Dorothy to the SMH Dramatic Society play *Murder Party*. Really excellently done, and I alone guessed who done it. Brian Davies was to the fore as a young detective, and the nurses in it displayed great talent. I really must make an effort and get myself organised, I should love to take part.

Saw Tony Oddie this afternoon. He told me he had just received a letter from you, which had been chasing him around the countryside. His hand is still very swollen and his arm is in plaster. Pretty poor prognosis I rather gathered. Barbara Emerson is on the sick list too, she's been warded in Ophthalmic for some time now with some form of conjunctivitis – she says she's fed up with her eyes, and Duncan and life in general. Also Peter has been sent to North Africa, and being in the regular Army is likely to remain there, even after the war. Still as she said, and as Dorothy and I say about twice a week, we'd rather have it the way it is, and after all we had as much chance of getting killed in the blitz as you have now. But it isn't awfully comforting.

Margaret came up this morning to see Eva off to Devon, and looked in at the flat on her way out to lunch. She goes back on Monday. She was funny describing your letter where you told them how you were singing *O come, O come, Emmanuel,* and nobody knew the tune except you. How did your solo in *Good King Wenceslas* go? I should love to have heard you. Margaret has also been knocking back cod liver oil and malt, and finds it is just the thing for keeping coldies away. Touch wood I haven't had a cold this year, all due to radiomalt, do you think I could interest them in a testimonial in exchange for a free supply (I get it free now anyway).

Dickson has started a rumour that Jim MacGavin has got the MC and is missing in Tunisia – but Dickson is always starting rumours, and this is a shocking place for them. Every day something new is going round.
Later

I've had a marvellous idea! Can't imagine why I never thought of it before. It's simply to take a one-roomed flat in the same block as Ma, and live out. I've got quite enough stuff to furnish one room, and then when you do get to Town we'll have somewhere of our own without bothering about hotels and squashing in with Ma. Approve? The only snag is that there most probably won't be a flat free for some time. As for mun, they pay me more if I live out, and the extra just about pays the rent. Excellent. I'm so thrilled, thinking about it! I'll just get the bare necessities, and then when you come we can choose things together to add to it. Won't it be fun, having something of our own, even though it's only one room (bathroom, kitchen and usual offices also of course). Darling, write soon and say you approve, I'm so looking forward to getting on with it.

Goodnight my dearest dear –
All my love always darling,
Doris

Lindo Wing,
SMH, Paddington

January 18th, Mon.

My darling,

Your Air Mail of Jan 7th arrived today. Very welcome after a gap of ten days or so. Thank you dear for it, although I was disappointed not to receive the sonnet. Nobody has ever written poetry for me before – at least not to my knowledge. There's not a great many words that rhyme with Doris, except Boris and Horace (and perhaps forest!). I was thrilled to think of your party, and I imagined you all having a noggin together to many more happy years. My best to all the boys, and I'm looking forward to knocking back a few with them at the Fountains on our next leave. Pity you didn't contact Hugh Richardson, I'm sure he will be very pleased to see you, he's an awfully nice type, although he would call me 'Popsie' at the top of his voice in public places – anyone less like a popsie than me! I see reports in the newspapers every now and again about Beetle's Wagon going to and from, so I suppose you are doing much the same thing.

Had a long letter from Mig Walker today. Michael has left Kenya, being relieved by Baskerville – and he is now at a camp outside Plymouth waiting for his shore job, which Mig has a suspicion is going to be at Stornaway in the Hebrides. She herself is in pod, and hopes to produce in July. She says that if they do go to the Hebrides the brattie will probably be born clad in Harris tweed and speaking Gaelic – I'm hoping to see her soon, so will get all the low-down. She was rather funny about knitting small garments – apparently there is a great shortage of baby wool, so she is buying pinks and blues ad lib, and says she will have to make the things in stripes then it won't matter if it's a boy or a girl. Nice people they are, we must definitely keep in touch. I wish they could get settled in this part of the world and then I could see something of them.

We had a couple of air-raids last night – very few planes, but the barrage was terrific, Portsmouth's was nothing to it. A few bombs appeared to be falling, but it was very short, and not much damage that we've heard of. I was quite incredibly shaken by it, and was much more frightened than I've ever been before – I suppose it's really a question of getting used to it. The second raid was at 5 a.m. Dorothy and I both dressed, and I packed my small bag with a pair of pyjamas, a lipstick, my marriage certificate and your photograph, and felt much better! The all clear went at 6 so I went back to bed. But don't worry about me darling, I feel safer here than anywhere, and I can always go down to the tunnel, and Dorothy is here to hold my hand. Luckily she holds the same views as I do about getting dressed and being ready with clothes on instead of waiting for the bomb in a night dress. I don't think we'll get any more, they had to do something because we bombed Berlin the night before, but it wasn't much of an effort.

A long mad letter from Jill yesterday, among other things she has begun again with 'Elmer' who is 'so VITAL' in capitals, underlined. Also she is going to Haslar to visit a charming Commander called Sloane, but don't tell Elmer, and Gerald Turner is coming down for the week-end, but don't tell Sloane! I don't know where I am with them all – I've written and told her to do nothing until I have inspected all the contestants. She's coming up for the day on Monday week, to 'hear all the noos', which certainly isn't very much, and will probably degenerate into a session of 'lowies'. She collects the lowest lowies I've ever heard – no doubt from Elmer – I wouldn't put anything past Elmer!

George has had a filthy cold again, in spite of the Tabs Eastonii Co I've been forcing down his throat. He looks so washed out. I think l'affaire Pamela shook him a good bit, although he won't admit it. He says he's through with dolls, and won't believe me when I say he'll probably marry someone in no time at all. I hope he does. I think marriage improves everybody – although I don't know whether it's improved me, I certainly feel better for it. Life is so much more worth living, isn't it, when you've something definite to live for, and someone too.

I'm going out with George for a noggin tonight – actually I'd much rather go to bed, but he's keen to go even though he does have a cold, so I don't want to disappoint him. I'll try and stick to Cables and the Great Western, but I suppose he will want to move to the 'Clickety Click' or some other low haunt. Funny he can't stay long in one pub, but thinks the whole joy of the evening is to go from pub to pub and have a pint or two in each.

I had a compliment paid me last night (says she vainly) – Mr Juler told me I had looked very nice at the New Year's Eve Dance. Wasn't that sweet of him? I was so pleased.

10:30 P.M.

Well, the evening was not a great success! Poor old George had a touch of D & V without the V, and was keen to get home as soon as he could. Apparently he consumed two cascaras last night, which were his undoing. He says it's all due to being ashore, and he's never coming ashore again, although he admits that being at sea is not much better!

Well darling, I'm going along to find out if there is any tea being brewed, and then I'll be crashing the swede. We're ten days into our second year darling, and it's going to be even better than the first. The thought of having you here for weeks and months on end is more than I can bear to think about – I do long for it so much.

Dear heart, more than ever your very loving wife,

Doris X X X X X X

The Manse, Cheam

Sunday, Jan 24th

My darling,

I'm sitting in front of the Manse fire, just underneath the Mediterranean map, and wondering where you are at this moment. The Med looks very vast from here, I hope you are not having to stoodge around it too much.

I came down yesterday afternoon, and return this evening after a very pleasant week-end, spent in the usual manner in sleeping, eating, and (yes, truly) taking Timo for a long walk over the Downs. I went to the kirk this morning and assured everyone that you were in good form. I was also somewhat embarrassed by being asked how the baby was. She is very well as far as my somewhat inexperienced eyes could see, although the family are very worried because she doesn't make any noise. Also the air raids upset the food supply, and she is half on the bottle and half on her mother. But I think things are improving. Marian is going home on Thursday, and Mrs Gilbert is going to stay on with them for a week until things get settled. I'm bitterly disappointed that they won't let me go, I think I'd be doing a lot more good helping Marian than nursing neurotic types on the Wing.

Your father seems much better, and preached very well this morning. They have a new doctor called Strachan, and he appears to be very conscientious and efficient. Timo is in terrific form, and rushed about barking madly at the top of his voice. He still goes out and gets lost periodically, and is a great worry to your parents. When you get your shore job we must try and have him with us if it's possible. He's very affectionate, and sits on anyone's lap if they will stroke him. (He's lost at the moment, but no panic).

Yesterday was Jack Suchet's wedding, a very excellent party, only lacking your presence. Dorothy and I togged up in our best, and made a triumphant exit from the Hospital gazed upon by odd nurses, Jack Harvey, etc. We arrived at the Mirabelle at about 12:30, and proceeded to knock back a couple of sherrys, and conducted a somewhat questionable conversation with Maurice Nellan, the theme of which was, should men throw in the sponge as far as women are concerned when they are married. I missed the end of the conversation, but I wasn't terribly interested – I've met Maurice Nellan before!

The lunch was terrific, and just for spite, and in reply to your tales of fried eggs and spinach omelettes, I'll tell you what we had. A most enormous hors d'oeuvres, with quantities of luscious fishies, including bits of lobster wrapped up with anchovies – a boiled chicken with rice, brussels, potatoes, beans, carrots, asparagus, mushrooms (honest boss, no exaggeration), cream and wine sauce. Then a fresh baby fig with cream & jam, wedding cake, coffee – my mouth is watering all over again!

I sat at a rather isolated bit at the end of the table, and had a long and very interesting conversation with Wing Commander Jimmy Jeffries. Nice chap, I don't think I've met him before, but he seemed to know all about you. We talked sailing, and Mary's people, and more sailing, and a good time was had by both. Other guests – about 40 in all – were mostly Joan's relations, Sister Hepworth, McElligott, Duncan and Audrey, Dick Willcox and Sadie, and one or two oddments. Old Jack was pretty quiet, I don't think he'd had enough to drink. He made a nice little speech as also did Dr Gage. They went off at 2 to Lynton! Hope they have decent weather, it has been perfect these last few days, and this afternoon on the downs it was lovely, very blue sky, and sun, and a few clouds, and warm enough to go without a coat.

This time last year we were at Ealing, remember? Very odd place, remember trying to empty the wretched radiator of the car? And the policemen in the bedroom?

<u>Cont. Monday</u>

Very amusing journey back last night. An army officer just back from Tobruk, two married dolls from Wales, very chatty, and a Canadian Air Force chap. The conversation flowed freely, and ranged from crossword puzzles and London policemen, to the attractions of Wales and Scotland. It turned out that the Army Captain was being stationed at Dolgelly, and there was much argument between the relative beauty of North and South Wales. I stood out strongly for the North, and held forth as though I had lived there all my life! Anyway it passed the time (I came back the long way from Belmont) and the journey passed in a flash.

The Medical Society is having a debate on Thursday. I don't think I'm going to be able to make it, which is a pity. The subject is, 'That women should be admitted to British Medical Schools on equal terms with men'. The proposer is Prof. Pickering, with Brimblecomb; the opposer the 'Lord' Dickson, seconded by Abel. I bet Dickson will come out with a few low cracks, he thinks women are complete nitwits and no good at anything – at least that is the impression he gives. I often feel I'd like to have half an hour alone with Dickson with a Higginsons Syringe and about six pints of boiling en-sap! I expect Bourne will be there, he's very hot on the subject, and is always writing to the *Times* about it. I've never regretted not getting my wretched first MB so much as I do now. Even if I did start again, and you would let me start, I don't suppose I could make the grade, my brain has got so rusty. I'll have to sit back and help you to get all the honours. Fellowship first, I think Edinburgh FRCS is the thing to go for – and then a London MD, and then General practice – see I've got it all planned out, and I'll be your dispenser, secretary and drive the car; and you can take little Horace on your rounds so that by the time he gets to Mary's he will know what's what –

BREAK FOR <u>2</u> LETTERS! YIPPEE!!

Well, I've read them through three times – first with a rush, second very slowly, and third just to make sure I hadn't missed anything. Sweetheart they are so lovely to have, every letter gives me the same thrill as the first one I ever had (I wonder if you remember that one?) These were numbers 60 and 63 – I wonder what became of 61 and 62, or did the numbering go adrift between the two? They were written on Jan 8th and Jan 15th, so I'm sure there must be something in between the two. I was half expecting to hear from you today, because your last letter came on Monday last week, but I didn't go and look in the Lodge for them, because there are never any there when I do that.

Darling how clever of you to buy me some bedroom slippers – just the berries. I've been meaning to get some but have been loathe to spend the coupons, and I've been contemplating buying half a sheepskin and organising a pair out of that. Also the invisible panties sound very exciting – I'll keep them for our Mediterranean cruise! I've been very good, saving coupons like mad, and have got a large lump of them in hand for kitting up in the spring – can't go to a shore job with a shabby wife. I really do feel that this much talked of shore job is getting nearer – I'm sure once North Africa is cleared up they will send you all home – anyway you could apply couldn't you, if they appeared to be forgetting you? I saw Fish Watson on Saturday, very resplendent in his uniform – I don't know where he is going – he looked very new and shiny braided. You will be quite an old hand, familiar with all naval terms and customs.

I expect you have read the account of the Russian Convoy battle and the sinking of the *Achates* – the Lieutenant Loftus Jones who describes it was a friend of my youth in Guernsey. He's actually younger than me, and younger than George too, but I remember him very well. He had a twin brother, also in the Navy, who was killed early in the war – they used to live down the road from us, and did a lot of sailing. I wonder if you have contacted Hugh Richardson yet.

Darling I'm so sorry my letters aren't getting to you – it's pretty poor. I've written lots, Air Mail type proper, Air Letter cards, and ordinary 1½d type. I suppose you will get them all in a bunch. Do tell me if it's not worth sending Air Letter cards, because I've been sending them since the beginning of Jan and they say they have priority over ordinary Air Mails. Also I'm afraid my numbering has gone adrift too, so you'll have to open them all first and line them up in order. I'll try again though, and make this one number 60.

Please finish the sonnet, or if you can't, send me as much as you have written.

The best way to get rid of the Bishop is to have a measles scare, or say you found a cerebro spinal germ in the drinking water. You could of course push him overboard, or poison his soup (though that's a bit messy) or just all pretend to be skitzy, he'd soon go then.

Dear Roger, I feel so happy for getting your letters. I'm so terribly glad that you'd don't mind being sentimental, and don't put on a 'strong silent man' act. I can't tell you how much it means to me to hear from you and to know that you are loving me all the time, as I'm loving you my darling.

Goodnight my most dear and precious husband,

All my love to you sweetheart,

Doris X X X X X

February 1943

Churchill was in Cairo on 2 February when he heard the news that General Paulus and his entire force had surrendered to the Red Army at Stalingrad. Russian determination and the Russian winter had thwarted Hitler's dream of conquest, just as they had thwarted Napoleon 130 years before. Churchill was fully aware of the significance of this event. It was Germany's greatest military defeat, and it cheered him up no end. Following a very jolly evening at the British Embassy, he travelled on the next day to Tripoli to meet with General Montgomery. That very day Montgomery's forward troops had marched into Tunisia towards another confrontation with General Erwin Rommel. Finally Churchill flew to Algiers for a meeting with the American General Dwight Eisenhower, the overall commander of Operation Torch.

Engine trouble on the Liberator delayed their scheduled midnight departure, and Churchill's whole party had to get off the plane and wait for many hours before they could finally take off. Sir Alexander Cadogan was not a happy camper. William Manchester writes,

Cadogan, having now experienced the travails of long-distance travel in an unheated bomber, pledged to his diary never to be "dragged around the world again in these conditions, which are filthy. I don't think PM has ever looked into our plane or realises how beastly it is". ... Cadogan was correct in describing the beastly discomforts and dangers of flight, but he was wrong about Churchill. Churchill had known full well ever since his first flights to Cairo and Moscow six months earlier how beastly such journeys were, and how necessary.[1]

Churchill finally got home on 7 February. He had been away for almost four weeks. It had been a long, exhausting trip, and he was feeling poorly: 'I was more tired by my journeying than I had realised at the time, and I must have caught a chill. A few days later a cold and sore throat obliged me to lie up.'[2]

Churchill gave a report to the House of Commons on 11 February on the progress of the war and the Casablanca Conference. It would be his last speech in the House for over a month. On the evening of 16 February his temperature shot up alarmingly and his doctor Sir Charles Wilson was called in. He diagnosed pneumonia, which was confirmed by an X-ray the following day.

John Colville said of Sir Charles, 'He seldom treated Churchill's ailment himself but always knew the right specialist to summon.'[3] In this case he summoned Dr Geoffrey Marshall of Guy's Hospital, an expert in respiratory diseases.

In his detailed examination of this episode, Professor Allister Vale writes:

> Marshall described his entry into the Prime Minister's bedroom as being filled with important men and tobacco smoke. Winston was chesty and feverish and Marshall had difficulty in clearing the room before he diagnosed pneumonia. 'You will have to relinquish the conduct of affairs for a fortnight', Marshall pronounced. 'How dare you', retorted Churchill, 'the war is at a critical stage.' 'Very well', Marshall replied, 'but you know what we call this illness, we call it old man's friend because you fade away so gradually that you arrive in the next world before you know you've left this one!' 'Am I as ill as that?' said Churchill. 'You certainly are.' 'Very well, then I'll do as you say.'[4]

The two physicians prescribed a period of bed rest, plenty of fluids and treatment with M&B, a new anti-bacterial medicine. The patient would need skilled nursing care, and Sir Charles turned to St Mary's to send their best. Doris, a recipient of the Gold Medal for Excellence in Nursing and the daughter of a former Dean, a position now held by Sir Charles, was the obvious first choice. On the evening of 19 February she was told by Matron to go immediately to the Prime Minister's residence.

'I went straight away in a taxi,' Doris later wrote to Churchill's official biographer Martin Gilbert, 'and was met by Sir Charles who said, "Glad to see you, nurse. I must warn you, the Prime Minister doesn't wear pyjamas" – and neither he did. [Only] a silk vest, velvet jacket with a diamond V on the lapel and slippers of velvet with PM embroidered on the front'.[5]

Churchill was suffering from a pneumococcal infection caused by bacteria called *streptococcus pneumoniae*, which infected the lungs and caused fever, loss of appetite, chest pain and difficulty breathing, and could damage the heart. The condition, usually called strep pneumonia, was potentially life-threatening to the elderly or to people who smoked or were heavy drinkers; Dr Marshall knew that the Prime Minister was a high-risk patient. There was an ever-present risk of pleural empyema (a build-up of pus in the pleural cavity) which could lead to serious lung damage. Edward Fitzroy, Speaker of the House of Commons, who was five years older than Churchill, was suffering from the same ailment and was in critical condition.

It was important to reduce the fever, and Doris had been trained to do this: 'I had to give him a tepid sponge as he had a high fever. This is a nursing technique for lowering the temperature by evaporation from the skin. WC took great interest in this, and I knew that if the temperature didn't go down I would have very little authority. Luckily it did.'[6]

The next morning, 20 February, her friend Dorothy Pugh arrived to take over the day-time nursing duties. Dorothy wrote in her diary, 'Quiet day, really very little to do. It all feels rather strange and unreal but no doubt I shall soon get used to it.'[7] As the senior of the two, Doris had the more responsible position of night nurse. It was her job to monitor the patient throughout the night, and to use her judgement as to whether to wake Dr Wilson, who was sleeping downstairs, should his condition deteriorate. It was decided that Dorothy should live in as it was a rush for her to get there from the hospital early in the morning. Each day the two nurses would exchange notes after Doris's night shift, usually having breakfast together before Doris returned to St Mary's to catch up on her sleep. At 6 pm the team of doctors had a consultation with the patient, after which Doris would take over the nursing duties.

The Prime Minister's wife Clementine Churchill was more concerned about her husband's health than she let on. She had written immediately to their youngest daughter Mary (later Mary Soames), who arrived for a short visit on Sunday, 20 February. The two women went to church together and in her memoir Mary writes, '[Papa] is pretty ill. I was shocked when I saw him. He looked so ill and tired – lying back in bed ... I found the house frightening – nurses' caps, kidney bowls and bedpans.'[8]

A doctor today has an arsenal of antibiotic drugs he can use in a case of the haemolytic strep pneumonia from which Churchill was suffering, but in 1943 the use of such drugs to treat bacterial infections was in its infancy. Alexander Fleming had discovered the antibacterial properties of the *penicillium* mould in September 1928 when, returning to his lab at St Mary's after being away on holiday, he observed a bloom of mould on a Petri dish which had inhibited the growth of the *Staphylococcus* bacteria inadvertently left in there. (The story goes that the mould had blown in through an open window from the Fountains pub and brew-house across the street.) He made a culture of the active ingredient and called it penicillin. However, Fleming failed to develop his discovery. Craig and Fraser explain: 'The problem that Fleming then faced was to isolate the active ingredient in the mould if it was to be of any use in treating vast numbers of patients; this needed the skills of dedicated chemists. Fleming, being a bacteriologist did not have these skills ... he could not get anyone interested or a chemist who would extract the active ingredient for him. This fact raises the question ... [of] whether his retiring personality failed to get across to others the enormous significance of his discovery.'[9]

For over a decade his work and success remained unrecognised. It was not until 1939, when other scientists became involved, that the effectiveness of penicillin became apparent. The American pharmaceutical company Merck began commercial production, and in December 1942 survivors of the Cocoanut Grove nightclub fire in Boston were the first burn victims to be treated with the new drug. Jack Suchet worked closely with Alexander Fleming on the use of penicillin in the treatment of venereal disease. Nonetheless, penicillin remained difficult to manufacture and was in limited supply until early 1944, when, with the backing of the US Government, large-scale production became possible. For the remainder of the war it was used with great effect on wounded Allied soldiers, saving many thousands of lives. Doris and Roger's friend Graham Jones had been taught by Fleming how to grow penicillin cultures, and in a Prisoner of War camp in Germany he arranged an informal trial of the drug through the International Red Cross, which he used to treat his fellow prisoners during an epidemic of pneumonia. Alexander Fleming was made a Fellow of the Royal Society in March 1943. Many awards followed later in recognition of his work: he was knighted in 1944 and was co-winner of the Nobel Prize for Medicine in 1945.

In the 1930s, however, the treatment of choice for bacterial infections such as cerebrospinal meningitis, septicaemia and pneumonia were the so-called sulpha drugs. Antibiotics such as penicillin, which are derived from micro-organisms, kill the disease-causing bacteria, but sulpha drugs, being chemical compounds, act by inhibiting their growth, thus helping the body's natural defences to rally and mop them up.

Gerhard Domagk, a German scientist working for the Bayer pharmaceutical giant in the early 1930s, had found a promising anti-bacterial compound contained in a red dye. In December 1934 Bayer was granted a patent for their new product, which they called Prontosil. French researchers subsequently showed that the active ingredient in the dye-based Prontosil was a group of chemical compounds called sulphonamides. (Alexander Fleming is alleged to have told Doris's friend Duggie MacLeod that 'he had something much better than prontosil to offer, but nobody would listen to him,'[9] according to Craig and Fraser).The venerable British chemical and pharmaceutical company May & Baker got into the action in 1936 to find a patentable sulphonamide. They enlisted Dr Lionel Whitby, pathologist at the Middlesex Hospital in London, who isolated a variation called sulphapyridine. It was given the number 693 in the May&Baker series, and was thereafter always known as M&B693.

By March 1938 large-scale clinical trials had proved the effectiveness of the new drug, and the following year a more powerful and less toxic variation, sulphathiazole, was introduced as M&B760. This was the drug that Churchill's doctors chose to use.

Doris later wrote to Martin Gilbert that on her first night with the Prime Minister, 'Geoffrey Marshall ... put him on a course of M&B760. Chemotherapy had only just started with the sulphonamides, and the results, though good on the whole, were still uncontrolled ... WC was fascinated by this and demanded to know exactly how the drug worked so that he could recount it to all his visitors.'[10]

Painful urination was one of the more distressing side effects of the drug, so potassium was given at the same time to prevent crystals of uric acid forming in the kidneys. Doris administered this in the form of potassium citrate (Pot Cit). He complained of head pains, so each night Doris would rub his head with oil of wintergreen (methyl salicylate), a concentrated form of aspirin which could help reduce the fever. 'This became something of a ritual every evening', Doris wrote, 'and he would sing an old music-hall song while I was doing it.'[11]

To maximise the effectiveness of the drug, it was important to take it at regular intervals and to maintain a constant level in the blood. Churchill's blood count was closely monitored, since tracking the white count daily is an indication of how well the infection is coming under control, particularly the levels of two specific components, neutrophils (often called polymorphs) and eosinophils. Churchill took a keen interest in his illness and always wanted the doctors and nurses to explain what they were doing. He found the composition of his blood particularly intriguing; in late night conversations with Doris, when he was relaxed and chatty, he would talk about the 'pollywogs' and 'eowins' which were his names for the two types of indicator cells. (Churchill loved to play with words and often made up his own. 'When I use a word ... it means just what I choose it to mean,' said Lewis Carroll's Humpty Dumpty; Churchill might well have said the same thing. 'Pollywog' is an old-fashioned term for a tadpole; 'Eowin' is his own invention.)

Since 1732 the Prime Minister's official London domicile has been at 10 Downing Street, in the City of Westminster, just a short walk from the Houses of Parliament. King George II gave the property to the First Lord of the Treasury, Sir Robert Walpole, who is usually recognised as the country's first Prime Minister. He designated the house to be the official residence of future First Lords, and it is in this capacity that successive Prime Ministers have used the house.

Although there had been earlier buildings on the site, the residence known today simply as 'Number Ten' mostly dates back to 1682 when Sir George Downing put up a row of fifteen rather poorly-constructed terrace houses on the north side of what would later be called Downing Street. Walpole employed the eminent Palladian architect William Kent to combine what was then Number 5 with an elegant and substantial mansion directly to the north, whose previous occupants had included the Duke of Buckingham and the Earl of Lichfield, and to renovate the interior to create a single grand dwelling with the entrance on Downing Street. In 1777 the famous black front door with the lion's head knocker was installed, and the house was renumbered as Number 10. In 1796 the present Cabinet Room was created, and further interior alterations took place throughout the 19th century. The adjacent house, Number 11, was designated as the official residence of the Second Lord of the Treasury, the Chancellor of the Exchequer. By 1906 the house had electric lighting, baths, telephones and a lift, although the building continued to be heated by coal fires until central heating was installed in 1937. In that same year the conversion began of part of the upper floor to create a private flat for the Prime Minister.

With the threat of hostilities increasing, construction began in 1938 of a large underground complex in the basement of the New Public Offices (now the Treasury Building) on Great George Street at the top of Storey's Gate. This imposing neoclassical-baroque Edwardian edifice was close to Downing Street and, because of its internal steel construction, it was deemed sufficiently strong to withstand aerial bombing. The basement was heavily reinforced and equipped with everything necessary to accommodate key personnel and to provide an emergency government centre in the event of war. Called the Central War Rooms, this complex included kitchens and canteens, dormitories, an operating theatre, broadcasting equipment and a Map Room – the nerve centre from where the progress of the war could be continually tracked.

There was also a Cabinet Room, where Churchill declared in May 1940, 'This is the room from which I'll direct the war.'[12] A former broom cupboard was turned into a transatlantic telephone room where Churchill could talk to President Roosevelt on a secure line. To discourage eavesdropping it was disguised from the outside as Churchill's private lavatory (WC's WC, perhaps?). There was also an office and bedrooms for the Prime Minister and his family. Churchill hardly ever slept overnight in his underground bedroom, though his daughter Mary sometimes used the one designated for her mother.

Although Number 10 was strengthened with steel beams and metal shutters and an air raid shelter had been installed, the blast waves from nearby bombs caused considerable internal damage during the London Blitz. It was determined that the old house was too vulnerable to future bombing raids and that it was unsafe for the Prime Minister and Mrs Churchill to continue living there. A suite of rooms immediately above the underground complex was adapted to provide living quarters and office space. In October 1940 Winston and Clementine took up residence in this flat, called the Annexe.

Most accounts suggest it was a rather dreary place, and Churchill continued to spend part of most working days with his staff at Number 10; there was relatively sheltered access to Downing Street through the adjacent Foreign Office building. Clementine did her best to turn the Annexe into a home. Wrote Mary, 'My mother soon made the gaunt, unprepossessing rooms look almost pretty by painting them in pale colours, hanging many of their own pictures, and using much of their own furniture.'[13] In fact it wasn't that bad. The flat was up a half-flight from street level, and the bedrooms and lounge overlooked St James's Park. High ceilings made the small rooms seem less poky, although they probably were rather dark; today the dark brown woodwork is painted white and efficient modern lighting has replaced the dim lamps of wartime.

It was to the unobtrusive entrance to this Annexe, at Number 2 Storey's Gate, that Doris came on the evening of 19 February. It may have been safer, but the Annexe was hardly ideal accommodation. A corridor along which people were constantly passing connected the front door with the offices of the Prime Minister's staff and ran through the middle of the living quarters. Churchill's study, where Doris and Dorothy worked and rested, was next door to his bedroom, but the bathroom was on the other side of the passage. Visitors 'would occasionally be astonished to be confronted by a figure enveloped in an enormous white bath towel crossing back to the bedroom from the bathroom,' wrote his secretary Elizabeth Layton Nel. 'Mr Churchill was always equal to these moments, and the visitor would be put at his ease by a stately greeting from the towel-clad figure.'[14] A staircase with a decorative banister connected the flat to the warren below, where Dr Wilson would spend the night in one of the cell-like bedrooms.

Getting the Prime Minister to stay in bed was one thing – getting him to rest was quite another. On 22 February Dorothy noted, 'Fairly busy day. PM kept finger on bell pretty well all day ... PM told me that Tunisia will be OK now.'[15] Churchill wasn't going to let a little thing like pneumonia slow him down, for the war certainly wasn't going to wait on his recovery! He was already accustomed to working in bed, it was his standard *modus operandi*. 'All my work had come to me hour by hour at the Annexe,' he wrote in *The Hinge of Fate*, 'and I had maintained my usual output though feeling far from well. But now I became aware of a marked reduction in the number of papers which reached me. When I protested the doctors, supported by my wife, argued that I ought to quit my work entirely. I would not agree to this. What should I have done all day?'[16]

Even the King wrote urging him to slow down: 'My dear Winston, I am very sorry to hear you are ill, and I hope that you will soon be well again. But do please take this opportunity for a rest, and I trust you will not forget that you have earned one after your last tour, and you must get back your strength for the strenuous coming months.'[17] Lacking his usual vigour, the Prime Minister put up only a token resistance: ' ... we reached an agreement on the following lines. I was only to have the most important and interesting papers sent to me, and to read a novel... On this basis I passed the next week in fever and discomfort, and I sometimes felt very ill.'[18] For a week he did indeed cut back on his workload while he (presumably) read his chosen book, *Moll Flanders*: ' There is a blank in my flow of minutes from the 19th to the 25th.'[19]

Doris was pleased to find that one of the perks of her new assignment was plentiful and delicious food, for she had a hearty appetite and enjoyed a good meal. She found the restrictions of rationing extremely irksome. (She later recounted that one day early in the war, her godmother, the wealthy and elderly Mrs Walter Agnew, had invited her for luncheon at the venerable London restaurant Simpsons in the Strand. Doris went eagerly, with visions of Simpsons' famous roast beef and Yorkshire pudding dancing in her head. Her heart sank when the old lady ordered lightly poached eggs for them both!). Many of her memories were associated with what she had eaten at a particular place or time, but she had the figure of a slender ectomorph and she rarely put on weight, though she did not always see that as a good thing.

Clementine insisted that she and her husband be issued the same kind of ration book as everyone else. However, the Prime Minister was expected to do a certain amount of official entertaining and to maintain an appropriate standard of living, and allowances were made for this by the Ministry of Food in determining Downing Street's rations. Both the Chequers estate and the Churchill's private residence of Chartwell had farms which supplied his household with milk, butter, cream, eggs, chicken, pork and an assortment of fresh produce. Fresh oranges were a rare treat for most people; they were brought in from America and usually given only to children, but enough fruit was apparently available for the Prime Minister to have fresh-squeezed juice daily. Norma Major writes: 'The need to offer endless hospitality made enormous demands on resources and the limitations of the ration books caused great concern both at Chequers and No. 10 ... There were requests for extra diplomatic coupons for butter, margarine, cooking fat, cheese and tea and a shortage of soap meant that Miss Lamont [the curator] was having trouble keeping the house clean for the guests, and the guests clean in the house. If the rations were stretched a bit, so was the ingenuity, although early arrangements for supplying Chequers with fresh eggs were not strictly in accordance with Ministry of Food regulations.'[20]

Churchill was a renowned trencherman to whom a good dinner was almost a sacred occasion. An unabashed carnivore, he had no time for vegetarians: 'Almost all of the food faddists I have ever known, nut-eaters and the like, have died young after a long period of senile decay.'[21] Fortunately he had an outstanding chef, Mrs Georgina Landermare, who could work wonders with limited ingredients. His daughter Mary writes that members of the public would send him presents for his birthday: 'people sent him delicacies of every kind – not only grand and sophisticated presents of oysters or rare vintages, but more homely and just as much appreciated gifts of butter, cream and eggs.'[22]

Historian Andrew Roberts and Phil Reed, Director Emeritus of the Churchill War Rooms Museum, recently recreated for the BBC the Prime Minister's wartime lunch, which they served in his private underground dining room. The menu was: Native oysters; Petite Marmite; Roast venison with mushrooms; Ice cream and raspberries; Stilton; Apples, grapes and walnuts; Pol Roger champagne; Chardonay; Claret; Port; Cognac; Cigars. So much for austerity! For the same BBC programme the John Lewis store served in their staff canteen a typical square but unexciting British Restaurant meal: Skilly soup made of grated carrot and oatmeal; Cottage pie; Carrots and swede; Apple crumble. The contrast could not be greater.

There could never be any shortage of alcohol, for Churchill's consumption of drink was legendary, though it rarely had any ill effects. On his first visit to Washington in 1941 a bemused dinner guest observed, ' ...he consumed brandy and scotch with a grace and enthusiasm that left us all open mouthed in awe. It was not the amount that impressed us, although that was quite impressive, but the complete sobriety that went hand and hand with his drinking.'[23] He was very particular about what he drank and when he drank it. On that same visit he had instructed the White House butler, 'I must have a tumbler of sherry in my room before breakfast, a couple of glasses of scotch and soda before lunch, and French champagne and well-aged brandy before I go to sleep at night.'[24] The champagne was always Pol Roger; just recently I saw a sign outside Oddbins wine store in Notting Hill Gate advertising Pol Roger as 'Sir Winston Churchill's favourite'. He told the granddaughter of the eponymous vintner, 'I could not live without Champagne. In victory I deserve it. In defeat I need it.'[25]

In fact, the hard drinking was probably exaggerated and part of a deliberately cultivated image. As Clementine Churchill's biographer Sonia Purnell points out, his morning whisky 'was heavily diluted and sipped so slowly it lasted until lunchtime.'

She continues, 'he relished reports of his drunkenness, which lent him an air of machismo.'[26] However, even a life-threatening illness could not cure him of the habit. Dr Wilson and Dr Marshall had prescribed plenty of fluids for their illustrious patient, because sulphathiazole does not easily dissolve in tissue fluids and drinking several glass of water daily will alleviate some of the side effects. Doubtless they did not have champagne and brandy in mind, and it is most unlikely that the atypical fluids chart that Doris described in her letter of 23 February met with their approval!

Doris was fascinated by Winston Churchill, as was almost everyone who came within his orbit. Although he had been born into the aristocracy, he was one of those rare people who (to paraphrase Rudyard Kipling) could walk with kings and never lose the common touch. Churchill was immensely popular with the British public, and was dedicated wholeheartedly and single-mindedly to the goal of total victory, a goal he pursued with astonishing determination and vigour. He could be a demanding and sometimes capricious taskmaster for those who worked for him, and he expected others to keep the same erratic hours that he did; but everyone knew that he pushed himself at least as hard as he pushed them. He was often brusque and inconsiderate of others. Doris recalled that one day 'a new secretary came into his bedroom to take notes, and appeared a little flummoxed by his appearance. "And who is this?" he demanded, "I don't want you, go away!"'[27]

However, he could also be thoughtful, charming and appreciative, as Doris herself found out: 'He was very kind to me – interested to know that my husband was a doctor in a destroyer in the Russian convoys, and he arranged that I should see the underground Map Room at Storey's Gate and the Cabinet Room at 10 Downing Street.'[28] (In fact Roger's ship was no longer escorting the convoys in the Arctic but was now stationed in the Mediterranean). She was impressed by his concern for the fighting men and women: 'Even when most ill ... he would ring up Bomber Command in the early hours of the morning to find out how many casualties we had (not how many bombs had been dropped) and how many planes had got back safely.'

According to his long-time private secretary John Colville, '[Churchill] had a great liking for young people, of either sex, and he treated his Secretariat as if they were his children.'[29] Wrote Doris: 'He had some fresh eggs sent to him from a primary school, each one with a child's name on it, and <u>each</u> child had a personal thank-you letter.'[30] By most accounts Churchill was a kind and honourable man, and although he could be crafty when it was expedient and ruthless when he had to be, he was without malice. He inspired great loyalty and affection in everyone from the most junior secretary all the way up the King himself. His personal bodyguard, Inspector Walter Thompson, served him devotedly for eighteen years. Frank Sawyers, his 'man', was Churchill's long-time valet and saw him more intimately than anyone except Mrs Churchill and the medical team, but Sawyers refused to capitalise on the experience and never publicly revealed anything about it.

Writers and contemporaries alike have commented on Churchill's remarkable energy and a robust constitution somewhat at odds with his appearance. No one doubted his physical courage. He had been a brave soldier; he craved adventure and the frisson of danger. To the consternation of Inspector Thompson, the Prime Minister often walked in the park or climbed up onto the roof of the Annexe during an air raid so that he could see for himself what was going on, seemingly oblivious to the bombs falling all around. Churchill was a short endomorph with a slight lisp, and perhaps this air of invincibility was also part of the public image that he wished to project.

Churchill was not a man to hold a grudge. Although he had profoundly disagreed with Neville Chamberlain over the policy of appeasement, he knew that the former Prime Minister was a decent man of strong principles. When Chamberlain died of cancer a few months after his resignation, Churchill delivered a moving and sincere eulogy in the House of Commons.

Churchill had a small circle of close friends whose advice he respected and whose companionship he enjoyed. These included the Canadian-born newspaper tycoon Max Aitken, Lord Beaverbrook, and the charismatic young Irishman Brendan Bracken, who had been a supporter of his since 1923. Bracken, a master of communication, preferred to wield his considerable influence behind the scenes, although he did serve as Minister of Information from 1941 until 1945.

Anthony Eden was another scion of the British upper classes, who had won the Military Cross for valour as young officer in the First World War while still only a teenager. During most of the 1930s he had been a supporter of Chamberlain's policy of appeasement towards Hitler, and it was not until 1938 that he moved towards Churchill's camp. He was appointed Foreign Secretary in late 1940 and became one of Churchill's closest confidants, a faithful lieutenant and, many years later, his successor as Prime Minister. Doris noted that Eden was a regular visitor both at Downing Street and Chequers.

Churchill was fortunate to have for his top civilian scientific advisor the German-born physicist Frederick Lindemann, known as 'the Prof'. Lindemann had a brilliant mind, an impressive grasp of complex data, and the ability to explain it clearly and cogently. Churchill listened attentively to his analyses and stored the information in his prodigious memory, allowing him to make quick and accurate decisions when required. Together the two men formed a living 'department of statistics', an important asset in the war effort, and in recognition of his worth Lindemann was elevated to the peerage in 1941 as Baron Cherwell. They had been friends since the early 1920s; 'the Prof' was an intellectual with many of the same interests as Churchill, and he and the Prime Minister saw each other almost every day.

Equal in Churchill's esteem was General Sir Hastings Ismay, his Chief Staff Officer and principal military advisor, known to everyone by his nickname 'Pug'. He was constantly by the Prime Minister's side. Patient, tactful and universally respected, Pug Ismay played a vital role in making the administration of the war run smoothly. Mary Churchill called him, 'the indefatigable puller-together of so many threads'.[31] When Ismay published his memoirs in 1960, Churchill wrote the frontispiece in which he acknowledged Pug's invaluable contribution: 'In the first volume of my *Memoirs of the Second World War* I wrote, "I had known Ismay for many years, but now for the first time we became hand in glove and much more," and I am glad again to record my tribute to the signal services which Lord Ismay has rendered to our country, and to the free world, in peace and war.'[32]

Above all, Churchill's rock was his wife, his 'dearest darling Clemmie'. 'My ability to persuade my wife to marry me [was] quite my most brilliant achievement,' he was quoted as saying to friends. 'Of course, it would have been impossible for any ordinary man to have got through what I had to go through in peace and war without the devoted aid of what we call, in England, one's better half.'[33] The sentiment was genuine, although he never fully appreciated Clementine's unique contribution to his success and his well-being, and the personal cost of her devotion. They corresponded extensively when they were apart, and Winston nearly always found time to write long letters home. According to Boris Johnson, '[Clementine] curbed his excesses, she made him think more of other people, and to be less self-centred, and she helped to bring out what was lovable and admirable in his character.'[34]

Somewhere in Whitehall

Sunday, Feb 21st, 2 A.M..

Darling heart,

You will observe from the somewhat cryptic address that I am not in my usual position, and certainly up beyond my usual bed-time. Reason being that on Friday evening I was summoned to the Matron and asked if I would go straightaway to a case, a very important case under the care of the great Sir Charles Wilson. So along I came, and here I am my second night on, and by the looks of things the beginning of many nights. I can't say much now, but I'll let you know full details later. Put two and two together and you get V for Victory. Dorothy is on day duty, so we feel we are really doing something for the War Effort at last. Everyone here is charming to us, and The Patient is all he is cracked up to be. 'Nuff said.

Other news is just nil I'm afraid. Except that Ma has given in her notice to the DH Evans' corsets and bought the canary bird a husband, so I expect she will spend the next few months trying to produce hatchable eggs.

I'm sitting in front of a fire trying hard to keep awake. We have a congestion of the right base and a haemolytic strep infection – not so good at all, and of course obstinate as a mule. Will sleep with one pillow, and keeps popping out of bed to go to the bathroom, watch me put a stop to that!

Darling I <u>do</u> wish you were here to share this thrilling time, and the honour too, with me. There's so much I want to tell you, but I'll store it all up for when you come home.

'Scuse this scrap, but I'm just about propping my eyes open, and in any case I must go and deal with M&B. Which has suddenly caused me furiously to think that they have put him on the wrong one!! What an awful thought, but surely 760 is sulphathiazole, which is for staph? Or is it me that's mad? I wish they'd get old Goose on the job, he'd fix it. <u>Later:</u>

M&B dealt with, and scrumptious paté sandwiches consumed with many cups of tea. Gets a bit lonely about this time, but there are some lovely marine sentries dotted about all over the shop. I think I'll have another cup of tea.

I'm sitting at a large desk in the study, and gazing at an enormous map of the world fixed on the wall ahead. Your spot looks so many miles away, I wish you were nearer.

I must stop all these morbid thoughts and settle down to some reading. Last night I didn't sleep a wink all night, and finished *Blythe Spirit* and Dorothy Thompson's *English Journey* – not bad? Tonight a most charming young man brought me in 10 *Life* magazines and 3 *New Yorkers*, so I think I'll start on them.

Lots more later darling. Just now I love you and love you.

My own sweet, all my love always, D.

10 D. Street, London

Monday, Feb 22, 3:30 A.M.

Hello darling,

Still here, but I think there's a turn for the better, so it may only be for a few more nights. I slept solidly today, so I'm having a pretty boring night – I've read one book, and can't bring myself to do any sewing. I keep nipping down the corridor to read the tape machines. All the latest news comes in, and is stuck up on a notice board by my efficient marine friend. He says he's always forgetting to take it out when the piece of paper is finished, and the whole issue gets jammed up. However that hasn't happened tonight, and I've had the latest dope on Tunisia etc. The only snag is I can't hear the bell down there, and have to come whistling back to see if it's ringing.

He's had two Seconal tonight, and has only woken once since ten o'clock – then it was to have his temperature taken – and finding it had gone down two degrees after I had sponged him at nine, he said I should have a bar to my gold medal. A further bar was awarded for being able to find him some cold jellied consommé without having to wake anyone up, so I gather I am approved of. I only pray the temperature will be down when I take it again. The trouble is that feeling a bit better he thinks he is cured, and will probably walk down the corridor to have a bath with only a towel round him in the morning.

We had the M&B expert, Dr Lionel Whitby, up from Bristol today – he did a blood count, and all is well. Poor old Charles W had to explain M&B from beginning to end, its effect, composition and varieties, and then a complete account of the composition of the blood, and the reaction of the white cells to M&B treatment. The old boy doesn't miss a thing, and foxed CW by asking what was the proportion of blood at the surface of his body when his temperature was 102.

(Interrupted by Mrs C wanting a look at his chart. Lucky I hadn't got my feet up and my cap off!) Made her a cup of tea and explained the relations of pulse to temperature etc. Charming woman. Had cup of tea myself, several cups in fact, also delicious chicken sandwiches, very tasty. Dorothy does better than me though – being on day duty she has all her meals here, and also sees all the many famous folk who call to see him.

It was rather funny this morning. We decided that he should have a bedpan, bottle, and also a long mackintosh for the tepid sponges he's so fond of having. So I was sent back to Mary's in an enormous army car to collect the things. Matron twittered away and produced a collection of new articles for me to choose from. Sister Bloss, not to be outdone, produced a fine sputum pot from the Wing. I haven't persuaded him to sit on the bedpan yet, but he thinks the bottle is a great improvement on the pot!

Later, 5:30 A.M.

Been having a long chat with the old boy, he's been telling me his daily habits, did you know that he stays in bed until 12, sleeps from 3 to 5, never goes anywhere before 5, and never goes to bed before 2. What a man. He also tells me that he hates cigars, and never smokes more than a quarter of one! (Believe that or not). We have also discussed the progress of the war, and the Beveridge Report, give me a little time and he'll get my views on the Rushcliffe Report on Nursing! I'm sure this is a golden opportunity but I can't seem to get going. He's not particularly clear-headed during the night and is apt to ramble off at a tangent.

The temperature went up at 5, and he is very concerned to know why – it's so difficult to cope! Not like an ordinary 'Albert' or 'Princess' Ward type where you pretend it's exactly what you expected, and if they drink up their 5 pints a day they'll do fine. I tried to persuade him to take some Ovaltine at night, but he declares he hates 'pap' – can't stand milk or porridge, kind of 'steak and beer' for breakfast type.

Enough for now. I'll write again tonight. All my love to you darling, thinking of you so much my sweetheart.

Always and ever, Doris

10, Downing Street, Whitehall.

Feb 23rd

Darling Roger,

Isn't this a beautiful address! I feel I want to write to Richard on this paper in answer to his letter from the White House! But I might say something the Censor objected to, and the letter would come back here, and then I would feel a fool!

Dearest, you would laugh if you could see me now. I'm in the PM's study, sitting in that odd-shaped chair he sits in for his photographs, and using a blotter stamped 'First Lord, Cabinet Room' on the outside. An enormous desk, surrounded by telephones with different coloured receivers, pots of glue, pens, paper etc., and maps of the world round the walls. The study is next to his bedroom, and there is a connecting bell, which usually goes off with a loud buzz about 2 A.M., just as I am getting my head down.

He usually requires me to bath him at night, and he holds court to Sir Charles, one or more secretaries, and any odd visitors who may be around, while I'm doing it! Tonight he had his bath earlier, so I hadn't so much to do. I rubbed the top of his head with Meth Sal, administered dope, M&B and Pot Cit, had a serious conversation about bowel action, and with the help of his man fixed him up generally. His temperature came down to 99, which is the lowest it has yet been, so Sir Charles had to be fetched from his bath to look at it. I hope to goodness it doesn't go up during the course of the night, but I'm afraid it will.

He's very interested in his blood count, which is done every day, and now talks knowledgeably about 'pollywogs' and 'Eowins'. Actually he is a lot better now, but it's been a fairly bad haemolytic strep pneumonia, and might have developed – after all he's 68, although he doesn't look it. 'Ah – Charles' is charming, and not a bit condescending. We get on very well, and laugh at the Old Man's whims and fancies quite a lot. He is staying here all the time, but I've not had to call him up yet, and I send him a written report with his breakfast.

It will be an anti-climax going back to the Wing! We are treated awfully well, and Dorothy during the day-time has the most sumptuous meals. She sleeps here at night, but I go back to the flat after my shift. If we stay for any length of time we are going to change over, but I'm really quite content to stay on nights, although keeping awake all night with no one to talk to is a bit of an effort. The secretaries are charming, and the head man looks in every night to see if I've got everything I want, and supplies me with piles of American magazines. They are all quite glad of this break, because when he is well they all work till about two in the morning and start again soon after eight. There's a great deal to be said against a parliamentary career!

Darling I'm longing to see you, and tell you all about it. I can't write very much, you'll understand that.

One thing that might amuse you is his fluid intake chart, it goes something like this:

> Champagne oz 10
> Brandy oz 2
> Orange juice oz 8
> Whiskey and soda oz 8
> Etc.

Doesn't that make your tongue hang out?! There seems to be no lack of alc here, and Dorothy gets a glass of wine with her dinner.

Just going to make myself a cup of tea and settle down with some sandwiches and a book. I'm reading *My Early Life* by Winston Churchill, which I thought very appropriate for the occasion. It's very entertaining and most amusingly written.

Thinking of you all the time sweetheart darling, this being without you is very hard, but I'm so proud of my husband, and perhaps now you will have reason to be a little bit proud of me.

Tell Richard's American friends to pull their trusses up and get started. Everyone here is very confident of eventual success, but setbacks are so discouraging. Take great care of yourself my dear love,

Always and every your own,

Doris

Same, Westminster, London

Friday, Feb 26th, 1:30 A.M.

Darling Roger,

Still here, but the Patient is greatly improved, and all the nursing now is to appear at the correct hours with the correct doses of M&B, Pot Cit, etc., take temperatures and prepare orange drinks – even the latter is not strenuous, as the butler prepares the tray for me, and all I have to do is cut up the oranges and squeeze them! Also of course I deal through the night with the 'bed bottle' which is thoroughly approved and considered to be a 'great comfort, but bad for one's inhibitions'. He has difficulty in manoeuvering it without spilling part of the contents in his bed, and he demands to have his mattress turned at odd moments during the night.

Dorothy and I are now in full occupation of the study, and tonight we were laughing like drains at the PM's desk. There is a neat line of medicine bottles at one end, flanked by two glass jars containing the day's specimens of urine, two packets of M&B, and various charts, temperature charts, fluid charts, etc. Further along comes my knitting – a pair of baby's booties – then a tray containing cups of tea, sandwiches, etc. Can you imagine all that on Hitler's desk!

I expect we shall be here until Monday at least. He may be going away for a few days, but I shouldn't think he would need us then, the pneumonia has settled very quickly, and the only danger is that there may be an empyema, but they will know that by Monday. Did you know that

The signed photograph that Winston Churchill gave to Doris, March 1943.

Doris in 1942; portrait by Angus McBean. (© Houghton Library, Harvard University)

Roger Miles RNVR, 1942.

Doris and Roger at St. Peter's Church, Vere Street, 8 January 1942.

Above left: Roger with his best man, his brother Richard Miles RNVR.

Above right: Wedding guests: (L to R) Ranald Hanfield-Jones (H-J), Barbara Ward (later Lady Jackson), Richard Miles, Jill Hippisley, Ted Miles, May Clayton Greene.

Doris and Roger's marriage certificate, January 1942.

Above left: Doris and Roger with Timo the dog, 1942.

Above right: May Clayton Greene with George and Doris, 1918.

William Henry Clayton Greene FRCS, with Zachary Cope (L) and Arthur Dickson Wright (R). (Courtesy of Imperial College Healthcare NHS Trust Archives)

Above left: Polly Guy with George and Doris, 1928.

Above right: Roger's mother Annie Jones at her graduation from Aberystwyth University, 1903.

Doris in charge of a stall at the local fête, Jersey, 1936.

Left: Roger as Clytemnestra in *Agamemmon*, Bradfield College, 1934. It was his bravura performance that prompted Sir Charles Wilson to invite Roger to become a medical student at St Mary's Hospital. (Courtesy of Bradfield College)

Below: Roger and Richard, 1937.

Above left: May Clayton Greene with Hector, the Chow dog she rescued from occupied Jersey, 1940.

Above right: Sub-Lieutenant George Clayton Greene RN, 1939.

Below: Doris, George and May, 1940.

Above left: Doris with Jill Hippisley in London, 1941. (Courtesy of Juliet Fitton)

Above right: May, St John Ambulance volunteer, 1941.

Below: May, George and Doris in London, 1942.

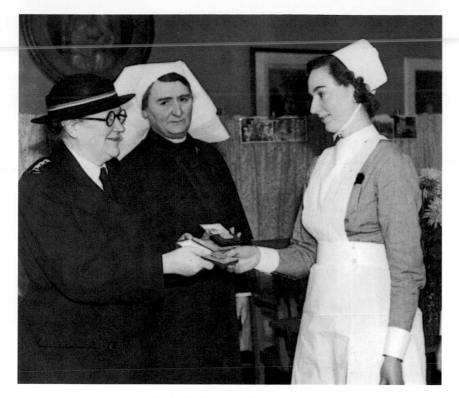

Above: Doris receives her Gold Medal for Excellence in Nursing from Miss Ruth Derbyshire, Head of the British Red Cross and a former Matron of St Mary's Hospital, while the current Matron, Miss Mary Milne, looks on. (Courtesy of Imperial College Healthcare NHS Trust Archives)

Right: Doris's Registered Nurse Certificate, June 1941.

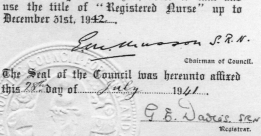

Reg. No. 110628.

It is hereby Certified that

Doris Clayton Greene

was admitted by Examination to the General part of the Register maintained by the General Nursing Council for England and Wales, on

27th June 1941

and that she is entitled in pursuance of the Nurses' Registration Act, 1919, to take and use the title of "Registered Nurse" up to December 31st, 1942.

Geo. Musson S.R.N.
Chairman of Council.

The Seal of the Council was hereunto affixed this 28th day of July 1941.

G. E. Davies S.R.N.
Registrar.

Above left: Cartoons drawn by Doris, included in her letter of 16 January 1943.

Above right: Winston and Clementine Churchill returning to 10 Downing Street, June 1943.

Below: HMS *Tartar*, in which Roger served in the Mediterranean campaign, 1942/1943.

Winston Churchill with President Franklin D. Roosevelt in Casablanca, Morocco, 22 January 1943. (Courtesy of the Franklin D. Roosevelt Library archives)

Above left: Jack and Joan Suchet's wedding, 23 January 1943. (Courtesy of David Suchet)

Above right: Bearded Roger, 1943.

Winston Churchill's temperature chart, 18–24 February 1943.

Feb. 22nd.
Good night. Seconal ʒi given @ 9.50. ı Taxol ı
M&B 760 ʒiii @ 9 pm. Bathed.
Slept well from 10.15 till 5 am, waking
once @ 1 am for some cold consomée.
T 101⁶ 98/30 @ 9 pm.
  99⁶ 92/28 @ 1 am.
  100⁶ 94/28 @ 5 am.
Slept from 5.30 – 7.30 am

Above: Doris's notes on the condition of The Patient on the night of 22 February.

Left: Dorothy Pugh, circa 1937.

Postcard showing Chequers in the Second World War. Doris's room is on the upper floor facing the front. (Courtesy of the Chequers Trust)

Above left: Doris's signature in the Chequers' Visitors' Book, 15 March 1943. (Courtesy of Chequers Trust)

Above right: Inscription in *War and Peace*, given to Doris by Clementine Churchill, March 1943.

Right: Inscription in *My Early Life*, presented to Doris by Winston Churchill, March 1943.

Above: A 6d air-letter from Doris to Roger, written at Chequers 11 March 1943.

Below left: Vicky's christening, September 1944. Standing: Roger, Marian and Ted Miles. Seated: Annie with Sally, Doris with Vicky.

Below right: Doris and Roger with Vicky, Gillian, Lesley and Geoffrey in 1951.

M&B, particularly sulphadiazine, did predispose to the formation of an empyema after pneumonia? That's why he's been having sulphathiazole, which acts more slowly but is safer.

The Dean is in bed with a temperature, so Dorothy has to supervise the X-raying tomorrow. The Old Man got very annoyed because the Dean went out to the Royal College most of the day, and ordered Dr Marshall to go over his chest and pack him off to bed. He sleeps down below in the honeycomb, and I went down tonight past packets of sentries, marines and whatnots, but he had gone to sleep so I left it at that. So I've got three patients now, because Mrs C burnt her hand two nights ago, and I dress that for her every night. Hope they pay us well!

I rang up Marian this evening and had a long chat, so long in fact that I almost missed my bus to come here. The baby is very well and putting on weight steadily and at the approved speed. John has been in bed for three days with flu, and poor Marian has been a bit hard-pressed coping with everything. I told her that's what it is to be a wife and mother, and she said rather menacingly, 'you wait and see'.

She was telling me about the offer your father has had to go to a church in Torquay, which he is seriously thinking of doing. It seems an excellent idea to me, far less work for him to do, I believe it's a very small church, and the best climate he could have for his condition. From a purely selfish point of view I should miss them terribly if they left Cheam, and it's awfully convenient having your home so close when you come. I'm afraid if they went as far away as Torquay we shouldn't be able to keep in touch nearly so easily, but still that's a minor point. It would be much better for them. As Marian said, *Tan-Y-Craig* is magnificent for holidays, but it's not exactly the kind of place they can retire to. What ages it seems since we were there, and what lovely fun it was! Remember going into Aberdovey on the bus, clad like a couple of pirates in trousers and oilskins?

I see Brian Davies around the place, and he always says hello very politely. At the moment he is producing some one-act plays for the Dramatic Society. I toyed with the idea of putting in for a part, but didn't after all. Too shy perhaps, I don't know. Anyway it's as well that I didn't because there wouldn't have been much chance of going to rehearsals on this job.

I seem to sleep most of the day, in spite of spending most of the night in an extremely comfortable leather armchair with my feet up and my head down. The PM is most considerate, and always the first thing he asks when I come on duty at night is how I have slept; and when I've tucked him up and wished him a very good night, he says he hopes I'll get some sleep too. I usually have a quick zizz from 4 or 4:30 to 7, but I wake up feeling like tripe, so I don't know if it's altogether worth it. He's very keen on people getting enough sleep, and we have long talks at night about that and many other subjects. Last night it was religion and dreams, and the night before was mostly political, very interesting.

Darling I think I'll finish on this bit of paper so it will go Air Mail (although I'm convinced that Air Mails are a ramp). I'm missing you altogether too much sweetheart, and wanting you very badly. I love you dearest, with all my heart and soul.

Always and ever,
Doris

Tonight's quotation by WSC: 'With twain he covered his face, with twain he covered his feet, and with twain he did fly.' He had plenty in reserve for acceleration.

Same place

12 M.N., Saturday Feb 27th

Darling heart,

Easter draws on apace, and events in North Africa look very hopeful, so I'm allowing myself to do a teeny weeny bit of looking forward to having you home before very long. After all, four days in eight – nearly nine – months, I mean to say! But don't come back for a week or so, because we are going to the country, the whole household, cooks, secretaries, wives, and his 'two guardian angels' – which should be extremely pleasant, there won't be a peanut to do except to give him his tonic regularly, and see that he gets his sleep, by fair means or foul. I imagine the Dean is coming along too, so it should be a very jolly party! Imagine us all playing poker together in the evenings. Nice countree walks too, at least round the garden – I hope the weather stays fine. I wish I could get hold of a camera or sumptin and send you a picture of Dorothy and me pushing the Old Man around the grounds in a bath chair. (I can't exactly see that happening though – he says he never goes out of doors if he can help it.) We reckon to be there about a week, after which I am sure he will be able to do without us very well.

I've got the nights all fixed now, and I can get in a pretty good zizz between 12 and 6, and if I do go in to him at 6 with my cap over one eye and hair on end, he's usually too sleepy to notice. You can't imagine how difficult it is to stay completely awake all night when there's no one to talk to. I'm reading an excellent book called *Death and Tomorrow* by Peter de Polnay, but even that fails to keep my eyes open.

Darling I haven't managed to send you any little books and whatnots for ages, I'm so sorry. Are you getting enough stuff to read? I know your mother sends you papers and things, and I hope the Times Book Club is doing its stuff. I recommend *Death and Tomorrow* for your list, it's about the fall of France, and very good as far as I've got.

What a stupid little letter this is, but it's been so nice talking to you. I'll pack it off and write some more tonight (it's now 6:30 a.m.).

All my love my darling, bless you for all you mean to me.

Always and ever your most loving wife

Doris

Westminster

Monday, March 1st

Darling Roger,

No letters for a fortnight, so there should be a good big bunch at any moment now. I spread the last lot all over the Desk yesterday night, and read them all through again. Sweetheart I hate to think of you cooped up for all these months in your wretched little box, I think it's wonderful that you haven't developed acute claustrophobia by now – I'm sure I should have! I'm thinking of you now sitting at your desk – I wonder if you are, it's 11:30 P.M., just about your bed-time – with my picture in front of you, or am I stowed away? I should have given you one you could have stuck on the wall (bulkhead), and then I could have revolved with the ship with no trouble at all.

You know I've never had any qualms that this slice of your life was going to alter you in any way, but I see now that it's bound to, and that after it's all over we won't be able to go back to being the people we were before the War, or even the people we were a year ago. I believe that settling down together is going to be pretty tricky, and that we will both have to make a lot of allowances and adaptations. I know we'll do it all right, but I know that life is not going to be the one mad lovely rush that our all too short and precious time together has been so far. So forgive me darling if I sometimes seem a bit dull to you, and remember that I warned you.

Awful moralising, but I just felt like that. Forget it, and just remember that I love you as deeply and as truly as I ever did.

Our Patient is making rapid strides to health, and is taking me with him to the country for a few days, which will be very pleasant. My job will be to see that he does his breathing exercises, give him his tonic, and be there when he wakes up at night. I think we go on Wednesday, and I imagine I shall be there over the week-end, but not much longer. The Matron was saying tonight, I wonder what your husband will say when he hears what you have been doing while he's been away. I'm longing to hear from you, but I suppose it will be some time before I'll get your answer to these last few letters.

> Wash me in the whitewash on the wall,
> Don't wash me in the water
> You wash your dirty daughter,
> Wash me in the whitewash on the wall.

That is one the Patient's many songs – he sings a lot, rather tunelessly, and at the top of his voice – that one is sung while being bathed or washed in bed, and is very disconcerting! As he gets better so his cigars get larger, and tonight after dinner he was smoking one that I swear was over a foot long – a mammoth and enormous ceegar! I wish I could get one for you – perhaps if I admire them enough he will give me one. It would last you about a week. Also some of his Napoleon brandy wouldn't come amiss.

Jill came up today, and we had lunch together. Unable to get any food anywhere else we went in to Cables, and the Girls rallied round and gave us an excellent lunch for a very small sum, enquiring tenderly after you, Tibbie in her usual way saying, 'How's my lady? And how's my husband?' They are nice souls, and I promised we'd go there for a meal just as soon as you came back.

Jill is continuing to have a very gay time at Oxford – 'five dances, four cocktail parties and three dinner parties in a fortnight, my dear' – but is anxious to be afloat. She thinks she will wait though until the European part of the war is won, and then when Singapore is 'opened up again' she'd like to go there in a hospital ship. Nothing like having things planned out. She's anxious that I should go down to Oxford and see her, but there's so much I want to do, and so little time to do it in. I intend to hold out for a good bit of time off when this show is finished, after all I've missed two week-ends, and 12 hours on with no time off gets pretty wearying. D'you think I dare ask for a week? I don't see why not.

It's midnight, and the Old Man is still working away, with a couple of secretaries and several whiskeys. I will take my courage in both hands, and suggest very firmly that it's quite time he went to sleep. I can hear most of what's going on, and from the laughter it sounds like lowies!
Later:

Well, I made my appearance, and it's not lowies, but his latest speech being read to Anthony E. However he submitted like a lamb, and took a Seconal, so in about half an hour he should be beginning to feel sleepy. By that time I'll be feeling like getting my head down too!

Ma is going back to Evans, in a very superior capacity. She's on the Head Dame's staff, and does all kinds of things like checking stock and organising queues and departments where they are short-staffed. She has knocked her hours down to 11 to 4, so she really feels she should be able to cope. I told you that she had bought a husband for The Bird, didn't I? We have the same trouble again, and you can't move in the flat for fear of disturbing the wretched things! Makes me sick!

No more news from George, but I think we should be hearing soon. It shouldn't take him much more than two months to get to NZ, and he's been gone about six weeks now. It will be a great relief to know he has arrived safely.

Dr Geoffrey Marshall, who is looking after the Old Man, with the Dean of course, is also looking after poor old Jocylyn Swann – he's in the Royal Cancer Hospital, and is in a very bad way. I wanted very much to go and see him, but Marshall said he honestly didn't think he would recognise me, and he's being kept pretty well under with Medinal. Isn't it terribly sad – he was such a dear old thing – not all that old either. The Speaker of the House of Commons is ill too, with this same kind of strep pneumonia, and is not expected to recover.

Rather morbid account of deaths and diseases I'm afraid. There's an awful lot of it going round though, it starts as a cold or chill, and before you know where you are it's a cracking pneumonia with a soaring temp. Daddy Swann's of course is a ca of the lung, I think I told you about that before.

It's Tuesday now, 8 A.M., and I'm just about to tuck in to a scrumptious breakfast – we may be poor, but we do see life!

Darling, I'm just living for some more letters from you – my life and my moods these days are regulated by the post. Thank you again my dearest for writing such magnificent letters, they are such a great joy to me, and thank you darling for loving me, and for giving me so much happiness. My own dear husband, all my heartfelt love always,

Doris

March 1943

By the beginning of March Churchill was much improved, although still quite weak. The Annexe rooms were dark and sunless, and Clementine was anxious to take her husband to Chequers, the official country residence of Britain's Prime Ministers, where the fresh air and sunlight would speed his recovery. It was initially suggested that both Doris and Dorothy should accompany the Prime Minister and Mrs Churchill to the country for his convalescence, but Sir Charles deemed that the Patient was sufficiently recovered to require only one nurse. Doris was the one selected, and on 3 March she travelled in the Prime Minister's convoy to Chequers without her friend.

On that same day the Right Hon. Edward Fitzroy, Speaker of the House of Commons for fifteen years, died of the strep pneumonia that he had contracted at the same time as the Prime Minister. He was buried in St Mary's Church Westminster, where in July 1946 Winston Churchill unveiled a stained glass window that had been placed there in his memory. Churchill was aware that he might well have shared the same fate. He wrote to Mrs Fitzroy, '... I hope you will forgive my not writing in my own hand (as I am still in bed) this letter to tell you how deeply I sympathise with you in the great loss you have sustained, and how profoundly I share in the esteem for your late husband and in the sorrow at his death which are so universally expressed. After I made my speech three weeks ago today, on my return from my journey, I went and had a few words with the Speaker in the Chair. He had enjoyed the speech and had been interested by it, and we had a cordial and pleasant interchange. This was the last time I saw him, for both he and I were almost immediately struck down by a very similar attack, from which I suppose my being five years younger helped me to recover.'[1]

Chequers is a large Grade 1 listed country manor set within extensive grounds in the Chiltern hills near Aylesbury in Buckinghamshire, about 40 miles from Number 10 Downing Street. For nearly 100 years it has been the official country residence where the current Prime Minster can entertain visiting dignitaries, meet with members of the government, or just relax. Although almost everyone in England recognises the name, few ordinary people know what the place is like; the estate is very private and has never been open to the public. The estate is an ancient one, but the house that stands today was built by William Hawtrey in the 16th century, in the early years of the reign of Queen Elizabeth I. In the early 18th century the estate came into the possession of a descendent of Oliver Cromwell, and the house today contains an important collection of Cromwell memorabilia.

In 1909 the Conservative MP for Fareham, Arthur Lee, and his wife Ruth, a wealthy American heiress, negotiated a lifetime lease on Chequers. The advertisement in Country Life described it as a

> ... beautiful old house with many historic associations and restored and partially rebuilt in 1566 ... situated in the centre of the Park of about 100 acres, and ... approached by two drives with entrance lodges. It is of Tudor character, in red brick with old stone mullioned windows, and presents a pleasing and dignified appearance. The House contains a lofty central hall 33ft square, with gallery, dining room 37ft x 21ft, drawing room 37ft x 21ft, fine library 83ft x 16ft, morning room, smoking room and boudoir and there are some 30 bed and dressing rooms ... extensive stabling, and shooting over 2,700 acres including some 600 acres of covert.[2]

The Lees' first task on taking over their new home was to restore the outside of the house to more closely resemble the Tudor original by removing pseudo-Gothic additions and the stucco that had been plastered over the red brick exterior in the 19th century. Over the next few years they lovingly and expertly restored the interior. It was a massive undertaking, for the place was in a poor state of repair and, in Arthur Lee's words, 'an orgy of Victorian Gothic'.[3] They also laid out the lovely gardens, which, like the interior, remain virtually unchanged today.

Chequers served as a military hospital during the First World War. Meanwhile, the owner of the estate had fallen heavily into debt, and in 1917 Ruth and Arthur Lee were finally able to buy the freehold and own the place outright. They had no children of their own to inherit it, and sought a way to preserve their creation in which they took such pride. Sir Arthur (he had been knighted in 1916) was well aware that the war had turned the old social order on its heels; he foresaw that future Prime Ministers would not be drawn from the landed aristocracy with country houses of their own. In a far-sighted act of generosity, he donated Chequers, 'this house of peace and ancient memories', to the nation as 'a place of rest and recreation for her Prime Minsters for ever',[4] along with the entire contents of antique furniture, artworks and historical artefacts. A Trust was established to ensure that the house and its treasures would be maintained as close to their current condition as possible. It was formally handed over to the government in 1921, and David Lloyd George was the first of a long line of Prime Ministers to take advantage of the Lees' altruism. Mrs Margaret Thatcher would later write in her memoirs, 'I do not think anyone has stayed long at Chequers without falling in love with it.'[5]

Doris was charmed by the fact that, despite its grandeur, the old house felt very much like a home. She was given a room overlooking the courtyard, on the upper floor adjacent to the Prime Minister's, with a connecting door. One night soon after they arrived he called out to her to come to his window: 'Look Nurse, those are our boys going to Germany, we can rely on them.' Overhead passed a flight of British bombers from nearby RAF Abingdon heading east at the start of the Battle of the Ruhr.

Her duties at Chequers were not onerous: 'it was a question of making him do chest exercises and giving him various medicines ... I also had to rub his head with wintergreen oil.'[6] She was on call through the night, but in the daytime she had an opportunity to explore the house and its beautiful surroundings. The weather was mild and dry. Doris loved the outdoors and she enjoyed being able to take long walks in the countryside of the Chiltern Hills, a pleasure she was denied while living in London.

Twice during her time at Chequers Doris passed through the old market town of Amersham, about 10 miles away. (This picturesque location has featured in several films and popular television series, including *Midsummer Murders* and *Agatha Christie's Poirot*, starring David Suchet, the son of her dear friends Jack and Joan Suchet). The 17th century Griffin Inn had been a busy stopover for coaches travelling between London and Oxford before the advent of the railway. Nowadays an Italian restaurant occupies the historic building, but in the inter-war years it was a popular meeting place for many clubs and civic organisations. In the 1930s the town's Victorian workhouse was converted into a hospital affiliated with St Mary's; during the Blitz it was one of the Sector 6 overflow facilities. Roger had apparently spent time in Amersham during his medical training, and the Griffin seems to have been his regular pub. However, I have been unable to find out anything about his drinking companion Reggie Seed.

There was plenty of congenial company for Doris at Chequers. A contingent of the elite Coldstream Guards provided tight security for the Prime Minister. Domestic servants were scarce, so the house was staffed by the capable, energetic and amiable women of the Auxiliary Territorial Service (ATS). All of Churchill's secretaries had accompanied him to Chequers, and Doris became friendly with Elizabeth Layton, a bright and articulate young Canadian woman of about her own age.

After dinner there would be a film show in the Long Gallery, attended by visitors and staff alike. 'He loved watching films, particularly newsreels', Doris recalled, 'and was delighted if he featured in them – "Look, Pug, there we are!"'[7] *Desert Victory* was a new documentary celebrating the victories of General Montgomery and the 8th Army at El Alamein and Tripoli. Churchill was very impressed and sent a copy to President Roosevelt, who responded that '*Desert Victory* is about the best thing that has been done about the war on either side.'[8] Churchill was following events in North Africa with close attention. In Tunisia, the advantage had see-sawed back and forth between the forces of the Allies and the Axis throughout February, but gradually the enemy was being squeezed into an increasingly small enclave. On 9 March General Rommel returned to Germany for medical treatment; he would never return to North Africa.

Winston Churchill was a master of the written word and as compelling an orator as Cicero. He attributed his facility with the English language to the fact that he had received a thorough grounding in English grammar and syntax while being held back in a lower class at school In his autobiography *My Early Life* he writes:

> By being so long in the lowest form I gained an immense advantage over the cleverer boys. They all went on to learn Latin and Greek and splendid things like that. But I was taught English. We were considered such dunces that we could learn only English. Mr. Somervell, a most delightful man, to whom my debt is great, was charged with the duty of teaching the stupidest boys the most disregarded thing namely, to write mere English. He knew how to do it. He taught it as no one else has ever taught it ... . It was a kind of drill. We did it almost daily. As I remained in the Third Fourth three times as long as anyone else, I had three times as much of it. I learned it thoroughly. Thus I got into my bones the essential structure of the ordinary British sentence which is a noble thing. And when in after years my schoolfellows who had won prizes and distinction for writing such beautiful Latin poetry and pithy Greek epigrams had to come down again to common English, to earn their living or make their way, I did not feel myself at any disadvantage.[9]

Churchill delighted in wordplay, and thousands of his pithy retorts, neologisms, witticisms and puns are enshrined in the English lexicon. He had always been an insatiable reader and as a young man 'I had picked up a wide vocabulary and had a liking for words and for the feel of words fitting and falling into their places like pennies in the slot.'[10] He didn't use a speech-writer; those powerful and unforgettable phrases were all his own. 'He prepared his speeches at Chequers', wrote Doris, 'often in the bath (he was proud of being able to turn the taps off with his toes). He took immense pains with them, waltzing around in his bath towel and going through them with Charles Wilson or Lord Cherwell'.[11] Said John Colville, 'He knew how to move hearts and emotions.'[12] It was these speeches, delivered in his unmistakeable voice in the House of Commons or on the wireless, that kept the British people going. 'For millions of people', writes Boris Johnson ' ... he deployed his rhetorical skills to put courage in their hearts and to make them believe they could fight off a threat more deadly than any that they had ever known.'[13]

Clementine's hope that her husband would be able to have a rest at Chequers turned out to be wishful thinking, for now that he was feeling a bit better Churchill carried on 'business (almost) as usual'. According to Norma Major, 'Nobody came to Chequers expecting a long night's sleep.'[14] Letters, minutes and memoranda kept his secretaries busy. Every day there were visitors – Cabinet members, advisors and friends. Churchill's travels and illness had for some time kept him from the Prime Minister's regular weekly meetings with the King at Buckingham Palace so, on 8 March, King George came to Chequers to call on *him* instead, causing great excitement among the household. It was an active day, for that evening Churchill thought he was coming down with a cold and Sir Charles Wilson, who that very morning had taken his seat in the House of Lords as Lord Moran, was forced to rush down from London. Fortunately the threatened cold did not materialise.

When Doris finally left Chequers she was invited to sign the Visitors' Book, and the previous entries on the same page as her signature indicate who had come to see the Prime Minister in the past few days: 'Rab' Butler, Minister of Education; Sir Orme Sargent, Deputy Under-Secretary to the Foreign Office; James Stuart, Chief Whip; Sir Kingsley Wood, Chancellor of the Exchequer; Baron Keyes, a former Admiral of the Fleet and another of Winston's old friends; Sir Stafford Cripps, Minister of Aircraft Production, and Mrs Cripps; Lord Cherwell, the 'Prof', and David Montgomery, the teenage son of General Bernard Montgomery. 'He was especially fond of Monty', Doris recalled, 'and had him and his son to stay for a weekend.'[15] The signatures of the Foreign Secretary, Anthony Eden, and the King of Greece were on the preceding page.

Meetings would go on late into the night. Doris wrote that one evening, 'I had to march into the dining-room after dinner (all male) and present him with a ruby-red capsule on a silver tray, to be told, "The price of a good woman is above rubies".'[16] The capsule was a sleeping aid, a barbiturate called quinalbarbitone, more commonly known by the brand name Seconal. Churchill claimed to sleep soundly, but Lord Moran writes in his memoir, 'He is, of course, a little *naïf* when he preens himself on not losing a night's sleep in the war; he forgets that he takes precautions each night to prevent such a mishap, in the shape of a red tablet.'[17]

For Clementine Churchill, a visit to Chequers was rarely relaxing, and this time was no exception. Although the day-to-day running of the house was the bailiwick of 'the charming, efficient and diplomatic Scottish curator Miss Grace Lamont'[18] (as Mary described her), it was Clementine who had the constant responsibility of maintaining the Prime Minister's household, whether at Downing Street, Chartwell or Chequers. She was always 'on duty'. It was a responsibility she shouldered with grace and fortitude, for all her married life had been devoted to ensuring that her husband was free to concentrate on the weighty matters that demanded his attention. History does not sufficiently acknowledge her importance, because without Clementine, Winston would not have achieved his full potential and the world today would a very different (and almost certainly a poorer) place.

She was born Clementine Ogilvy Hozier in 1885. Although her grandfather was an earl, her mother Lady Blanche Ogilvy had caused a scandal with her many love affairs and was scorned by polite society. Clementine and her siblings had an impecunious upbringing and were starved of maternal affection. When Clementine was fifteen she entered the local grammar school in Berkhamstead, where the teachers recognised and encouraged her academic abilities, and she blossomed in this nurturing environment. She even hoped to go to university, but this idea was too avant-garde for Lady Blanche and was firmly quashed. Her mother's straitened circumstances meant that Clementine had to earn her own keep after she left school, first by giving French lessons and then by dressmaking. In her biography, Mary writes touchingly of her mother's young adulthood and her meeting with Winston. 'Clementine's social life was strictly rationed by sheer lack of money. But she was then, as later, immensely fastidious, and had simple good taste, and so, despite the not inconsiderable difficulties, Clementine soon became remarked upon for her beauty, charm and natural elegance.'[19]

In March 1908 Clementine was invited to dinner at the home of her mother's aunt Lady St Helier. She was reluctant to go – 'she was tired, she had no suitable gown ready, and no clean gloves.'[20] But it was at this dinner that Clementine met the rising young star of the Liberal Party, already a controversial public personality, Winston Spencer Churchill. The attraction was immediate and mutual. Winston was delighted to find a beautiful, well-educated young woman who was interested in politics, 'a woman he could talk to rather than worship,'[21] writes Sonia Purnell. He was eleven years older than she, but Clementine was captivated; 'I feel no one can know him, even as little as I do,' she wrote to Winston's mother Jennie, 'without being dominated by his charm and brilliancy.'[22] In April Winston joined the Cabinet as President of the Board of Trade, and Clementine got her first inkling of what life might be like at the centre of national events. It both excited and troubled her. On 11 August Clementine accepted Winston's proposal of marriage, but as Mary writes: 'Even during these few weeks of their engagement, public life laid constant claim to his time and his interest. Already she saw the face of the only real rival she was to know in all the fifty-seven years of marriage that lay ahead – and for a brief moment she quailed ... it was the warmth of Winston's swift reassurance, and the force of his own supreme confidence in their future together, which swept away the doubts that had beset her.'[23] They were married on 12 September at St Margaret's, Westminster.

Winston and Clementine had five children, four of whom grew to adulthood. Their third daughter, Marigold, died of septicaemia of the throat in 1921 when she was just a toddler. 'My mother never got over Marigold's death,' wrote Mary, who was born a year later, 'and her very existence was a forbidden subject in the family. Clementine battened down her grief and marched on.'[24]

She had the intelligence and determination to have made a good career for herself, but like so many women of the time Clementine Churchill sublimated her own ambitions in the cause of her husband's success. Her daughter states that her mother 'focussed all her energy and interest upon Winston, his career and their home.'[25] She commiserated over his losses and cheered his victories, and there is no doubt that he loved her deeply and relied on her counsel and support. But she was by no means subservient. Clementine was the only person who was not in awe of Winston and could stand up to him. Sometimes they argued fiercely, and she wouldn't hesitate to tell him off when she felt that he needed it. The exigencies of his life meant they were apart much of the time, and she was frequently made ill by the stress of it all. Winston, however, was not always as sympathetic as he might have been or aware of the sacrifices that she made for him.

'Clementine was by nature shy and reserved,' writes Mary. 'The shyness she soon conquered, and the civilized education she had received, and her lively intelligence, amply equipped her for the political and social world into which her marriage brought her.'[26] She did not seek publicity, but when her husband became Prime Minister of a country at war she 'stepped up to the plate' and became the compassionate and human public face of the Churchills. With no official role to play, she carved out one for herself. Winston hid nothing from her and she had an intimate knowledge of the conduct of the war. Every day she and her assistant Grace Hamblin read and replied to dozens of letters from the general public, and in many cases Clementine spent hours trying to solve someone's particular difficulty or injustice. She visited the London air-raid shelters, and, appalled at what she found, harangued the appropriate ministries to improve the sanitary and sleeping conditions. She stepped up her charity work, becoming President of the YWCA's Wartime Appeal. Working with Mme Agnes Maisky, wife of the Soviet Ambassador, she launched the Red Cross Aid to Russia Fund, a job that would take up much of her time and energy. At Winston's side Clementine toured the bomb-ravaged districts in London and the provinces, scrambling over piles of rubble and commiserating with the victims. Everywhere the couple were greeted with cheers and applause.

The people loved Clementine for her grit, her elegance and her empathy, and it was in no small part due to his wife's efforts that the Prime Minister's popularity soared. Her contribution received belated official recognition when in May 1965, just a few months after Winston's death in January, the Queen conferred on her a life peerage, and she took her seat in the House of Lords as Baroness Spencer-Churchill of Chartwell.

Clementine complained to Ivan Maisky, the Soviet Ambassador and husband of her good friend Agnes, that Winston was a terrible patient who ignored what the doctors told him and continued to work even with a high fever. President Roosevelt had been ill with a fever at the same time as Churchill; his also had been cured with sulphathiazole. On 17 March he wrote to the Prime Minister, 'Tell Mrs Churchill that when I was laid up I was a thoroughly model patient, and that I hope you will live down the reputation in our Press of having been the "world's worst patient".'[27] Lord Moran protested at Churchill being called a bad patient: 'He is, of course, nothing of the kind ... Winston has no intention of dying if sheer will-power will keep him going. Besides, no intelligent man, properly handled, can ever be a bad patient. On the contrary, when Winston is sick he does what he is told, provided, of course, that he is given a good reason.'[28] Doris found him (usually) co-operative. He hated being ill, and she had been 'very impressed by his immense vigour and enthusiasm, his determination to get over his illness as soon as possible.'[29] On 9 March Clementine wrote to Mary, 'Papa is progressing very slowly but (I hope and believe) safely through his convalescence to his normal strong state of health.'[30] It did not take him long to bounce back, and by 15 March he was sufficiently recovered no longer to need nursing care.

Doris returned to London, to her family and friends, and the familiar routine at St Mary's. After the week's leave that she had insisted on, she was back in the Lindo Wing as Ward Sister. As well as the boils and the bedpans there were more parties, engagements and weddings. The genial Welsh nurse Esmé Rees had recently married an airman and was a welcome addition to 'Married Alley'. Despite the inevitable let-down after her 'most amazing three weeks', Doris continued to 'box on' with her usual combination of practicality, humour and optimism.

The war dragged on, with no obvious indication of a speedy or favourable outcome. On 9 May Doris wrote to Roger that she had received a much-delayed letter from his colleague Ivan Jacklin (one of St Mary's star rugby players); in a poignant twist, Jacklin was lost at sea just four days later. In the Atlantic, German U-boats were inflicting crippling losses on Allied shipping. German forces had launched a counter-offensive in Russia and retaken the city of Kharkov. The Nazi SS liquidated the Jewish ghetto in the Polish city of Krakow and stepped up its programme to exterminate all the Jews in the occupied countries of Europe. Although US planes and ships had inflicted a significant defeat on the Japanese in the Battle of the Bismarck Sea in early March and had seized the strategic initiative in the Pacific, progress was slow. Only in Tunisia, where Allied troops under General Montgomery and General George Patton had broken through the German defensive line, was there clear hope for an immediate victory.

Churchill was back in the House of Commons on 16 March. On 21 March he made a stirring speech to the nation, broadcast on the BBC. 'Let me first of all thank the very great number of people who have made kind inquiries about me during my recent illness,' he began. 'Although for a week I had a fairly stiff dose of fever which, but for modern science, might have had awkward consequences, I wish to make it clear that I never for a moment had to relinquish the responsible direction of affairs.'[31]

Although Churchill remained confident that the Allies would ultimately prevail, he warned his listeners that the war would not be over soon. What lay ahead was unknown, and he would not commit future governments to impossible expenditures and programmes: 'Nothing would be easier for me than to make any number of promises to get the immediate response of cheap cheers and glowing leading articles. I am not in any need to go about making promises in order to win political support or to be allowed to continue in office.' The first and immediate task was to win the war. 'The day of Hitler's downfall will be a bright one for our country and for all mankind. Bells will clash the peal of victory and hope and we will march forward together, encouraged and invigorated and still, I trust, generally united upon our further journey.'

He then went on to lay out his vision for a four-year post-war plan. Although the speech contains echoes of a parochial past, his ideas were compassionate and far-sighted. He imagined a future world institution representing all nations and founded on the concepts of 'freedom, law and morality'. He proposed a national insurance programme, investment in British agriculture and improvements to infrastructure and industry. 'We must establish on broad and solid foundations a national health service,' he said. Equal opportunities for all must be secured. 'We must make sure that the path to higher functions throughout our society and empire is really open to children of every family ... All cannot reach the same level, but all must have their chance ... Facilities for advanced education must be evened out and multiplied. No one who can take advantage of higher education should be denied this chance.'

His plan proposed broad advances in social welfare, but Churchill was no socialist. Free enterprise was to be encouraged: 'We do not intend to shape our plans or levy taxation in a way which by removing personal incentive would destroy initiative and enterprise,' he explained. 'The modern State will increasingly concern itself with the economic wellbeing of the nation, but it is all the more vital to revive at the earliest moment a widespread healthy and vigorous private enterprise without which we shall never be able to provide in the years when it will be needed the employment for our soldiers, sailors and airmen to which they are entitled after their duty has been done.'

At the end of his speech he informed his audience, 'I have just received a message from General Montgomery that the Eighth Army is on the move and that he is satisfied with their progress. Let us wish them Godspeed in their struggle and let us bend all our efforts to the war and to the ever more vigorous prosecution of our supreme task.'

Winston Churchill would go on to win the war, but he would not be the one to implement his vision for the peace.

CHEQUERS
BUTLER'S CROSS·AYLESBURY
BUCKS

March 4th

My darling,

Why did you never tell me what a scrumptious place Amersham is?! We passed through yesterday on the way here, just the main street of course, and I was most impressed. I hadn't realised that these places, Amersham, Chalfont etc. were so rural. I had imagined a kind of suburban Ealing-type place with many cement villas, but what I saw of it looked perfectly charming.

The journey here was magnificent. Two cars, I came in the second with a private secretary, naval ADC and the detective. We kept buzzing a fire buzzer and shooting out a 'Police' sign as we jumped lights and went the wrong side of islands with alarming abandon. We whistled down in just over an hour, and I arrived to find my bags had come down earlier and had been unpacked for me, and everything laid around in true country house style – I haven't discovered yet where everything has been put!

The place is staffed by ATS and guarded by guards, police, etc. The ATS are frightfully efficient, and rush around – they do everything, cooking, waiting etc., and are extremely good at it. I'm certainly living on the fat of the land and look like putting on pounds before I get back to Mary's.

It's rather lonely without Dorothy, but there is a very amusing Canadian secretary with whom I have meals. The other secretaries and guards officers etc. are all most pleasant and there is a film show every evening, to which the whole staff, visitors etc. go. Tonight we had a magnificent film of the attack of the 8th Army, from El Alamein to Tripoli, and the Old Man's comments are worth listening to! He's most awfully thoughtful too, and is always urging me to take my cap off and get my head down. The routine went a bit adrift yesterday, and I somehow got a bit behind on the sleep, owing to him being rather like ADW as far as time and punctuality are concerned.

However I've just about caught up now, and am feeling in great form. It's a lazy life really, except that he usually wakes at about 5 a.m. and requires jelly and whatnot, but apart from that there's only tonics and breathing exercises, and upholding the honour of Mary's by looking as decorative as possible!

This morning I took a walk to the nearest village, Butler's Cross, about a mile and a half away – and when I returned my nose had taken on its usual country hue!

Sawyers, the valet and man of all work, is my slave for life (I don't quite know why) and is forever bringing me trays of tea, apples, and nips in with buckets of coal all day long, so that by the evening the fire in my room is halfway up the chimney. The place itself is, for one accustomed to a modest way of life, incredible. It is <u>the</u> old-fashioned type country house, down to the brass cans of hot water and four-poster beds (even the penny houses are unusual). Enormous central hall with a gallery and bedrooms opening off that. Masses of oak panelling, oil paintings, tapestries, polished oak stairs and brocade curtains. The rooms themselves, except for the drawings, dinings, etc., are not large, and are awfully comfortable. They have a most attractive rush matting covering to some of the floors, with rugs on top. Of course far too much stuff, packets of china and whatnots scattered about, and enough odd bureaux and chairs and things to furnish a large hotel.

Strictly speaking I don't suppose I should be telling you all this, so keep it under your hat.

<u>Friday morning</u>

I think it's Friday now, but I lose count of the days in this place. I managed to have a much better night last night, and slept on the bed from 1 to 7 with odd awakenings in between. Very muddly dreams about you and the Old Man, but principally about you. You were on the point of arriving all night, but you never quite got here. Very annoying, the old boy rang his bell just as I had reached the station to meet you. Dear Roger, I hope it won't be too long before I really go to a station to meet you, I'm missing you such a lot.

I ransacked the library yesterday to find something to read. Very odd selection – a volume of *Modern Surgery* (written about 1860) next door to Gibbon and Tennyson's *Poems*. I've embarked on Somerset Maugham's book *Of Human Bondage*, which I've always meant to read. So the time passes pleasantly enough, reading, writing and knitting, broken by intervals for very sumptuous meals and energetic country walks. Today there appears to be a fog and also a sharp frost, so I don't think I'll leave my nice fire before lunch. It's a bit too early for many flowers, but there are heaps of crocuses out, enormous great things, and snowdrops.

My breakfast has just arrived – to make your mouth water I'll tell you what it is – grapefruit (<u>reel</u> one), boiled egg, toast, butter, marmalade – I'm afraid when I get back to St Mary's I shall turn up my nose at my victuals!

I'm going to pop this into the first dispatch bag going up to London this morning. I've got an extra set of Air Mail stamps, so I'll risk it being too heavy – if it is that's just too bad!

Darling heart, keep well and safe won't you – I do worry awfully I'm afraid – your canoe is <u>so</u> small! I'm loving you sweetheart, and thinking of you all the time – I have little thinks about you at most odd times and places, chiefly in the bath and when I get into bed. It's going to be such marvellous fun when you are back again – even if it's at our old friend the Paragon. All my best love my darling,

Always and ever yours,
Doris

Somewhere in Bucks

Saturday, March 6th

My darling,

I was so thrilled to have your telegram which came here yesterday. Just for a moment when I opened it I had a wild hope that it might mean you were back in England, but I didn't really believe it was that. Anyway thank you dearest very much for sending it, and I'm awfully glad to know that you have had some fairly recent mail.

At long last they have decided to let us send Air Letter cards to ships in your part of the world, so I'll lay in a store – they are so much simpler than Air Mail proper, where you have to go and have the thing weighed in the Post Office every time, and you can really get quite a lot on to them. Let me know how they compare in rapidity.

We've got a wonderful organisation of hours of work here, with 'staggered' sleep, which sounds awful but really works out very well.

The Old Man's theory is that no one was meant to work twelve and fourteen hours at a stretch, and that if you go properly to bed and sleep for a couple of hours in the daytime, you can work till the small hours with no trouble at all. That's my theory too, and it works very well.

My day really begins at 7 P.M. when I'm called with a cup of tea and the evening papers (all of them). I have a bath and dress up in the armour, and by 8 I'm all set for dinner. If I can persuade the Patient to do his breathing exercises before he gets up for dinner I do, but his usual excuse is that he is too tired or too busy (too lazy really). At 8:30 a large and very scrumptious dinner in housekeeper's charming sitting room with two secretaries. This goes on till about 9:30, when I lay a tray with a glass of water and two minute radiostoleum capsules on a large glass plate, and march with same into the dining room. I have to time my entry to coincide with the finishing of the coffee, so that he takes the things before he starts on the brandy. Very tricky sometimes!

After dinner every night we have a film, the whole staff, guards, policemen, guests, family all go, and as it's a talkie apparatus which doesn't break down (touch wood) it's usually very pleasant. Some of the films are rather stupid and if the OM doesn't like any of it he comes out with some pretty cutting remarks. As dinner is never over much before 10, the show hardly ever ends before midnight, and you can see the poor audience sitting patiently, absolutely dying to go to bed!

From 12 until 1, 2 or 3 the Patient usually puts in some solid work, and there is much telephoning and rushing up and downstairs with dispatch boxes. While he was ill I used to make an appearance at intervals and murmur that it was 'twelve o'clock, sir' or 'one o'clock, sir', without I must admit a great deal of success, except on one occasion when he packed up like a lamb, but I think that was because he wanted to spend a penny.

The ritual of 'settling down' for the night is gone through, and I am instructed to 'take that thing off your head and get some sleep'. This I do after partaking of coffee and sandwiches. I can't go right into bed, because if he were to ring it would take too long to get dressed, so I take off all starched appurtenances, shoes, belt, etc., and creep in between the blankets. So far I have managed to wake before him in the morning, so I have been able to whip in as soon as his bell goes looking all spruce, but I'm terrified that one morning the bell will go while I'm still asleep, and in my haste I shall go in without my collar or some other vital part.

The morning I either sit by my roaring fire, or go out for a walk, coming back at lunch time to supervise the breathing exercises. The afternoon I can do what I like, and then at 3, 4 or 5 we both go to bed again (sounds suspicious!) until dinner time, when the whole thing starts again. Not a bad way of life you must admit. I don't know how much longer it's going on for, but I'm not complaining! Everybody is extremely kind, and I live like a queen.

The weather continues to be heavenly, and the country around is lovely, with enormous beech woods and very pretty lanes. I had a funny walk yesterday, quite embarrassing really! I started off up what looked a very promising lane, and strolled along, not taking very much in. After I'd been going for about five minutes I noticed rather a lot of soldiers in groups beside the road, and then lots of army lorries parked, with soldiers sleeping, eating, peeling potatoes. This went on for about a quarter of a mile, and my progress was accompanied by the usual assortment of whistles, noises, 'good afternoons', etc. The further I got the more soldiers there seemed to be, and the lane just went on and on! I'd gone much too far to turn and walk all the way back, so I just kept plodding on, hoping that I should be able to find my way back by another route, and visualising myself tramping the roads until midnight. It was a physical impossibility for me to turn round and go back the same way! Luckily the lane was clear of the Army after about 2 miles and led to a track through a glorious beech wood. This I followed, and by great good luck it came out right where I had started from. But next time if I see any soldiers I shall go the other way!

Talking of soldiers there is a troop of guards outside my window having a very terrifying bayonet practice at the moment. Very fierce.

This weather is wonderful, you know those lovely days which start off misty and frosty, with a very pink sky. By lunchtime the sun has come right out, and the sky is very blue, and all the buds on the trees are beginning to open – heavenly. How I wish you were here to enjoy it all with me, everything is a hundred thousand times nicer when you are here, just because it's you. Dear darling, I'm still wondering how it all happened, and still thanking God that it did. What a waste of time life would be without you.

Give my love to Beetle when you see him, and tell him he really should follow the general example and get married.

Sweetheart I'm loving you more and more, and thinking of you so much.

God bless, my darling,

Always yours,

Doris

Two fine letters just arrived, 75 and 76, I'll answer them tonight. Love, sweetheart – D.

WENDOVER·2176

CHEQUERS
BUTLER'S CROSS·AYLESBURY
BUCKS

Tuesday, March 9th

My dearest,

I had such a charming letter yesterday from Ivan Jacklin. He said he had written to you and told you all his news which you would no doubt pass on. Wasn't it nice of him to write? He's in another ship, HMS *Express*, which I gather is the one you see cracking through the waves at the beginning of the *Gaumont British News*. I couldn't think who the letter could be from with 'Maritime Mail' on the envelope, as it wasn't from you – it was written on Dec 26, so I take it he is quite a way away.

As you can observe I am still here, and beginning to get a wee bit restive. I thought I might possibly get away about now, but there doesn't seem to be any signs of it. Yesterday he thought he was starting a cold, so there was a great flap with inhalers, Doren's Powders, nose sprays and whatnots, and the Dean leapt down complete with toothbrush and dinner jacket. However no panic, and when this morning I asked him how he was feeling I had the terse reply, 'no cold'. So that's all right.

Yesterday was a great day, because the King came to see the Patient! Great excitement. A guard of honour was formed, and marched around for some time, finally settling in three long rows right in front of the door. After about 10 minutes they realised that no car would be able to get near the door, and no one would be able to get in or out, so they were forced to re-form, which they did with a lot of remarks to and from the ATS staff who were watching out of every available window. The poor guard had to stand there for an hour and a half, and the Lieutenant in command told us that they were pretty mutinous by the end. I'm not surprised, it was very cold. We didn't see much of HM but it was a big thrill just the same.

Today, with the PM's blessing, I'm going up to Town. The dear Dean (soon to be Lord Moran of somewhere, so I gather from 'below stairs' as it were) has kindly consented to give me a lift in his barouche driven by Lady W. Hope she can drive.

Later

My fears were justified. She can't drive. However no harm was done, except that Sir Charles was somewhat late for his meeting owing to the fact that we got mixed up with swarms of troops with leaves and things twined round their tin hats, in the process of having a battle. With much to-ing and fro-ing, and backing here and there, we eventually emerged unscathed, and reached the old city in about twice the time it usually takes.

I went to Mary's and saw all the girls. The Matron was charming, and told me to sit down – unprecedented move on her part! Apparently the Dean had told her a lot of guff about us, and she was feeling pretty pleased. We had quite a chat about this and that, and she asked if I had heard from you, and thinks it's very nice that you should know all about it. I had lunch with Dorothy in the dining room, and I must confess was not much tempted by the muck there after the scrummy food we have here. I must suggest they make this a permanent position! I arrived back this evening in state in the PM's own car, and the driver stopped for some cough drops on the way, guess where? Right outside The Griffin in Amersham! If your friend Reggie Seed had been there I'd have gone in, as it was I just gazed upon the place where once you had knocked it back!

A grand packet of mail when I got back. Two from you, or one rather in two envelopes, of Feb 28th, so that's quite rapid. One from Marian, and a postcard from George in New York, saying he was hoping to see Richard. It was sent on Feb 13th, so it's not been too long coming. I knew your letters were waiting for me, because Dorothy told me that she had forwarded them yesterday, so I had a lovely feeling all the way coming back. They were good too darling, and lovely to hear you so cheerful.

The old boy asked if I had enjoyed myself in London, and said he would like me to stay here another week – suits me, except for the early rising I find it very comfortable. At this moment I can smell a succulent odour as of roasting chickens! The Matron has sent me down a dozen new aprons, which was very thoughtful of her, so I can blossom out every evening in white and shining armour! It's very odd dressing up in uniform in a private house, but I'm getting used to it. More later – that succulent chicken won't wait!

1 A.M.

I'm beginning to rival your record for films, only the ones we get are usually goodies and no technical hitches. Tonight we had Ralph Richardson in *The Silver Fleet*, very excellent and most moving.

I was right about the chicken, but we had wild duck in aspic, which was equally tasty! The food seems to get better and better, and I'm becoming a most disgusting glutton. I'm just pushing back hot coffee and biscuits, while waiting for the Patient to finish his whiskey and come and do his exercises before going to bed. There's going to be trouble over the said exercises I foresee! As I was away he's only done one lot today, and he will argue – quite rightly – that 1:30 a.m. is not the time to be doing exercises. I wonder who will win – somehow I don't feel much like arguing tonight. I'm so tired I could go to sleep standing up. Sawyers, the 'Man' and I stand around and offer up fervent prayers that he will come up to bed, but from the sounds coming up from below there's a pretty animated conversation going on. The party is exclusively male, and how males talk!! Now they've turned on the wireless, or gramophone or sumptin', and *Praise the Lord and Pass the Ammunition* is echoing round the sacred rafters of the Great Hall.

Darling heart, as usual I am awfully happy tonight after these two fine letters from you. Tell the old tubes and screws to hurry up and get rusty, or to drop off or sumptin. If I have to live much longer without you I shall disguise myself as a troop and come out in the next convoy. I 'spect the crew is getting a bit mutinous with no leave, hardly, for almost nine months – nine months!

Do you know that poor little Horace's due date was March 11th? Tomorrow. I've just remembered. You might have been in quite a flap just now if all had gone well. But I should have hated you being so far away. I'm afraid when we do have one you will have to be standing by to hold my hand. Oh my sweet, if only you were here now to hold my hand. I'd never let you go. I do want you so terribly.

Later

Well I won the argument and the exercises were duly performed. As a matter of fact it wasn't an argument at all, I just said, 'you've got to do some more exercises,' and he said, 'no I won't, I'm too tired'. So I said no more, and in about five minutes, during which time I did my best to look reproachful, he said, 'Oh well, if you want to you'd better do them.' If I wanted to!! Anyway they were done. There's still some consolidation apparently, and of course he thinks that the M&B has cured him completely, and won't realise that it's going to take weeks for it to clear up.

I must pack this up now – hope it won't take too long to reach you. I'd send you a ceegar band but it might make it too heavy. That's all I've got so far, but tell the Captain I'll fix him one of the big torpedo-shaped ones before I go. I send you lots and lots of love my darling – no extra charge in the mail – and enough kisses to last until you come home – millions of them.

Goodnight my dear love,

God bless and keep you safe and well.

Always yours my darling,

D.

Same

Thursday, March 11th

Darling,

Two more letters today. This has really been a record week. I'm sad though at the little PS in the second one saying no more Air

Mail for a while. Still these two have been very rapid, 6 and 7 days, counting the forwarding from London. Yes, I'm still here, until Monday I think. Your letters came down in state in the dispatch bag from No. 10!

About the financial side of Miles and Miles Inc, of course do exactly what you like. I've not touched the allotment at all, and £11 something goes every month to buy Savings Certificates (15), the rest just mounts up in the bank. If you make it £10 I shall go on buying the certificates just the same, and the rest will just go into your account instead of mine. I haven't been to the bank lately, but I think we are doing very nicely. When I get back to Town I'll have a good look at what's going on. When you're away I spend very little, and my pay, which is some seven pounds odd per month, is quite enough. Poor darling, nobly trying to exist on £1 a month pocket money! The only thing is shouldn't somebody be doing something about my Income Tax? Tell them you must come home and see to it.

I'm terribly sorry your Chief Engineer is leaving you. I hope I shan't miss him if he does get as far as Mary's – I don't know Guy Yates, but no doubt George does. I wonder if he plays chess – I can see you playing lonely games with yourself. I'm afraid it won't be so easy to introduce the Chief to 'the boys' as all the ones I ever knew have gone, or are married and rush home to their loving wives every evening. However I'll do my best. I'd like very much to see him.

I've heard from Peter Baly's Wren about Jill. See how these things get around! Don't cut your beard off, not while you're sunburnt anyway. But if you stay out there during the summer you will find it very hot, won't you.

I've done the right thing by Mrs C. I've been tending her hand where she burnt it on a hot water bottle – in fact I brought some Tulle Gras down from Mary's on purpose. She came to my room the other day to have it dressed, and found me reading *Anna Karenina*. She asked if I had read *War and Peace* and I said no, I hadn't been able to get a copy. So the next thing I knew she had given me a lovely copy, suitably inscribed by her and Madame Maisky, she has a lot which she sells for her Aid to Russia Fund. Wasn't that very nice of her?

Just been tucking the old boy up for the night. It's quite a performance, and involves undressing him, plying him with cold soup, soda water, sleeping tablet, and trying to make him do the breathing exercises he avoided earlier on! Poor old boy, you know it's taken it out of him and he says ruefully that he's not the man he was. After all he's 68. But it'll take more than this to get him down. Sometimes I wish it was someone else here instead of me, which is sheer cowardice. I've got awfully fond of him in spite of his occasional tantrums and rather overbearing ways. He's very sweet to me, and always thanks me so nicely when I do anything for him.

I'll write more when I get back to Town, and that'll be nothing to all I'll have to tell you when I see you. Roll on the day! Darling darling darling, I'll put my arms around you and never let you go, and what would their Lordships say to that?!

Sweetheart, dear precious husband, I love you and adore you always

X X X X X X X X X X Doris

Chequers

Saturday, March 13th

My darling,

I seem to have got into a habit of sending everything by Air Mail lately, so I'll send this in the ordinary post so that when you do get a sea mail it won't only contain letters from bank managers.

My time here is almost over, and I must admit I'll leave with great regret. It's been a really lovely holiday – nothing to pay, lovely weather and wonderful food – what more could I want? There is even congenial male society in the form of two officers in the Coldstream Guards who accompany me to the nightly film, and with whom I take a stroll around the grounds occasionally. Very properly they address me as 'Sister', which makes me feel about a hundred, particularly as neither of them looks more than 21. However they are very pleasant and most amusing. We have violent arguments about everything, and to my delight I find that I can hold my own very satisfactorily!

More royalty yesterday, and more mistakes by the wretched guard of honour. This time it was the King of Greece, who came to lunch. Two other guests also came, and the guard, not knowing if the car rolling up the drive contained the King or not, gave two Royal Salutes to the wrong people before he eventually arrived.

Meals here are most extraordinary. You very rarely start lunch before 2, and don't finish till 3, and as I have breakfast at 8 you can imagine that I get a bit hungry by lunch time. Dinner is timed for 8, but by the time we've got the Old Man up and dressed, and he's had his sherry, it's nearer 9 by the time we start. Still, I don't complain, although the poor cooks do!

I'm trying to make up my mind to go out for a walk before lunch, but I've got a grand fire in my room, and I'm half-way through *Anna Karenina* – a most absorbing book – it's very difficult! If I don't go out this morning I don't suppose I shall get out all day, and it's a lovely day, although a bit cold. Yesterday it was so hot that I got quite sunburnt, also I lost my way. Thinking I was walking along a ridge which would bring me back to the house, I found after about two miles that I was going about 90° in the wrong direction, and was forced to walk all the way back. I want you here to direct me.

There are some lovely walks round here. The house is in a long, flat, shallow valley, and to the East there is a ridge, beyond which is a huge plain with Wendover about 3 miles away, and Aylesbury beyond that. It's lovely country, enormous meadows, and lots of beeches and elms, and lovely Georgian houses. Of course you know what it's like from being at Amersham. I like Wales better, but this has a lot of charm. I'd so love to have one of the houses round here – red brick, white painted windows, and lovely gardens with lawns and yew hedges. I think it makes such a difference the kind of place you live in. Although at the moment a 2x4 with you in it is all I aspire to, I hope someday that we will have a really lovely home of our own.

Have you ever watched cows walking about? I'm watching some from my window now, and they walk in a most peculiar fashion, moving their back legs like sticks.

The problem of what to do this morning was solved, I went into Aylesbury in an enormous car to fetch the food for the week-end. Extremely pleasant drive sitting back in the barouche like a queen, surveying the lesser mortals who have to walk. Home just in time to do the old boy's exercises before he got up, and then sumptuous eats. It's a lazy life, but it's done me a power of good. I bought a beautiful picture postcard of this place which I'll send to you when I've shown it to the family – I could only get one, so don't lose it.

The ATS staff here are awfully sweet, and they all call me 'Ma'am' and rush to do things for me. Thoroughly spoiled I am!

Just off now to my countree walk, wish you were coming with me. I often imagine that you are beside me, and I have long conversations with you, rather one-sided ones I'm afraid. Darling there'll be so much to talk about, won't there? There's so much to tell you, and packets for you to tell me I'm sure. Do you know that it's 8½ months since we had time for a proper conversation? Your first day home I'm going to be completely selfish and keep you all to myself. You won't mind darling will you? Just one day with nobody else at all, and we'll talk the whole time, well, almost the whole time.

Goodbye sweetheart, take care of yourself my dearest,

All my love always,

Doris

Lindo Wing, SMH

Monday, March 15th

Darling Roger,

Back again in the old homestead after a most amazing three weeks. Now that I'm no longer on the spot, as it were, I can give you a lot more of the lowdown. I didn't like to write much when I was there, somehow it didn't seem right to say too much about what was going on.

Had a very touching farewell this morning, he thanked me very kindly for all I had done for him, and made me sign the Visitors' Book – Doris Miles SRN, next to Anthony Eden and five away from the King of Greece!! I was presented with a signed portrait and a signed copy of *My Early Life*. When I thanked him I said I would be able to show them with much pride to my grandchildren. He asked if I had any children (with some surprise) and said, 'Oh, plenty of time, I'm going to make a speech about it' – and proceeded to tell me exactly how many old people there would be in 30 years' time. He is most amazingly natural, and the whole time he treated me more as an intimate friend than a nurse. He would talk on the phone when I was in the room, and have 'Most Secret' documents lying around the bed. I'm afraid though that this illness has set him back more than he thinks.

Darling, I wish so much that you could have been there, even invisibly, to watch the goings on! I used to undress the old boy every night, it was quite a routine peeling off first the rompers, then the long silk pants, and down to the little silk vest in which he slept. Very clean man though, two baths a day and a complete clean set of clothes after each one – I shouldn't like to have had his laundry bill. And dear, don't <u>ever</u> become so busy that the only time you see your wife is at lunch, at dinner and when you are in the bath!

I was deposited at Mary's by a huge army car, and kindly welcomed by the Matron. She asked me what I would like to do, and I said I'll have a week off, thank you very much. She was a wee bit stunned by that, but gave in without a murmur, so I'm off until next Monday. As a matter of fact now it's over I feel extraordinarily tired – kind of reaction I suppose – and also I didn't get much sleep, although I didn't notice it at the time.

There was a grand letter from you waiting for me when I got back. No. 80, of March 8th. Your numbering is magnificently organised these days, except that some of the early 70s are still missing. I've had them all in order most neatly. I'm so glad you've had some form of picture taken <u>at last</u>! Send me results <u>immediately</u>! My camera takes a 120 film, if you can bring one back it will be fine.

Of course I remember the week-end you were on leave from *Trinidad*. I was thinking about it too. Never in my life, before or since, have I felt quite so utterly desolate after you'd gone. It's rather stupid to say this, but I think women do perhaps get the worst of a war, because there is absolutely nothing they can do about it except 'box on', and that does sometimes become extremely difficult. I'm quite convinced that if women governed every country in the world there wouldn't be any wars.

What a lot of tripe!

Duncan has gone to Portsmouth, Surg. Lieut.(P/T) Gregg RNVR, and Brian Brierley goes next week. Jock Morrison was up last week, but I missed seeing him. He is nicely placed at Southend with wife and young Ian. Tilly Turner has gone overseas with the Queen Alexandra Nurses, so look out for her in the pubs of Nord Afrique.

We had a letter from George today from America, written on the boat on Jan 30th. There was only one other passenger, a Sub-Lieut of the New Zealand Navy, and the doctor who was working his passage. Most of the time they spent playing bridge, and poor George invariably loses. They also play chess, at which he occasionally wins. The rest of the time is spent in walking round the decks and eating enormous meals. He says it's a real rest cure and that he is getting very fat. I wonder how long it will be before we see him again. Years I'm afraid.

Ma says to thank you very much for your letter, and to tell you that she will write to you when she gets a moment off from cleaning the flat and coping with the canary bird. Poor Marigold (the lady bird) came to a sad end the other day, she got caught between the two cages, and was found dead in her bed the next morning. Examination revealed a haemothorax death being due to loss of blood – poor little peanut. She was buried with much sorrow in the window box. The poor little husband sings all day at the top of his voice. What with him, the piano-playing dame next door, and Captain Sykes' wireless this is a lively place! No sign of a flat yet, but I'm still hoping. I'm going down to Cheam tomorrow for a few days, and on Thursday we go en famille to Glennis Montague Smith's nuptials.

A very odd thing I wanted to tell you about Chequers was the policemen. The place is guarded by a whole mass of Coldstream Guards, and a posse of Metropolitan policemen. These are known locally as 'Snow White and the Seven Dwarfs', and they look utterly ridiculous walking about the lovely grounds as though they were on point duty at Marble Arch. They even wear the old-fashioned helmets – I laughed every time I looked at them! The place is also crawling with detectives in bowler 'ats, led by a powerful and important person called Inspector Thompson in the biggest bowler 'at of them all.

I was shown the historical treasures before I left, which include a life-mask of Cromwell, and the ring belonging to Queen Elizabeth which was sent on her death to James in Scotland. It's an amazing thing, with a kind of miniature locket on it which opens, and has images of Elizabeth and Anne Boleyn inside. Of course the place is simply stacked with antiquities, flags, pictures and whatnots, but the Ring is the most important. Living there is like being in another world – I didn't even know what day it was most of the time, and I didn't hear the wireless news the whole time I was there.

Darling, what sweet things you say to me – you know you will make me quite swelled-headed, and I'm sure you endow me with many virtues that I don't possess. Being married to you has been so wonderful that I feel almost a different person. How lucky it was that you didn't go to Thomas's, and that I failed my 1st MB!

Dearest I love you so much, my most precious and dear husband.

All my love,

D.

Cheam

Thursday, March 18th.

Darling,

Two marvellous letters from you yesterday, Nos.81 and 82, which were all the more welcome because they were quite unexpected. They really do appear to be pulling up their trusses at last about the mail situation – about time too! I meant to write to you last night, but I must admit that I was so tired I just rolled into bed and slept solidly and soundly for a good twelve hours.

Today I escorted your parents up to Town for Glennis Montague Smith's wedding. It was in <u>our</u> church, St Peter's, and they even had our hymn (one of them). She looked very lovely in white with all the trimmings, and the groom was in his No. 1s (he's a naval surgeon), very good-looking, but not nearly as nice as you. His name is Michael Woodward, and he has a shore job at Portsmouth where he is going to work for his DA.

The reception was at Claridge's, and not very nice really. Too many people, too little food and drink (Miaow!). We made a nice little gossipy circle with the Hollidays. Marjorie was there, and Graham, whom I'd not met before, and his wife. Marjorie said that Keith was somewhere around the Mareth Line, having been first into Benghazi and first into Tripoli. Apparently his first job in Tripoli was to deliver the wife of his billet-owner of a son! He said it made a nice change. Mr Goldspink made a very fluent speech including such rolling sentences as 'Down the vista of the years'. All very touching.

Ma had a letter from George today, which had come by Air Mail, but which had quite obviously been in the drink on the way. It was written from New York where he seems to be spending some time, and some money! His descriptions of the dolls are very funny, and he says their hair is worn any length from three feet to eight yards. He didn't say how long he was staying but appeared to be digging in very comfortably.

I wish I could correct my faults as you suggest by telling you what they are, but I'm afraid they are too deeply fixed. The chief and most oppressive one that I battle against is laziness, sloth, idleness, or what you will. Terrible fault it is too, and I never seem to conquer it at all. You will have to beat me with a stick to cure me.

Look dear, don't bother to send me any more powder and things, because I am really very well stocked, and also there is a considerable increase in cosmetics here, and I can get more or less as much as I want. So you save the mun for that dinner we are going to have at the Ivy.

Timo is very well and sends his love. He is sitting beside me just now chewing a very long bone and making a great deal of noise. If we ever do get ourselves organised into a house in the near future I'm going to steal him away from the Manse – he's a sweet little dog, but very stupid I'm afraid, no tricks, and an awful yap!

I wonder where you are tonight my darling – I can imagine you sitting here with me in front of the fire, with your shoulders all hunched up, and I have a great longing to stroke your hair, but restrain myself because you probably wouldn't like it a bit. Then as the parents have gone to bed I might sit on your knee, and we would be very sentimental. Dearest, I wait very patiently for it.

All my love, darling heart,
Doris

The Manse

Saturday 20th March

My darling,

We've had yet another wedding present – from the Tweddles. When I came here on Wednesday it was laid out on the bed to greet me, and until I had seen your mother I didn't know whether to go into raptures or be rather rude. However her first remark about it was 'it looks just like a banjo' – which made everything all right. I'll draw it for you – it's a most useful kind of thing, but not a very lovely specimen. However when we have a hall it will adorn it very nobly.

It looks something like this:

mounted in fine black oak with a fluted end, the business part in chromium Got it? Yes, a barometer cum thermometer for a'telling of the weather. I've written thanks to Mrs T and thanked Mr T personally, so do write straight away darling, will you?

I don't want to nag, but while we're on the subject of writing, have you written to Anna yet about the portrait? There's plenty of mun in my bank to pay her if there's not enough in yours.

I met Mr Barnard yesterday in Belmont. He shook me warmly by the hand and had chatted away for about five minutes before he admitted that he hadn't the least idea who I was! Very apologetic when I told him, and would I convey to you his very best and kindest regards, and hopes the naval dentists are not ruining your magnificent teeth.

Latest rugger news – Tom Kemp captaining Cambridge in the Inter University Past and Present match, and Peter McRae is playing in the England and Wales match today. I haven't seen any rugger at all this year, but if Father feels up to it we aim to go to the seven-a-sides. It would be lovely if you were back in time for that. No more squashing into the back of Ian McLean's car this time though. I believe Dickson still goes to rugger matches on four wheels, but everyone else goes by humble bus or underground.

How are you doing for exercise? Don't please get fat – it would be the case of Jack Spratt and his wife in reverse, and I'm afraid even the good food of Chequers hasn't increased my weight at all. You ought to walk round the ship many times every day, but I suppose you'd be liable to fall over ropes, sailors and whatnots if you tried.

I've been most energetic and have taken Timo for long walks over the Downs. You wouldn't know me, so enthusiastic I am to go walking! Very good we are too, and obey all commands to come to heel and not to chase dirty stray dogs and non-existent rabbits. Johnny is here too, and is growing very affectionate – he's sitting on my lap at the moment and keeps butting his head against my hand, which accounts for odd writing. He's getting a very stolid kind of cat, and your mother thinks he is not quite all there. Timo rules him with a firm paw, and eats Johnny's food under his nose if he feels like it.

I'm going to attempt to send this by 5*d* Air Mail, will you let me know how long it takes? I have a nasty suspicion that I am being done down and that 5*d* Air Mails go by sea, so I'd like to check up.

We're off now to Marian's to see my niece, and then tomorrow back to Mary's and the Wing to do Sister for a week. I wonder if you will walk in one day – I often imagine that you will, and how the girls would stare at my handsome husband. My very handsome and beloved husband whom I love very much –

Always yours, D.

Lindo Wing
St Mary's Hospital, W2

Monday, March 22nd

My darling,

Back to the old address again, and it's just as though I'd never been away. The usual querulous types of patients and Bloss agitating around in the background. The wretched woman has removed most of the nurses off the floor and stocked it with new ones, so now nobody knows anything about any of the patients, me least of all. Who cares anyway!

The three back numbers were waiting for me this morning, 72–74, and very delightful reading they made. They were of Feb 15, 18 and 20th, so they had taken their time, but it's nice to have a few in hand by the sea-route which turn up unexpectedly when there are no rapid Air Mails arriving. 72 was a real long one, describing the first *Tartar* Brains' Trust and your visit to the Allies Hospital. You say the only English surgeon they had heard of was Dickson Wright, but you omitted to say whether it was fame or notoriety – I suspect the latter. I haven't seen the dear man yet, but I anticipate a fair amount of pumping at any minute now. It will be interesting to see how little – or how much – he will succeed in getting out of me.

The £10 sounds good. We will save it up and not squander it on riotous living – or will we?!

Also in the post today was an Air Mail from George in Noo Yoik, and a long letter from Isabel Drummond. Tomorrow I will go to Perry's with my cheque book and purchase an assortment of wedding, christening and birthday gifts, which we owe all round. Isabel sounds frightfully thrilled with life, although her fiancé is about to go abroad, and she will stay on at the Hospital when married. I think a nice little gift from us would be in order, don't you? Then I must find something for Glennis, and if I can't I'll send them a cheque. A christening present for our niece Sally, who has very kindly asked me to be her godmother. I rather hanker after a tiny pearl brooch as being out of the usual run of spoons and mugs.

She is growing rapidly, and looking much more like a human being now. I fed her yesterday, and did the necessary with the nappies – she's an extremely well-trained baby, and has an enchanting dimple in her right cheek. She appears to like her aunt, anyway she didn't yell, and seemed quite content to kick me in the stomach while she dribbled down my neck! John is terribly proud of her, and has created most marvellous structures in the nursery to hold the bath, and various things. She's not really awfully like anybody, and her eyes look just like a china doll's – ready to roll out at any moment. Marian sent you a photo of her I believe, but you can't tell very much by that. Anyway she looks a pretty good model to me.

George's letter, enclosing sketches of his mates, was written on board, and he sounds very content and 'feeling much better for being back at sea'. The only thing that worried him was that the doctor, with whom he played chess, had all kinds of weird and wonderful rules he, George, had never heard of, and produced a book on chess to substantiate his claims. One rule which worried George very much was that if he got a pawn to the far end of the board he could claim a queen, in spite of the fact that he hadn't lost his queen, and could go on doing this until he had a whole team of queens. This seemed most unfair to poor George, but I believe it is quite legal; though to play an opponent with more than one queen must be a bit hard.

With great relish I am embarking on *War and Peace* which I intend to read very slowly, taking a very long time to digest it. For a wartime edition it's a very excellent one, with good historical notes. That period, the beginning of the 19th Century, has always been a favourite one of mine, and in my youth I used to read every book about Napoleon that I could lay my hands on. Another very fascinating period is the early 17th Century in France and England, with all the ramifications of the two Royal Families – if I could place one of them in relation to all the others I was very proud of myself. Do you know for instance who was called the 'Snow Queen' and whom she married? Question for your quiz.

Kind regards come to you today from your friend from Harefield, Dr Idris Jones – a very delightful man – we have a case of his, a sweet girl of 23, married, with an 18-month-old baby, and she has TB meningitis. Her father is an old Mary's man called Livingstone who had two sons in the Medical School (one now in the Navy). They are such nice people, and the father just won't see that it's TB although he is full of it himself. Terribly sad, and not a thing one can do about it.

Esmé Rees is married to her airman. He had three days' leave and then off to the Shetlands and she will be back next week, another addition to Married Alley, we are getting quite a crowd up here! Dorothy's away on holiday so I had rather a lonely return, particularly as I arrived a day earlier than the home sister expected, and I was greeted with a blank stare and 'well, I don't <u>think</u> your bed's been made up, and I <u>know</u> your room is not done' – charming place!

Will you take great care of the enclosed postcard please dear? I'd like to keep it, and I could only secure one. Isn't it a lovely place? My room is top right-hand corner, and the Patient's was next to it on the left. I wonder did you hear the speech last night. I imagined you listening to it. Rather good I thought, and he certainly sounded in his usual fighting form. One phrase I couldn't make much sense out of, and that was when he spoke of 'bringing the magic of averages to the rescue of the millions' – but perhaps it was over my head.

Cool I've found a letter I never finished reading!! Wonder how I came to do that? This letter business is certainly one way of learning what a person is like. Darling I'm more glad than I can say that you can write to me so freely and spontaneously all that you are doing and thinking. I can imagine some men just putting down the same old things day after day, and really getting quite boring! Although you do say mostly the same things, you say them so beautifully and sincerely that every time I read them it's like reading them for the first time, and every letter gives me as much joy and thrill as your very first ones did. I'm glad you like mine, although I never get down quite what I would like. Do you know that during the whole of my school days I never once wrote a respectable essay?

I can picture you writing in your box, or at your desk, I wish I could see you, how you look when you are writing to me. I usually look pretty stern, because I write quite a lot on duty, and it doesn't do for the Sister to look as though she spends her time writing love letters, so I act as though I'm writing a report on the patients or an order for more toilet rolls or sumpthin'. My pile of letters is getting a bit out of control – I think I shall have to find somewhere to stow some of them away. I want to read all through them again, but I never have time! It would take about twelve hours.

Darling, sometimes I miss you so much that I want to scream, and I feel like shaking Churchill and everybody and telling them to stop this fool war at once. I s'pose it will end one day, but it doesn't seem as if it's ever going to. I want you to come and kiss me, and I'd forget about everything, and think of nothing but you, and us, and being together.

Darling heart, I love you so much – my dearest Roger,

All my love always,

D.

Tuesday, March 23rd

My darling,

I've spent rather a lot of money today on Sally's christening present – I went to Perry's, and before I knew what was what I had written a large cheque for a very tasty platinum brooch set with a pearl, which they tell me is a real one. They are going to put her name on it, <u>and</u> they took 5 shillings off the price when I looked a bit dubious about it. I didn't manage any wedding gifties, but I think I'll send Glennis a cheque from us both. I tried in The Times BC to get you a *Bible of Today*, but they say it's out of print at the moment. On Thursday I'll see if Bumpers are more helpful.

Clive Sowny's engagement is in the paper today, to a WAAF. What years it seems since he was here. Alec Mathison is reported to have dropped anchor here for a short while today but I haven't seen him. Tony Oddie told me that he had been in, and had reported seeing you some five weeks ago. I wish I had seen him.

Duggie was asking after you today, and when I told him what I had been doing he very delightfully said, 'he couldn't have had a more charming person to look after him.' Dear Duggie – in Jill's words he is a 'real cuddle'. Others to welcome me back were Bourne and George Mathews. Dickson I've not met yet, but any moment now he'll be bouncing in.

The Tunisia business looks good from this end. I do hope it will be cleared up soon and you will be home again. I don't believe your work is as prophylactic as you make out. Mind you keep your tin hat on, and don't take your water wings off because it's hot. The only consolation I have for your being out there is that the Med is a lot better to swim around in than the Arctic Ocean.

Not much progress with the living arrangements I'm afraid. I've got my name down for a flat in Ma's block – everywhere else in that district is very expensive and there's no point in living out if I'm not near enough to borrow her brooms and things, and share the fire of an evening. I'll just wait and see what turns up. We have a bed, Marian has given us the base, it's a divan type, but as yet we have no mattress to go on top. We have sheets, blankets, pillow cases (no pillows) and an eiderdown which has accompanied me through my schooldays and my hospital life.

Willie Noble very full of himself – he has just been appointed Civil Consultant in Ophthalmology to the Admiralty – I asked him if he would appear in uniform, but he said no, somewhat regretfully! I was to be sure and tell you about it, and if ever you had anything wrong with your eyes you were to go to him. He'd fix you up with a nice pair of contact lenses in no time at all I'm sure.

I've embarked upon *War and Peace*, but have only managed the first chapter. Being a Sister is a lot busier than being a charge nurse, and you get blamed for everybody else's mistakes, even the theatre porters'. Still, I can take it.

I weighed myself yesterday, and to my great sorrow I've only put on ½lb in the last six weeks. What can I do about it? Other people can get fat. I think I'll have to be a cook for a bit, I'm sure that would do the trick – you would come home and find a nice white pudding for a wife, with little currant eyes! The lovely weather continues, and I have a mournful vision of an exceedingly wet summer. A miserable mood I'm in!

Darling I love you, more than ever when I'm in a bad mood. All my fondest love my dearest,

Always yours,

D.

Lindo Wing
St Mary's Hospital, W2

Friday, March 26th

My dearest,

Do you like my posh notepaper? It's a present from a patient, but rather solid I'm afraid, so I shall have to ration you if this goes by Air Mail. It's so smooth to write on that the pen tends to run on ahead of my thoughts, so many words may be left out.

Dorothy arrived back last night, and she said to tell you if ever you get near a place called Bone keep an eye open for her Roger. Esmé Rees comes back on Monday so Married Alley will be up to full strength.

More romances developing in the fold. Brian Brierley has become engaged to Nurse Mansfield – Australian, short and dark, used to be a very efficient instrument nurse on the Theatre. All very sudden and romantic I'm told. I wish Tony Oddie would find himself a nice wife, he's such a sweet thing and deserves one. I think I'll set about matchmaking! George always had the greatest scorn for 'matchmaking mothers and daughters' who laid plans for ensnaring eligible males. He used to be thoroughly rude to all of them. But I still think it's wrong that men should do the proposing – I think both men and women should do it. That seems to me to be the thing that makes men superior to women, that women must depend on them, and wait to be asked. It's all wrong! And I think one day it will be changed (says she smarting under the yoke of being an oppressed woman!). Darling I'm longing to have some arguments with you! I love arguing, but I'm awfully bad at it, and I can never say what I want to say. You should hear me arguing with Jill. She gets so worked up, and it's very easy to pull her leg. She used to be very politically minded, and we used to have fierce controversies over things about which neither of us knew the first thing.

We've got a bitch of a patient, a Russian, who makes a fuss about everything, and told one nurse she ought to be digging trenches in Russia – I'd like to tell her what I think she ought to be doing! I'm getting such a terrible 'social manner', I hope it won't stick. I butter up these horrible people, and smooth them down when they get cross – horrid females. I can hear the Russian Rose shrieking at her nurse now, so I suppose I shall have to go and calm her down. I wish she'd blow right up.

Our meningitis girl is getting better – it wasn't TB after all, and old Wilfred Harris has taken over, and I really think she's going to be all right. Isn't it marvellous!

Only one more page to say all the things I want to say to you. It would take a million pages to do that. To tell you how I miss you, and think of you at all times of the day. How much I love you, and feel your love all the time – it is a marvellous feeling isn't it? I've reached a kind of placid state, where I can go on waiting for you for a long time quite happily, knowing that the longer we wait, the lovelier it's going to be. Things are a bit dull of course, and the horrid gaps in the mail are so disappointing, but don't think I'm unhappy and miserable darling, because I'm not. I still get a thrill when I look at my wedding ring, although it's so permanent now that it has worn quite a groove in my finger, and I'm still delighted to think of myself as a 'Mrs!'

Thank you my dearest for all that.

Bless you my love,

Doris

Lindo Wing, SMH

Saturday, March 27th

My darling,

More honours for the hospital! Prof Fleming has been made an FRS and everyone is suitably impressed and pleased. I expect you have already seen that though, it was in the papers last week. It only remains for Dorothy and me to get our OBEs and the fame of Mary's is assured.

Ma has had a touch of flu (why 'a touch?'). I went round yesterday and found her flat, with all the usual symptoms, so I dosed her up with hot milk and aspirin – went round this morning and arrived just in time to prevent her from going out in the pouring rain to Camden Town, where she wanted to exchange one of her canary birds. I feel that wherever I go I should carry a first aid outfit, thermometer, Veganin, Dovers powders, calomel, and then when the occasion arose I could produce the necessary article from the bag. There's a nice little job for you – make me a handy container in which I can pack the various things. I don't quite know what you are going to make it of though, as I don't suppose you have much spare of anything on board.

Hospital rugger dance soon. We haven't been to a hospital hop together since New Year's Eve two years ago, when I disgraced myself with the oysters. I think the chances of my going to this one are pretty remote unless I can dig up some long-forgotten boy-friend – the trouble is that they are so long-forgotten now I don't know where any of them are. Pat Sames has a fine new job. Rumour was that he was going into the Army when his job here finished, but he has stepped into Jocelyn Swann's job at Prewett, and is fixed up in a house near Basingstoke. Very nice too – or is it?

Do you remember Joyce Fuller? She was a nurse here, and remembers you. She came in to see Dorothy and me tonight, has been married 2 years and has a babe of 11 months, and lives in Dover amidst all the shells.

It's Saturday night, and the drunks are rolling in to Casualty – there's an emergency medical waiting to be seen, and H-J has just started on an acute gall bladder aged 83. Added to this a suicide, soneryl poisoning, has just been admitted, also a fractured femur – what fun and games we do have to be sure, quite like the good old days when we used to have the welcome cuppa and Sister Jones used to come snooping round. Remember the night in Casualty I gave you stitch scissors to cut a man's trousers off with? You were so kind, and instead of throwing them at me as you should have done, went and thanked me, and got the proper ones yourself. You never knew how mortified I felt about that! Sister Jones often asks how you are, as though she loved you as much as I do.

Darling, how far we've grown in spirit since those days, and how much deeper and fuller our love is from knowing one another better. I love you my dearest more than I ever dreamed was possible, and in everything I do I think of you there all the time, and that makes this place bearable and the work interesting and even exciting. How lovely when we can work together and really share everything in our lives.

Beloved I do miss you so, and love you with all my heart and soul always,

X X X Doris X X X

St Mary's Hospital, W2

Monday, March 29th

Darling Roger,

An unexpected and very welcome letter from you this morning, No. 83, written the day after a 'do' which you say you will describe and then don't. I'm madly jealous of all the allied and other dolls, nurses, etc. But how grand to have met Steve. Do give him my very best, I've often wondered what had happened to him, and whether he was still in his tank lander. I expect he is glad to be out of it. Roger Pugh is also (or was) a member of the local vice squad and finds it pretty disgusting. I wonder what crack Dickson would think out on that subject. He was in great form yesterday – someone asked him why Bedford had beaten Mary's on Saturday, and he said, 'Oh, Kemp's married a nurse – daffodils are coming out, rugger goes to pot when the daffodils come out.' We had his opinion on the course of the war, and now know where everything and everybody in North Africa and Egypt are placed, and what the next moves will be. He threw out a terse inquiry about you as he whistled off down the stairs, but I wasn't giving anything away. He's getting stouter (actually getting a very fat tum) and the grey hair is turning to white and getting thinner. I can just imagine you and Beetle setting on to Steve in the middle of the clinical meeting – must have made the old brass hat boys sit up.

Very sad news today which has depressed the whole place. Barbara Emerson's husband Peter has been killed in Tunisia, terribly bad luck, and everyone with husbands out there is (are?) feeling pretty gloomy. I know you won't do anything so silly as to get deceased will you? It would worry me no end. Freda Field is pretty upset, because Dick is in the same neighbourhood as Peter was, and she went all hysterical this morning, which did nothing to brighten the atmosphere.

I bought another 53 Savings Certificates on Saturday, so now we are well away and approaching the 300 mark. We'll be so rich after the war that we won't know ourselves! I'm being very patriotic about clothes, and am literally going about in rags – the soles of my shoes are falling off and my stockings are one large darn. Don't think that I mind this – I rather like it, and it really doesn't matter two hoots whether I look smart or not. I'll look smart enough when you come home – you won't know me. 'All kitted up for the big refit,' roll on the day. I've got to the stage now where I can quite patiently go on waiting for months – and it rather looks as though I shall have to. Nine months since the Paragon. Can it possibly be as long ago as that? What a gloomy hole that was. Not one of our top-liners – I hope we won't have to go there again. Tell the captain your wife would like the refit to take place at Rosyth, about May 1st.

Which brings me to the subject of your birthday present. The *Bible for Today* seems to be out of print all round, so I'll think up sommat else for you.

Did you get the fountain pen your mother sent? I'm afraid you won't get anything out of the insurance for your pen and gold pencil, because it doesn't cover loss at sea. That is covered by the Gieves' insurance (which I have a nasty suspicion you never got organised). Mr Tweddle's part, as far as I can remember, deals with stuff actually in England, which isn't much help.

Darling I shall have to stick your things on to you, or only send you off with bare necessities – I hate to think how many socks you've had swiped!

Your mother came up to Town today, and came and had supper at the flat with us. It was so nice as we so rarely get a chance to show any hospitality to your most hospitable family. I put her on a tube at Baker St and she was going to catch the 9.18, so she should be home by now.

I tried to find a new 'lowie' to send you, but the only one I acquired was so low that I couldn't send it – one of Roger Pugh's, but still low!

You end your letter 'more tomorrow', so I hope there will be some. Regarding the further cheque from their Lordships in respect of books lost when *Trinidad* was torpedoed, I hates to dampen you, but don't forget that one at least of those books belonged to Lewises, and that I told them you would pay when your claim came through. At least I said I thought you would but that the claim might quite well take until after the war.

I envy you your omelettes, binders though they be. Eggs are still pretty few and far between. I've managed to secure a pot of marmalade and a tin of grapefruit against our possible stay in some joint which doesn't provide such luxuries. With great strength of mind I refrain from eating the marmalade. The food here gets bulshier and bulshier – if you see what I mean. Still I'd eat bread and water and like it if it would make the war end any quicker.

Must tuck down now, we are expecting a raid because we bombed Berlin on Saturday, but no panic. I think I'm a bit of a fatalist, and I always believe that things happen because they are meant to – like us getting married and when we will die. Is that because I'm superstitious? I suppose it all connects. Anyway I know that I was fated to love you and nobody else, and I couldn't have found anyone better if I'd had the choosing.

Darling heart, a very loving goodnight kiss and may you come back soon to

Your own loving wife, Doris

Here's some rosemary for remembrance

April 1943

'The spring of 1943 marked the turning-point of the war on the Eastern Front', wrote Churchill in *The Hinge of Fate*. '... the mounting Russian tide had swept the enemy back [to] ... the starting line of Hitler's offensive of the previous summer.'[1] In the Pacific, American fighters shot down the plane carrying Admiral Yamamoto, who died in the crash; Yamamoto had been the architect and leader of the Japanese attack on the US Fleet at Pearl Harbour in December 1941. Allied forces in Tunisia were closing in on the German and Italian forces, while from their base in Malta Allied planes inflicted heavy losses on Axis shipping in the Mediterranean. Churchill could now turn his attention to Operation Husky, the planned invasion of Sicily.

In the House of Commons on 20 April the Prime Minister told the Members, 'The War Cabinet ... [has] reached the conclusion that the existing orders on the subject can now be relaxed and that the church bells should be rung on Sundays and other special days in the ordinary manner to summon worshippers to church.'[2] Because people had become used to the idea that the ringing of the bells was the alarm signal in the event of invasion, they were still not to be rung at unusual times, at weddings or at funerals, but on Sunday, 25 April 1943, the British people celebrated Easter to the joyous accompaniment of the peals.

At first the public had found it hard to believe the gruesome reports of atrocities committed by the Axis, both in Europe and Asia. The first detailed and accurate story regarding the murder of hundreds of thousands of European Jews was buried on an inside page of the *Daily Telegraph* and had been largely overlooked. By the spring of 1943, however, the truth about what would later come to be known as the Holocaust could no longer be ignored. On 19 April, the eve of Passover, SS troops entered the Ghetto in Warsaw with the intent of rounding up the remaining Jews and transporting them to extermination camps. In a last-ditch, suicidal stand, the occupants fought with desperate ferocity in vicious street-to-street and house-to-house combat, attacking the invaders with hand grenades, Molotov cocktails and any weapons they could make or get their hands on. It was a courageous but ultimately futile uprising. By the end of the month German flamethrowers had destroyed most of the buildings. A few of the insurgents managed to escape, while thousands more sought shelter in the ruins and in the sewers.

At the same time, British and American representatives were meeting in secret in Bermuda to discuss the plight of the European Jews. Little was accomplished, however. Churchill was an outspoken opponent of anti-Semitism, and a strong advocate for a Jewish homeland in Palestine, but he had no input in the conference, which was attended by rather low-level officials. The participants did nothing to remove restrictions that would allow Jewish refugees to find a safe haven in Palestine, nor would the Americans agree to raise their own immigration quotas. The Bermuda Conference is widely regarded as a face-saving device so that the two governments could appear to be doing something, but the meeting did not save a single European Jew.

Doris's brother George had been cooling his heels in New York (with a marked lack of reluctance!) for several weeks during February and March, but was finally on his way to New Zealand. He had been in touch with Richard Miles during his stay, although he had not managed to get to Washington to visit him.

Richard was now sharing a house with the assistant Air Attaché, a Royal Air Force flying ace named Roald Dahl who had recently been shot down in the Middle East and invalided out of active duty. Richard wrote to Roger: 'My colleagues are a very varied assortment, and my particular associate is the assistant Air Attaché, who is one of the most remarkable guys I have ever met. He is a most undiplomatic diplomat, but gets on well with a lot of people over here because it is often the case that the less diplomatic the better.' Dahl had co-opted the RAF's tales of Gremlins, mischievous beings who took a perverse delight in sabotaging the planes and were responsible for all the unexplained mechanical failures, and had written a successful children's book from which Walt Disney proposed to make a film. Richard continues, 'He is a great lad, and is now engaged in writing a script for another film which is going to be a really big show, and I sit up all hours of the night with him, acting as his stooge and sounding board, arguing the characters and complicating the issue by "suggesting" themes of my own! It's great fun, and the other day we met the Producer and Author (both v. famous men) to discuss the whole thing. The Producer, a swarthy Hungarian type – can you guess? – found time to observe that I knew nothing whatever about film producing, but that did not prevent us having a very enjoyable lunch at his expense.' The proposed Disney film was never made, in part because of concerns over who owned the rights. 'The Gremlins are of course the property at large of the RAF,' according to Richard, 'and all the profits from these enterprises go into the RAF Benevolent Fund. Even so, I think they have helped to launch the lad as a writer, and he may go far. He has a completely screwy mind, and that seems to be the sort of mind to have these days.' After the war Roald Dahl did indeed have an extremely successful career writing children's books of a decidedly quirky nature.

Roald Dahl was one of many once and future celebrities who served in the British armed forces during the war. Others included actors David Niven, Dirk Bogarde and Alec Guiness; actor and film-maker Richard Attenborough; writer and comedian Spike Milligan; journalist Godfrey Winn; astronomer Patrick Moore, and writer Ian Fleming. Actor/director/producer Leslie Henson (a friend of Duncan Gregg) had, with Basil Dean, started the Entertainments National Service Association (ENSA) in 1939 to provide entertainment for the troops. During the course of the war dozens of stars performed for ENSA, including Vivien Leigh, Stanley Holloway and Vera Lynn. Both Mary Churchill, the Prime Minister's youngest daughter, and the heir to the throne, Princess Elizabeth, joined the ATS as soon as they were old enough, Mary as a battery gunner and the young princess as a truck driver.

In London, the most pressing question was what to do about The Beard! Roger had first adopted the hirsute look the previous summer, and it had been a constant theme of their correspondence for several months. Everybody at St Mary's who had seen the photograph that Roger sent to Doris had an opinion. The general consensus was that it had to go. Doris herself rather approved of the beard, although she did say it made her husband look like a somewhat disagreeable Eastern potentate. I think he looks a bit like a young King George V with a decent trim; the beard was neat and elegant, nothing like the scruffy stubble that young men affect today.

Lindo Wing

Funny, I never thought of writing across on this flimsy – in fact you could write in all kinds of directions to fill it up! Starting in the middle and going round and round, or from corner to corner. Might even try the old fashioned trick of writing one page and then writing across it, werry difficult to decipher though!

Your friend Dr Idris Jones has just been in – nice thing he is. He was telling me about a patient whose father said she had not passed water for 11 days – 'she probably got pressure of the bladder on the diaphragm and died of asphyxia'. His wife is having another infant in the summer, and after two boys they have great hopes of it being a girl.

I spent a coupon this morning, and bought me a succulent piece of pink silk for the manufacturing of underclothes – trouble is I've got so many things in the making that none of them gets finished. Is there anything you want? I might warn you that one of your shirts is in imminent danger of being transformed into a blouse for me – very simple process, often employed these days by couponless wives.

The Rugger Dance was held t'other night, and according to all reports was the loudest and drunkenest party there has ever been. Dickson went, but I don't think any of the others were there. The usual gang of nurses appeared the next day looking pretty shagged, and I believe the liquor situation was well in hand as usual. Sister Jones met Tank Symons on the stairs at 4:40 a.m. and describes him as looking 'very hairy'. She asked me the next morning if I had been dancing, but I informed her I was a staid married woman and didn't go in for such sports – it's awfully difficult to think up quick cracks to answer her with in the foggy hours before 8 a.m. I usually mumble at her on my way in to breakfast at one minute to eight, but I must admit she never attempts to make any sarcastic comments on my lateness.

I'm plodding on with *War and Peace*, but I don't think it's the kind of book to be read in bits like this – I think I'll wait until I can get a clear stretch, and really get down to it. Are the Times Book Club people sending you books all right? Because if they are not I'll go in and beat them up.

Remember a student called Livingstone? His father is awfully impressed because I am 'C-G's' daughter, and he said (you know how he kind of clips his words) – 'you married my very nice house surgeon'. I never knew you were his H-S, darling, did he beat you up? I told him how I urged you to be inspired by Willie, and mug up for Primary, but he agreed with you that it couldn't be done. So I won't nag any more.

We've got a delightful Judge in, patient of ADW's, Scots, and we had a long talk tonight about the glories of Scotland, particularly its golf courses – you'd have thought to listen to me that I had lived in Edinburgh all my life!! Dickson of course picks his brains about the Law and Judgery and, of course, knows things about all the great men of the bar. Funny, I no longer have the least bit of fear or awe of Dickson, and anything he could say wouldn't worry me in the least. Very odd, as I used to shiver if he so much as looked in my direction. Must be being married – gives you a whole lot of self-confidence you never had before.

The date of this letter by the way is April 2 – I forgot to put it at the beginning. I also forgot to put Darling Roger, so I'll put it at this end. Dear, darling Roger, I looks towards you and sends you all the love in the world.

Always and ever yours,
Doris

Lindo Wing

April 5th

My darling,

Lovely to have your flimsy on Saturday, No. 87, which took just 5 days, and so achieves a record for rapid mail. Saturday was a big day for the girls, and there were Air Letters in the same post for Dorothy and Freda, so we surmise that all the husbands are in the same spot more or less. And not a very healthy spot just now according to the *Daily Mirror*, however, you can't believe all you read in the papers. Congratulations darling on the wonderful small calligraphy, werry neat and tidy, and much smaller than anything I can achieve, but you wait till I get my mapping pen out, you'll need a magnifying glass to read it.

Don't bother to send me a watch strap dear, because George sent me a very nice one from New York a few days ago. We have discovered why he had the short stay over there – Ma rang up NZ House to ask if he had arrived, and they told her that his ship had had a 'spot of trouble' on the way, but that it had been fixed up and was away again. We had a couple of letters from him, and he seemed to be quite happy, and thought that New York was a very swell burg. I don't know whether he managed to contact Richard or not, but he said he was trying to.

The fruit sounds a grand idea. Make it all oranges with a lemon or two, and I'll make some marmalade out of it. If you can get the bitter kind of oranges they are better for the purpose, but any kind will do. No pineapples? Pretty poor. Peter Porter brought some back and gave one to Margaret, werry succulent it was. Otherwise dear, don't waste the mun on buying me things, far better save it up, and we'll spend it together when you come home (I've just spilled meths all over this, but it's dried successfully!)

We've had the most wonderful weather ever since Christmas. Today it's just like a perfect June day, and in spite of the fact that May is not yet out, I'm casting clouts in all directions with great abandon. I look out of my prison windows, and feel I want to rush off into the country and just lie in a vast field full of buttercups and do nothing at all; very lazy I am in my pleasures. On the other hand a swim in the sea, and a sunbath on the sands of Aberdovey would be equally pleasant, especially if you were there too – in fact it wouldn't be pleasant at all if you weren't there.

Oh dear, I do hate these flimsies! It's much more fun writing ordinary pages of letter. I'll send off some ordinary mail, so that you will have something from me that won't ruin your eyesight. By now you should have received the ceegars – I hope they came in good condition, think of me when you smoke them. Also dispatched is a birthday present for you which I have registered, so if you don't receive a registered package within the next six months let me know and I'll put in a claim.

Some lilies of the valley came for a patient today, and I spent a happy five minutes with my nose in them – the more I smell those flowers the lovelier they seem to be. If you come back in June or May I'll make you buy me a 'normous bunch of them and I'll do nothing but smell them all day. I think my sense of smell is one of my keenest senses. Nice smells give me quite a physical satisfaction, and nasty smells make me feel really ill. I wonder I ever survived my first nursing years in the sluices of Albert ward. I was quite sick once, literally, while cleaning one of them. What a subject for the last page of the flimsy!

I've just been having a row with a patient, a doctor who thinks he can order himself all kinds of treatment. He's the most neurotic man I've ever met, and is always going on about his bowels, throat, back and whatnot. Very firmly I declined to give him the SodaSal he thought he ought to have, and said I would ask Dickson – which means just nothing at all, because Dickson is more elusive than ever, and has taken to telling the patient what treatment he wants them to have and not bothering to confirm it with the Sister, which makes everything very difficult!

Beloved, how soon these flimsies come to an end. Your remark that I'd be getting lots of them was not awfully cheering as you are only allowed one a week. However, on we box, and there is no depression in this house. Look after yourself darling heart because you are very precious to me. It's a long and dreary wait my love, but the end will be all the lovelier for the waiting, and all our lives we will appreciate a love we had to fight for.

God bless you my darling and keep you very safe.

All my love always,

Doris X X X X

Lindo Wing
SMH, Paddington

Wednesday, April 7th

Roger my darling,

What a kind thoughtful man you are to send me the watch strap. It was sweet of you to hunt it up for me, many many thanks for it. I was so thrilled to have your letter so rapidly – it was posted in London this morning, although as a matter of fact I didn't look at the postmark

215

until afterwards, so hasty was I in opening the envelope. I hope very much that the two midshipmen will find time to look me up, although I'm sure they have plenty of far more important things to do in their leave. (By the way, 9051 is not the best number to use – the Wing number is 5081, and is a safer bet.)

Eric Norman dropped in again this morning – second time in two months – he is in a River Class corvette, and is just back from Gib, he said he just missed you, your boat having steamed in as he steamed out. But he met Tilly Turner and two other Mary's lasses now in the Queen Alexandra's on their way to North Africa. I wonder if you contacted them by any chance. This jealous wife feeling is very new, and very strange! I feel it must be rapidly got rid of. Not that I am a jealous wife at all, that would be horrible – but it's just that I so envy the people you are with, just because you are with them and not with me.

Dickson was here last night in the best mood I've seen him in for ages. I wish I could remember all his cracks but they come out so quickly, and anyway they look stupid written down. One was rather good. He was talking about the film *Desert Victory*, which Churchill thinks is so good. Dickson of course thinks that it's a very bad film – 'Too many corpses, and men's faces covered in grease. The Russians always have corpses too. They pickle them in formalin and use them in their films. We were the first to start it though. I was a corpse in a film during the last war. I wrote home and told them that the second corpse from the right in the third reel was me'.

The judge asked him if he knew anything about heraldry, something had been said about it, and Dickson said, 'Oh yes, very interesting subject. Have you got a coat of arms? I have – look, it's on my cuff link – "Truth conquers" and three leopards' heads'. That's all I heard, because I couldn't very well stand and listen any more, but he was very proud of his leopards' heads! Said his wife liked it, but obviously he was thrilled to bits with his coat of arms. He ought to have something more topical though, a pair of spencer-wells over a saphenous vein for instance. Be rather fun to invent one wouldn't it? Yours I think (no rudeness intended) might well be something incorporating a couple of chess men, a stethoscope and a glass of gin. H-J's no doubt would include a hand, a cricket bat and a kidney, while mine would have a bottle of cascara, a bandage and a cup of tea.

I expect you saw the great news of Tony Oddie's DSC. I think it's marvellous and I wrote to congratulate him today. There was a rumour that he's being invalided out of the Navy, but I don't know how true that is.

Your old friend Dr Lindenbaum has just been in. Vell, vell, vot do you think of dat?! Charming fellow.

I observe that you no longer talk of being home for Easter – I never thought you would be really, so I'll just tick the days off, and I won't begin to get impatient until June. Eric Norman was not a bit encouraging, almost as bad as George! The only consolation I get is that when you do get back they won't send you out in that canoe again. John Hill, did I tell you, is at Deal with the Marines, he couldn't take his four stacker for long could he? I think you are wonderful to have lived in your 2 x 1 for nine months without a moan – if it had been me I should have been a raving lunatic by this time, right round the bend and half-way up the road beyond. You're a fine person, and I'm very proud to be your wife. I tell all the girls who don't know you what a fine chap you are, so when you do come you won't mind if I show you off a bit will you?

The weather has changed at last, and we are having a fine old gale after three months of sunshine. I suppose from now on we shall have rain until the end of the summer – says she miserably, viewing new spring hat with veil. Anyway it's good for the crops.

Much later

Darling, I've wronged your little midshipmate – he rang tonight while I was out, and luckily a kind friend of mine answered and told him to ring the Wing tomorrow. Apparently he rang yesterday, and got switched on to all kinds of places before eventually they told him I was on duty and therefore <u>couldn't answer the phone</u>! Of all the bags!! This place is about the end. Wait till I tell them what I think about their organisation. The poor boy will think I'm completely uncontactable, and I'm so looking forward to seeing him. I hope he will ring tomorrow and not give up.

To revert for a minute to Winston, if you can bear it. Did I ever tell you how he rang his bell for me one day when I had just washed my hair? It was awful. My hair was half dry, and I had just set it and put in all the iron works when the bell went. I contemplated calling out 'I can't come, I'm undressed', but thought that wouldn't really do, so

I hastily removed all the curlers, tied up my hair with a bit of ribbon and bounced into the Patient in a pretty bad temper. He didn't notice a thing, just wanted me to undress him and put him to bed (4 P.M.) and had I noticed that he had had his hair cut? I said no, did he notice that mine was dripping down my neck? We parted good friends.

Dearest it's awfully late, I must pack this up before I reach the bottom of the page, I fear. It was lovely getting your letter today, hot from the oven so to speak, and I'm looking forward tremendously to hearing from the midshipmate.

Dear heart, here's a wee bit of lily of the valley for you, with lots and lots of love. It smells heavenly now, but I'm afraid it will be withered by the time it reaches you.

Goodnight my sweet and most precious darling,

Always all yours,

Doris X X X X

April 8th

My darling,

Isn't this fun, writing diagonally? I'm not sure what's going to happen when I get a bit lower down, and it's awfully difficult to write straight when there is no edge to steer by! But I'm not doing too badly!

Had a letter today from George, sent from New York on Feb 27th, enclosing a picture of himself and the boy he is travelling with, taken in company with an American doll and two American gangster types, on top of the Empire State Building – all looking extremely cold! He said he had been having a magnificent time, and was well qualified to act as a guide to the night spots of the town – I can believe it.

(I don't think I like writing sideways like this after all, it's making me feel sick).

Tonight there is a Medical Society meeting, and a talk by a Surg. Comm. Keevil, on 'Surgery in Tight Places in the Navy'. I'd like to go, but somehow I can't summon up enough energy to organise myself there, and I don't much like going to those things alone. Still I may yet make it. Remember the first Medical Society meeting you took me to? You told me you had never taken a girl to one until you took the girl.

Very flattered I was darling, and very proud to be The Girl. Prouder still when I can go to one as The Wife.

Today I went to Liberty's and spent much mun and many coupons on scrumptious silks for the adorning of my body. I had a lovely time, and will have occupation for many months in the manufacturing of garments. I've got some beautiful deep blue shantung silk, which is a dream. I keep taking it out of the drawer and stroking it, and gloating over it! It's not really an extravagance because there just won't be any more of it, and it will last for years.

I wrote to you yesterday to thank you for the watch strap, but that letter will probably take some time, so I'll thank you again now. It was awfully good of you dearest to bother about it. The midshipmate rang me this morning after vainly trying the hospital yesterday and the day before. He's not in Town just now, but promised to come and have a drink when he came up again. Our conversation over the phone was very disjointed, and eventually was cut off altogether – he said something about your watch which he had taken to the Goldsmiths, but I didn't follow much of that – you know how it is on the telephone, if you once lose the thread you are done for, and can't get the hang of the conversation at all.

Next Day

A bumper crop of mail today, your three letters of March 21, 23 and 24, Airgraph of the 14th, and also a long letter from George enclosing a picture of himself taken with a 'Deb' eating on Broadway. Poor boy said he sometimes wished he could wake up in Glasgow and see Pamela, because he missed her so. Your letters were lovely long ones, a real treat. Joe phoned over from the Lodge on purpose to tell me they were there, which I thought was very civil of him. There are lots of things to answer, and no space on this flimsy, so I'll write more tomorrow and push it off by Air Mail.

About your library books – they are baskets, because I specially told them not to wait until you sent one back before sending another. So today I went and beat them up, and now they are going to send you one every fortnight until you have three, and then another as soon as you send one back. Regarding the photograph, however bad it may be I was delighted to have it, and am even now poring over it, and wishing you hadn't shut your eyes at the last moment. I'm afraid many rude remarks have been made, and shouts of derision even, uttered about the beard – but pay no regard, if you like it you keep it (although I must admit you do look a lot like an Eastern potentate of the more disagreeable kind). Also after a year in HM Navy you still wear your hat like a plate – I'll be glad when you can give up that headgear.

Today met Surg. Lieut. Humphrey Juler in the street. We had a short conversation which unfortunately was completely lost because there was a pneumatic drill going about 10 yards away.

Lots of things to tell you darling, so I'll carry on tomorrow, and use the rest of this to thank you again for three lovely letters which have brightened my day so much. I'm going to read them all again before I go to sleep. Just studying the snap – dearest is your right hand completely as new? Because it's a most peculiar shape to me. May be the camera, I don't know.

Dearest Roger, I'm very happy tonight to have had these letters from you and thinking of you so much. My own dear husband, all my love is with you, and I'm just living for the time when I can show you just how much love there is. Goodnight darling heart.

Ever yours, D.

Lindo Wing,
SMH, Paddington

April 12th

Darling love,

Flimsy No. 2 arrived today. April 2nd it was written, so that's 10 days which is not as good as it should be. The last one took 5. Please go on with the ordinary mail, because they don't really take so very long, and are so lovely to have. I haven't ventured upon an Airgraph yet, but any moment now. I dislike them because they are so horribly public somehow, fancy having to hand your secret soul across the counter of a Post Office to be read by a discrumptious Civil Servant. I hope you have observed how well organised my numbering is getting these days. I have a very small diary, in which I record important events only, and all mail arriving and departing – works very well I find. I don't know what I shall do when I get to 100 – probably go back to No. 1 again.

The photograph has been shown around, and I'm afraid the general verdict was pretty poor. 'You'll have to make him get rid of that awful beard' is the usual remark. So with some regret your wife informs you that a clean-shaven husband will be more appreciated than a bearded one. Secretly I like it rather a lot, but not all the time, because I can't see all your face through it, and it hides your mouth which is the nicest part of your whole face.

I do hope that by this time you had had some letters from me. I've managed to get off something every three or four days I think, so there should be a packet somewhere. Did you ever get a rather nice set of maps I sent sometime in January, called *The World War in Maps?* I had a fine browse round in The Times BC the other day, but failed to find anything to send you – every other book seemed to be about the war, and I'm sure you are getting a bit fed up with that.

13th

A very pleasant letter from Tony Oddie today. He is at the RN Hospital at Chatham and has a ward with 46 gastrics to look after. He was very cheering about your rapid return as soon as things clear up, but I don't suppose his guess is any better than mine. I've got a jug full of lilies of the valley in front of me, and the smell is so strong – I shut my eyes and imagine I'm at home in Jersey picking them in the garden. Heavenly things – I hope you will be home before they are all over.

Barbara Emerson is back, she's been most awfully good about it. I wanted to write or say something, but so far I haven't managed to get started, and no amount of sympathy, and nothing that anyone can say, could possibly make any difference I'm sure. It's the one thing you have to fight out by yourself, and I doubt very much if I should make as good a job of it as she has.

Glorious wonderful weather again – the parks are all green and the daffodils are out. It's all pale blue sparkling sky, and a heavenly smell of spring. Sally's christening is next Sunday and I hope it stays fine for it.

Heard a story just now, but it's too long to write down, and anyway it wasn't very funny. My love to all the boys and girls when you see them. Must dash off and post this before mid-day. Darling love, I hope all is well with you, and life not too tedious.

Almost Easter again. I must try and make my way to St Peter's some time. Happy Easter to you sweetheart, and all my fondest love.

Always your loving Wife

Lindo Wing,
St Mary's Hospital,
London W2

April 30th

My darling,

The rain is pouring down, and it's a good old-fashioned April day, when you begin to regret all the winter woolies you have cast off with such abandon!

This morning Dorothy and I spent a happy two hours in our best hats at the Royal Academy Private View. We got there pretty early and were very glad we did, because by 11:30 you couldn't see the pictures for the people, and nobody seemed to be looking much at the pictures anyway. I always enjoy the Academy, although I think it's a pity that there are so many pictures, you feel rather swamped by the number. This time there were some very lovely ones, mostly on the small side, and no enormous life-sizes at all, economy I suppose. Anna has only one picture hanging – a lovely thing of spring flowers, very formal in design, but freer in colour than usual (says she as though she had lived in Chelsea all her life). I coveted one picture, a watercolour of a kingfisher in front of a waterfall, most lovely thing. A very good portrait of The Patient, *Profile for Victory* it was called, by Egerton Cooper. Dorothy and I stood and clucked happily in front of it, feeling very superior to everyone else. I feel a really personal interest in him now which I never did before. There's also a bust, just the head, in bronze (green) which I didn't like awfully – why make green heads anyway?

I'm going to Cheam tomorrow for the weekend – wish I could stay there, I'm getting so sick of this place, and feel like stopping in bed for a week. I'm tempted to ask for a holiday, but I don't think I should, because I'll be off when you come back whether the Ministry of Labour likes it or not. I'm getting all the old clothes spruced up for the great day. Darling, will you cut off your beard before you come back? Don't if you want to keep it, but you see I don't think of you with it somehow, and it does make you look so old. (Pay no regard to this wifely nagging – I've no right at all to ask you to remove the growth, if you like it you keep it and I'll like it too.)

This is a silly little letter – I'll push it off for 1½d and hope it will reach you one day. It's got all my love in it my darling sweetheart – how I wish I could give it to you in some other way than this. My own precious husband, just to write it down brings you so much nearer to me. I love you and love you,

Always yours,
Doris

A gram from George today, 'Overseas' saying 'Safe and well'

May 1943

With Allied victory in North Africa in sight, Churchill arranged a personal conference with President Roosevelt to discuss urgent questions regarding the next steps in the conduct of the war, and to iron out some 'serious divergences beneath the surface' before they could cause difficulties in the future. In *The Hinge of Fate* he writes:

> The doctors did not want me to fly at the great height required in a bomber, and the Northern route clipper seaplanes could not take off on account of late ice till after May 20. It was therefore decided to go by sea. We left London on the night of May 4, and went aboard the *Queen Mary* in the Clyde on the following day. The ship had been admirably fitted up to meet all our needs. The whole delegation was accommodated on the main deck, which was sealed off from the rest of the ship. Officers, conference rooms, and of course the Map Room, stood ready for immediate use. From the moment we got on board our work went forward ceaselessly.[1]

Among the Prime Minister's party were 'Pug' Ismay and the Chiefs of Staff, as well as many staff officers and military commanders, and Lord Moran. (Also on board were 5,000 German prisoners being transported to America, in what we can only suppose were extremely cramped quarters.) Elaborate precautions were taken to conceal the identity of the VIP passengers and ensure their safety. On 9 May ships of the US Navy provided an escort. The *Queen*

Mary reached her destination on 11 May, and by the following afternoon meetings were in full swing at the White House.

Trapped between the advancing armies of the British and Americans, the Axis forces in Tunisia surrendered on 13 May. More than 275,000 German and Italian troops were taken prisoner. Richard wrote to Roger from the British Embassy in Washington:

> My dear Herr Docktor!
>
> At the end of this exciting and happy week I feel bound to send off this note of heartiest congratulations to you and to all the guys in the vicinity in which you serve: great work and very pleasing it must be to feel that you have broken up the African party. I expect that the uppermost thought in the mind of any honest tar at the moment – as in fact it always is – is what about a spot of leave? I suppose there is now a reasonable chance of your getting some. Whoopee. I'll bet you just hate the sight of the Mediterranean by now, and won't have any enthusiasm about joining me on cruises after the war – 'to see where it all happened'.
>
> Anyway I think I would prescribe a short billet for you at this stage. For your wife's sake and to give the younger fellahs a chance. You have had a wonderful year and its time you piped down. I'm longing to see you again and see how you have reacted to it all.
>
> As you are aware Doris's little Patient is with us now, but I've not been able to see him yet. I hope I do, and in fact may do so this week.

In London, meanwhile, Doris was enjoying the unseasonably warm May weather and following with interest the finale of the campaign in Tunisia. She spent time with her friends, and was delighted to have a visit from one of Roger's shipmates and from 'Uncle Herbert', who was not really her uncle but her grandmother's elderly cousin at whose house in Hunstanton Doris had spent many pleasant summer holidays as a child. She missed fresh fruit so much that a gift of peaches from Guy Harben, Treasurer of St Mary's and a member of the Board of Governors, was a noteworthy event. Another noteworthy event was the awarding of the OBE in that year's Birthday Honours to the surgeon Arthur Porritt. Porritt had been a Rhodes Scholar and an Olympic medal-winning sprinter; he came to St Mary's in 1926 after doing his initial training at Oxford, and soon after qualifying he was appointed surgeon to the Prince of Wales, the future King Edward VIII. In March 1940 he had joined the Royal Army Medical Corps in which he served with distinction. He would later be appointed surgeon to King George VI, to Queen Elizabeth II, and have an outstanding career. He received many honours, including a knighthood in 1950, and became Baron Porritt in 1973.

On 14 May Doris, like many others in the country, tuned in to the BBC Overseas Service to hear the Prime Minister, her 'little patient', broadcast from Washington a tribute to the Home Guard in commemoration of the third anniversary of their founding. She had listened to many of his speeches before, but this time she had a rather more proprietary interest, noticing such details as his slight lingering cough.

A few days later, on 18 May, Richard wrote again to Roger:

Last night I went to the White House and met the Patient for dinner. He was in terrific form, was delighted to know that I was Nurse Miles' brother-in-law and asked me to remember him to her. He said that they looked after him wonderfully. Your dear old chief Charles Wilson was there too. I didn't know that he was now Lord Moran, but when that was all straightened up, he too sent his kindest regards and recalled the first time he met you at Bradfield and you walked home with him part of the way. Yes it was a great experience to see our two Number One men at dinner together and I've written it all up against a happier day when I will be seeing you again and can tell you all about it. Suffice to say here that I can never thank Mrs FDR enough for the fun she has given me, and that the great man seemed in absolutely perfect health, vigour and wit, and you can tell that to the Axis with my love.

I'm going to write off a line to Doris now to tell her what a good job she has done and give her all the news.

There was more good news in England that day. 'Torrent Rages along Ruhr!' screamed the headline of the *Daily Mirror*. Two nights earlier British bombers had destroyed several dams on the Ruhr river in Germany's industrial heartland using a new type of 'bouncing bomb' invented by engineer Barnes Wallis, causing catastrophic flooding in the Ruhr Valley. Although the disruption to German industry was not as great as the planners of the raid had intended, the loss of thousands of acres of farmland had a significant effect on food production, and repairs to the damaged mines, factories and dams kept construction workers and equipment tied up for many months and unable to work on other projects such as the Atlantic defences. The 'Dam Busters' raid was a propaganda coup and another massive boost to British morale.

The next day, 19 May, Churchill gave a rousing and somewhat jingoistic speech to a joint session of Congress, which was also broadcast overseas. 'I wonder if you heard the Prime Minister's speech today?' Richard wrote to his brother. 'It is tantalising to think of huge decisions being taken right under our noses and not being any the wiser than you as to what does America do next!'

What America did next was to pay heed to Churchill when he urged them 'to search our hearts and brace our sinews and take the most earnest counsel one with another in order that the favourable position which has already been reached both against Japan and against Hitler and Mussolini in Europe shall not be let slip'.[2]

In late May American forces ejected the Japanese from Attu in the Aleutian Islands. In the Atlantic German U-boats had been wreaking havoc, but more Allied vessels, overwhelming superiority in the air and improvements in anti-submarine technology combined to tip the balance, and in 'Black May' 43 U-boats were sunk, more than in whole of 1941. Admiral Donitz temporarily recalled the U-boat fleet; they never again posed such a serious threat. And having gained control over all of North Africa, the Allies could now move forward with the invasion of Sicily and Italy, which Churchill allegedly described as the 'soft underbelly of the Axis'.[3]

The advantage lay with the Allies almost everywhere, but it was slight. In early May the SS completed the destruction of the Warsaw Ghetto and on 16 May the uprising was officially over when they blew up the Great Synagogue – 13,000 Jews had died, 50,000 were captured and sent to extermination camps. Although some relief had reached the starving citizens of Leningrad in January, the city was still suffering under a protracted siege. Meanwhile, in a remote village called Peenemunde on the edge of the Baltic Sea, the Germans were testing a new rocket-propelled 'flying bomb', the V1, designed to rain terror on Britain.

It would be two more years and many bloody battles before the war in Europe was ended, and several months after that before the enemy was vanquished worldwide. However, the tide had irrevocably turned. This was not the end, but it was, at last, the beginning of the end.

Lindo Wing
St Mary's Hospital

Monday, May 3rd

My darling,

Your Easter Sunday flimsy arrived this morning – werry rapid flight. The Airgraph you mention as having sent the week before is still in the air. One husband of a nurse here sends her a whole letter written on a series of Airgraphs – continued in our next, kind of thing – but it must come rather expensive at 3d a time. Darling you sounded awfully fed up – I hope it was only a mood of the moment and that your usual joie de thing has returned. I can almost see you as you write, and it's so easy to tell what kind of a mood you are in.

I'm afraid I object to the poker-playing – get the Captain to give you a few lessons, because your knowledge of the game is certainly not up to the Navy standard, and if I know anything of NO's they will continue to let you go on losing for as long as you like to play. And losing all the time is so monotonous!

I had migraine yesterday, isn't that annoying? But I'm better now, although I can still see lots of black spots. Dearest, I wish you were here to make a fuss of me and 'kiss it better'. I'm afraid you are going to find me a very clinging vine in lots of ways.

Duncan was in on Saturday, but unfortunately I missed him. He's still at Portsmouth, and according to the general verdict very much improved. He had rather a good story about one naval rating he had to examine, who when he had finished kept asking him, 'aren't you going to tell the Captain I'm here?' When Dunc finally enquired why the hell he should tell the Captain the rating said, 'because I'm Godfrey Winn'. The Captain, on being told, said rather peevishly that they had enough amateurs and didn't want any professionals.

I've bought you a ticket in a raffle for a bottle of gin – if you win I'll keep the gin until you come home, and we shall be able to celebrate secretly and all by ourselves! I've been selling lots of tickets to the most unlikely people. It's Booths' Gin, guaranteed free from impurities. Trouble is you can't get anything to put with it, though as a hardened naval type I don't suppose you would worry much about that!

Esmé Rees is joining the Grass Widders of Married Alley today. Accommodation is getting quite difficult, there are now so many of us up there. I shall be very glad when I can sub-let my turret for a time, I'm getting a little bit tired of it.

I'm reading a delightful booked called *You Deal, My Lovely* in the style of James Hadley Chase and Damon Runyan – all about a G-man called Lemmy Caution who is chasing American thugs in London. Here is a bit of it: – 'I then get to work on this mug; I proceed to give him everything that I ever learned durin' my toughest moments. I invent new things for the boy. By the time I have finished with him he looks like somebody had throw him into the gearbox of a battleship that was steamin' backwards...' Well, it's a change from Mr Tolstoy. Trouble is I'll be writing to you like that before I know what's what.

Next day

Received today your Airgraph of April 22nd. So glad you have had some more mail, but I'm very disappointed that my parcel was not there, however perhaps by now it has reached you. I find those Airgraphs aren't so bad after all. I must get some.

Today I went to the Times Book Club to try and get them properly organised. They are the most muddle headed lot of mugs I've ever met. No idea at all. The head woman of course was not there – 'So sorry Mrs Miles, will you wait Mrs Miles?' I said no, I won't wait, but I'll come in on Thursday and mind you have things fixed by then. I did go in some weeks ago and thought I had got things organised, but apparently not. Still as long as you have something to read, and they say that you've got three books out.

I met John for coffee – he has very skillfully fixed my watch strap for me. I told you I think that George had sent me one from the US, and I thought I would wear that one and keep yours as a kind of reserve for when this one breaks – as I'm afraid it will. John put it on for me, and then we found that it wouldn't undo, so we spent a busy five minutes in Buzzards' trying to work the catch, I feeling rather like an escaped convict having chains removed. Eventually we got it working, and it looks fine. John has made a very good job of it, removing a link from both ends and soldering the chain to the watch itself.

I posted off a couple of *Country Lifes* to you today, they are not very exciting, but in one of them there is a picture of a room in Chequers which is rather pleasant. I also bought millions of hair combs today, so I'm enclosing one of them. I've been scratching at my hair for ages now with an old bit of bone with about two teeth attached. Like this

(honest)

We are having his lordship Guy Harben in as patient today. Something wrong with his knee. Terrific flap to have the room all pansied up. When asked by the Theatre Sister what he was going to do Dickson said, 'just a knee'. How very helpful that is! We plan to sell the old boy many tickets for our bottle of gin.

Went out on the toot, beer drinking, last night with an uncle of mine (age 80!!)

Darling I love you, for ever and ever

Always yours, Doris

St Mary's Hospital, W2

May 5th

My darling,

Not much news since my last letter. It's getting very warm here, and the days are slipping away quite rapidly. It must be about time I had another letter – or letters – from you, I should think. Actually it's just a fortnight since the first of the batch arrived. I'm sure by now that you will have had some of mine, and also I hope some of the parcels.

Isn't this great about us taking Madagascar? I believe George must be out on that job, and I know Jock Morrison is, in a troop ship I believe. What fun and games you are all having, and what awful bores you will be when you are all old and get together to tell your stories – 'When I was in Murmansk, old boy!' Actually I'm just longing to hear about it all, and envy you no end being able to get on with the job – I'm glad you joined the Navy, even though it's pretty lonely without you, and I'm very proud of my husband.

<u>Wed.</u>

Sad news today about Kirby. It always seems to be the nicest ones who go and the ones who can least best be spared. It's made me feel awfully depressed. I also had a row with a nurse on here last night and felt really miserable yesterday, but have since recovered.

I spend a very agreeable hour or so every evening watching the people in Praed Street from my window – a vastly entertaining business. I have an uninterrupted view from Cables to the Fountains and beyond, and you'd never believe the things that go on – it's like a pantomime. The comings and goings from the Fountains alone are very amusing, and I'm sure the house opposite is the headquarters either of an international spy ring or the white slave traffic, the comings and goings are terrific! I often imagine that you are walking down from the station, and try to estimate at what moment I should leave the window in order to reach the Lodge at the same time as you do. (I'm quite sure though that if you really were coming I should either be half-way to the station, or have fallen down the stairs and broken my neck!)

It's been so hot today, really mid-summer weather – what a waste, we ought to be at the hut, or by the sea – I keep meaning to start playing tennis, but I'm too lazy. This grass widowhood business is very odd – I feel kind of in the air, and just waiting. I can't seem to concentrate on anything, or get interested in doing anything or seeing anybody, and I must be awful to work with! It's been so much worse, darling, than I ever dreamed possible, but I suppose every wife goes through it, and it comes of being civilised and having world wars. Anyway I've no regrets at all my dearest, and although it was so short it was perfect and lovely. Thank you for loving me.

Goodnight darling heart. Thursday tomorrow, and another day nearer to seeing you.

God bless,

All my love, Doris

There was a little sparrer,
Flew all the way to Spain,
And when he had arrived there
He flew back home again.

And as he flew back home again
He met a bloomin' 'awk,
Who pulled all 'is bleedin' fevvers out
And said, 'Now you b— walk!'

L.W.

May 8th

Darling,

Alec Lay rang this morning, and I was at lunch – wasn't it annoying? I should so have loved to have had a word with him. He reported that Beetle was home and was coming up to see me, so I'm looking forward to that tremendously. And I says to myself, if he can come home so can Roger –

H-J throwing a party tonight. Where and how and why I don't know – Duggie is taking me, so it should be very pleasant.

Isn't this little book rather tasty? Don't lose it will you dear (usual cry, I'm afraid, but it's such a nice little bookie).

Lots and lots of love sweetheart,

Always yours,

D.

Lindo Wing
St Mary's Hospital
London W2

May 11th

My darling,

Very exciting news in the papers these last few days, everyone is terribly thrilled about the North African campaign, and generally pretty optimistic. I don't much like the accounts of 'much naval activity' and I'm afraid I get a bit worried, but then I think everyone does with any people in it. I know you hoped to get back when this business had been cleared up, but I've an idea you will be kept for some time yet. Never mind darling, the longer you stay now the more claim you have on that shore job when you get back. No mail this week yet, should be a nice fat bunch when it does come.

I've been going quite gay the last few nights, and have really been enjoying myself. On Sunday, Dorothy's first anniversary, we went to the Great Western Railway Hotel to have a quiet noggin to celebrate the occasion. However, before we had time to summon the surly waiter and order anything the bar had closed. So we thought we would have a cuppa. Even this was not forthcoming – you know what that dump is like! However, along came Mr Guard, who is the manager of the entire GWR and an old patient of the 3rd Floor – and after that everything was magnificent, vast gin and frenches and double scotches being whistled up with no trouble at all! He's the man to know.

Last night I popped down to Oxford and went with Jill to a WRNS dance at the Town Hall. I caught the 4:45 from Paddington and was in Oxford by 6:15. It was teeming with rain, and after struggling on and off buses we arrived at Jill's wrennery looking like a couple of drowned rats. However we overcame the wet by eating our dinner 'en negligee' with our hair done up in curlers, to the great amusement of the wardroom steward(ess?).

The dance was priceless. Being practically the only doll not in uniform I had a big pull, and as the proportion of men to women was about 2 to 1, I didn't lack for partners. These ranged from Royal Engineer officers from an army camp at Bicester, to Sea Cadets, RAF troops, undergraduates, and even a rather elderly Lieut RNVR.

'My steady', as Jill called him, was a charming lad in the Navy, doing a 6-month's short course at Trinity, and spending all his week-ends, and all his money, in Town trying to do everything and go everywhere. He came from Glasgow. I chatted intelligently about the Navy, and presumed that after he had done his six weeks at sea he would go to the King Alfred and become a Sub. Lieut. 'Oh no', I was informed, 'we are Midshipmen until we are 20'. Jill was very amused and accused me of cradle snatching. But I must say that the youth of the partners in no way detracted from my enjoyment of the dance. We drank fizzy lemonade out of bottles with straws, and ate large spam sandwiches. They told me very proudly of all the night clubs they had been to, and I recommended a place or two as being worth their patronage!

We returned to Jill's wardroom with a charming Norwegian officer ('but Doris, isn't it sad? He's married, but he doesn't live with his wife') and a very drunken Army Captain whom Jill didn't know from Adam, and who insisted on seeing her home. However he was successfully dealt with, and left high and dry on the doorstep, and we finished off the evening with some more noggins. Very pleasant.

This morning I did a very rapid conducted tour of Oxford. Apart from Magdalen Bridge and Tower, Jill's idea of the geography of the place is pretty sketchy, but with the aid of a map we managed to pick out the more important colleges, and walked up the 'High' and down the 'Broad' and observed all manner of undergraduates and -ettes – <u>werry</u> odd most of them. But the town itself is really beautiful, definitely high on the list, almost as high as Edinburgh (by the way, have you ever been to Winchester?) and must be visited again. I managed to skip round Exeter College, but I couldn't find a picture of it to send Richard. Cordial invitations to go down again any time – I hope we will be able to go together. A nice place or occasion is just twice as nice when shared with you darling.

Dickson was funny at the sale the other day. I had collected a few things to send to you, including a tube of brushless shaving cream. He observed this, and asked if you were going to shave off your beard, and was very interested to know if you washed the whole of your face or just the top half. I explained how time-saving a beard was, and I doubted whether you always had time to wash very well, but I thought you were as clean as most.

I think I told you that he did the auctioning, and among the things was a bottle of champagne – 'Given to me by a grateful patient, God rest his soul!' He hasn't been much on the floor lately, but he's still got his eyes skinned for any empty rooms to fill up with his old ligatures.

Dear, you must come back soon so that I can leave here because all my black stockings have got holes in 'em and I'd die rather than give up coupons to buy any more. So miserable not having any letters from you this week. I haven't missed on Monday or Tuesday for ages and when I don't hear I always imagine awful things happening to you – very stupid of me I know, but there you are, you shouldn't have made me love you so much.

Going to dinner with the H-J's tonight – very nice invitation to stay the night as well, which strikes me as being a pretty sensible idea. Guy Harben in his cups last night gave me two peaches, which I thought it would be rather a nice gesture to take along to Sunbeam. When he gave them to me he was so whistled that he obviously didn't know what he was doing, and I didn't know whether to take them or put them in the fridge and give them back to him the next morning! However greed overcame my conscience.

I see Winston has hopped off again – wish he had taken me with him! What an incredible man he is.

Darling, I hope you are getting mail reasonably well, and that you are all right. Don't get sunstroke or anything will you? I think of you so much, and so long for you to come back. Dear heart, all my fondest love,

Always yours,
Doris

P.S. Arthur Porritt has the OBE.

Lindo Wing,
St Marys Hospital, Paddington

Thursday May 13th

My darling,

I smell just like a dissecting room 'subject', having upset a bottle of formalin lotion all over myself. Feelthy! So I've surrounded myself with jars of carnations and roses to take away the stink.

Had a very excellent evening yesterday with Beetle. Really quite like old times. We went to the Fountains for a couple of pints before going on to a very tasty salmon mayonnaise at Cables, old Beetle and I both talking as hard as we could go, until eventually he lost his voice. Kay Powell (Haines that was) joined us later, so did Jack Suchet, and that strange little man, friend of Robert's, whose name I think is Coop. Very entertaining party. I hope to see Alan again before his leave ends. In any case I'll get him to take this letter along with him, in that way it may reach you rather more rapidly than by the usual route. Nothing to send with it I'm afraid. I hope he succeeds in getting you the alc you commissioned, but I'm afraid he will have rather a job. He was very optimistic about your getting ashore pretty soon, although he said that your engines never seemed to go wrong, whereas Peter Baly's were always packing up. Perhaps your new chief won't be quite so expert as the old one.

Dice, darling! I'm shocked! What would your parents think? I'll look around for a nice pair of loaded ones, that's what you want – 'bones', I think is the term, and I'm quite sure George is an expert.

I expect you have heard by now about Duncan's cross-Channel steamer with landing barges – poor old Dunc with his big ideas about getting into a carrier. John Hill is in Tunisia with the Marines, in charge of sanitation, water etc. Poor Marines. Shake John a bit though.

Had a pleasant airgraph today from your captain to thank me for the ceegar. I'm very glad they have been smoked to a successful conclusion. Doesn't it make you sore to think that C only smoked a couple of inches and chucks the rest away? You could set up a tobacconists shop on the ends alone.

Do tell Alan how very much I enjoyed the evening with him, and I hope it won't be very long before we can all resume the conversation over a pint or two.

Enclosed the note I had from Guy Harben when he went out, very civil I thought. He's certainly a most generous man. He wrote Bloss a marvellous letter saying how the lifts rattled, the doors and windows of the Wing rattled, the post office van rattled in the middle of the night ... but the nurses were never rattled. (Much!) I was rattled tonight when a patient showed me a rash in his groin and started murmuring vaguely about VD. What would you do, chums? However, with my usual calm I murmured soothingly to him and provided him with a large bottle of calamine, hoping the thing will have faded by the morning. Very tricky, though, you must admit.

Don't get worried about the clothing situation here. I have packets of coupons in hand for a fine new autumn suiting, and otherwise have plenty of clothes to wear out. I certainly don't give up stocking coupons for the black horrors, I wear my old ones all patched up until they are so bad they they drop off my feet. At the moment I'm in awful thick lisle things that I bought many years ago and never could bring myself to wear them before. But they serve, and they don't ladder so quickly as silk ones.

Jack Suchet was demonstrating very proudly how he had had a shirt renovated, a new front made from the back, and new cuffs from the tail, or sumptin – sounded very intriguing. I must get going on any oldie shirties of yours that I can find. By the way, darling, do you realise that you won't have a suit to wear when you come home? You'd better get Richard to send you one from the US. I expect you will be glad to get out of your uniform after a year's solid wear. Must be getting pretty shiny by now.

I'm still ploughing through *War and Peace*, only another 400 pages to go. Trouble is you take so long to read it, that by the time you reach the end you've forgotten what happened in the beginning. Bet you sixpence you would never finish it. I've been reading H. V. Morton's *Atlantic Meeting* at the same time. It's the story of Churchill's first meeting with Roosevelt and the Atlantic Charter. Very well written, you should put it on your list.

Mrs Juler was asking about you today. Humphrey is in HMS *Walpole*, North Sea I think. Old Juler is a sweet old boy and always calls me 'Mrs Miles' very solemnly. Bourne too was enquiring how you were, and I told him how you were using his Penguin book. He was awfully pleased and sends you his best things. Did you get your March and April *Gazettes?* Pretty poor attempts, I though. Carne (porter) was saying that there was no one now to edit them – 'wants Roger Miles back, he's the one for the job'. You should write something for them don't you think? *How to be a Surgeon Lieutenant, Tight corners I have been in,* or sumptin – I'm sure they'd lap it up.

Eric Norman was up again today, having come in triumph from sinking a submarine, and laden with goodies from Newfoundland. That's the job you should have had – leave every two months. Still, I think your work is probably more exciting than escorting convoys to and from across the Atlantic.

Later

It's our Thursday again, however many I wonder since the first one? A good big think about you tonight my darling, I feel in a very lonely mood, and you seem so very far away. Perhaps it's because I've had no letters this week yet, but I'm sure they will come soon, I know you've been very busy, Alan told me. God bless you, beloved, and keep you safe.

Always all my heart's love my darling,
Doris

Lindo Wing,
St Mary's Hospital, W2

May 15th

Darling Roger,

For the umpteenth time I've dropped my pen on the floor, and now I think it's really gone phut – it's behaving in the most peculiar fashion, and the nib looks something like this

so if I suddenly go mad and tear large holes in the paper you will know the reason.

Your letter of April 26th arrived very pleasantly and unexpectedly this morning. It's good to have the old sea-mail type, and it really doesn't matter that they take three weeks or so to get here. Glad the lily had some smell in it. The other bloom was a piece of rosemary, and was also sent because it smelled good.

Did you hear the PM last night from Washington? Still got a cough – he ought to have me there to keep an eye on him. Great speculations at home as to where the attack is going to be made. Oddly enough the rejoicing over the finish of the Germans in Tunisia is not very wild or very noticeable. People just say, 'News is pretty good, isn't it?' – 'Um. How are your pears doing this year?' I believe the church bells are going to ring a victory peal on Sunday, and the Home Guard are having demonstrations and things. Dickson of course knew all about it, and just how long the Germans could keep on fighting. He must have spies all over the place.

We are having a heat wave here, with the temperature nearly 80 in the shade! My week-end off thank goodness – I'm going down to Marian's, and intend spending my day in a deckchair in the sun. Guy Harben gave me another peach, which I shall suck with great relish. He also gave me £5 when he left, and a charming note saying how much he had enjoyed being here. I'm torn between spending the mun on something every extravagant and unnecessary, or buying some Savings Certificates. I know what you would tell me to do, but it seems wrong not to store it up till we can spend it together. What will probably happen is that I shall get into the Times Book Club and spend it all there.

You asked whether a condolence strip to Barbara Emerson would be a good idea. I rather think it would, although they're most appallingly difficult things to write. I saw Anna the other day, and she said she had had a letter from you – I murmured politely 'oh yes', but nothing further was said. I think we'd better wait until you come home, and then we can go and visit her. She has taken on Duncan's flat behind Sussex Gardens. They turned her out of her little suite in the top theatre as it's about to be opened up again. Stupid thing to do I think, I'm convinced the raids aren't over yet, and we'll see them transporting everything back to Lewis Lloyd when they start again. (Pen's doing very well, isn't it? Don't breathe – I'm expecting the whole issue to fall to pieces at any moment.)

Heard from Milton the other day. Stuck in the mud somewhere in North Africa., she says it's rather like living in a lake. Sounds awful. I've much to be thankful for working as I do in this luxurious central-heated mansion!! At least I haven't endured the agonies of cold that I usually do during the winter. No colds and no chilblains – quite a record.

We've another grass widow joined the ranks in Married Alley, Mrs Brian Brierley, once Nurse Mansfield. Her husband is in HMS *Brighton* – one of the American destroyers. He's not as lucky as you, shares a cabin, and the sick bay is like a box. But he has a leading Sick Bay Attendant who is quite competent. How is your little man? Have you succeeded in beaching him yet? I think it would be a good scheme if I disguised myself as your SBA and came with you. One Canadian dame did stow away in her husband's bomber and came to England with him – so the *Daily Mirror* says.

Next day

Sitting in Marian's garden in blazing sunshine watching John digging beds very energetically. The babe is very well, and looking more human every day – hope to send you some photos of her soon. Marian has everything taped, and throws her around with great abandon, while coping with house ducks, day-old chicks and two broody hens. I'm afraid you won't find me half such a capable person as your sister darling, and as I've told you many times, I'm shockingly lazy – our brats will have to bring themselves up.

Looking at Sally and wondering what she will be like, it's awfully exciting wondering how ours will turn out. I think four would be a good round figure, don't you? Two of each. I like washing out baths too, so we'll have to toss up for that job, but I'll keep you to your word about washing up!

I love thinking about it all darling, and what fun it's going to be, what kind of furniture we will have, and how we will plant the garden – I refuse to live in a flat. Likewise I refuse to live in London or Manchester or Hull. I'll have to send your bills out I expect, because you would probably forget about them, but I'm pretty poor at keeping accounts. Still, I expect we will manage all right between us.

Later

Back from Marian's to find three lovely long letters from you waiting for me. They were written before and on your birthday, and were real goodies, so good darling that they made me cry a little bit! I can see you so clearly writing them – and you can express it all so much better than I can – the dreadful aching longing to have you back again, and the lovely feeling of joy in my heart whenever I remember our love and how happy we have been. Our love is a kind of armour too against the rest of the world – just because you think of me as you do, nothing and nobody can hurt me or make me miserable. Because you believe in me I believe in myself and don't care what anyone else thinks of me. Darling heart, I pray that it may always be like this, and although we shall fail in lots of ways to live up to the ideal we have of each other, may our love stay as fresh and wonderful as it was when we were married.

Beloved, I'm thinking so much of you tonight, and dream that you are with me, holding me close in your arms. I'll write lots more tomorrow and answer your letters properly – just now I'll say goodnight my most precious husband, I love you and love you.

Always and for ever all my heart's love,

Doris X X X X X X

Act Three

In December 1943 Churchill was again stricken with strep pneumonia while he was visiting General Eisenhower's HQ in Tunisia. This time Lord Moran believed it was more serious and that Churchill's heart could be affected. Once again M&B worked its magic. Churchill praised the 'wonder drug' that had cured him: 'I personally have never failed to pay my tribute of respect and gratitude to M&B; although I am not competent to give you an exact description of how it works, it certainly has in my case always been attended by highly beneficial results.'[1] By the beginning of 1944 the Prime Minister was convalescing in Marrakesh and busy working on the plans for D-Day.

Allied forces had landed in Sicily in July 1943, and by early September they were on the Italian mainland. Mussolini, *Il Duce*, was overthrown, and Italy quickly surrendered. German opposition, however, was fierce, and fighting continued for months as British and American troops clawed their way north. They did not enter Rome until the beginning of June 1944. Just a few days later, on 6 June, the D-day invasion began. Thousands of Allied troops landed on the beaches of Normandy in Operation Overlord, the largest seaborne assault ever undertaken, and slowly began to push through France towards the German Fatherland. The small city of Chichester, where Doris and Roger would later settle with their family, had a walk-on part in the drama; General Dwight Eisenhower, Supreme Commander of the Allied forces, stayed briefly at the venerable Ship Hotel for planning meetings shortly before the operation began.

In answer to King George VI's enquiry as to where he planned to be on D-Day, Churchill told him that he wanted to watch the bombardment from one of the cruiser squadrons. The King responded that he would like to come too. With visions of himself leading the army into battle like his illustrious ancestor, Churchill opined what fun it would be to land with the troops on D-Day and perhaps get there ahead of Monty![2] As Boris Johnson delightfully put it, 'He wanted to show the world that he was truly a Marlborough, and not just a Marlborough Lite.'[3] Luckily, cooler heads prevailed as the King soon realised that it was not in the interests of the country for both the monarch *and* the Prime Minister to put themselves in harm's way, and he persuaded Churchill not to go. Reluctantly, Churchill abandoned the idea of accompanying the first wave. He did, however, spend the day of 12 June touring the landing beaches and meeting the military commanders, and the King himself visited the troops in Normandy a few days later.

In November 1943 HMS *Tartar* returned to England for refit. Roger was given a shore posting at Corsham in Somerset, serving with the Royal Marines. Doris joined him there, and to their delight she soon became pregnant again. (She was not at all deterred by what her brother-in-law Richard had written to his sister Marian when she was expecting Sally: ' by all accounts having a baby ain't all fun all the time!') In March 1944, Richard wrote to them from Washington DC:

My dear Roger and Doris,

Your letter of February 12 came in this morning. I am replying tonight, although it is past midnight, because there is to be a special bag in the morning, which is to carry a bit of civilian mail. Thus, if all goes to plan, this should prove to be the fastest bit of correspondence that has ever taken place between us.

Firstly about the <u>babe</u>. I won't volunteer a name, so much depends on the eventual colour of the hair, not to mention such details as gender, but do let me know precisely what you need most and is in short supply and I will contrive to get it. I have seen things advertised known as 'complete layettes'; without enquiring too exactingly into the details thereof, I will obtain one at once. It is most exciting and I do hope all goes well. So much depends on good staff work of course, and I hope that you my dear brother have not become so ham-fisted from attending your present charges that you have lost the necessary touch. I need hardly fear that this will be so, however, and I have the quite distinct impression from your previous letters that if devotion is the first requirement of married life, Doris will get all that she can possibly manage without suffocation!

Certainly you make married life sound a handsome thing and I am much encouraged. Still, it is rather awkward when you are so far from home. You can't just go off and marry the first American girl you meet in a drug store, and although I am acquainted with at least ½ million quite dazzling poppets in this part of the world, there has not been any excessive stimulation of the Miles heartbeat for a long time.

In 1944 Richard, now assistant to economist Redvers Opie, was an adviser to the British Delegation under the chairmanship of John Maynard Keynes at the Bretton Woods Conference, which laid down the parameters for the post-war world and led to, among other things, the establishment of the International Monetary Fund and the World Bank. He was a strong believer in the special relationship (a term coined by Winston Churchill himself) between the United Kingdom and the United States. When Churchill, on a visit to the US, asked what Britain could do to cement the bond and show the country's appreciation for the help of the American people, Richard suggested that this would be an ideal time for the UK to switch to driving on the right as a gesture of solidarity. Churchill immediately shot down the idea, arguing that it was essential that the driver be on the left so that his sword arm was free in the event of an attacker approaching on the opposite side of the road! And so today the UK still stubbornly drives on the left.

Roger and Doris's daughter was born on 17 August 1944. They named her Ann (after Roger's mother) Victoria (for the Allied victory they were sure was coming soon) Mary (for Doris's mother), but she was ever afterwards called just Vicky. Jill Hippisley was her godmother. Shortly thereafter, Roger was again posted overseas, this time to the Far East and Japan. Doris took her baby to the safety of the welcoming home of Roger's Auntie Nellie in north Wales until the spring of 1945, when she returned to Cheam to stay with her parents-in-law, Reverend Ted and Annie Miles.

Dorothy Pugh was still at St Mary's in late August 1944 when Winston Churchill was diagnosed by Lord Moran with a mild bout of pneumonia. Doris was obviously unavailable this time. Dorothy's son told me recently that the Prime Minister specifically asked for 'Mrs Pugh', and Dorothy was once again called in to nurse him. In early September she accompanied Churchill to the Quebec Conference on board the *Queen Mary*.

The adventurous Jill Hippisley did not wait for hostilities to end before setting out to sea. In February 1944 she was posted to the hospital ship *Oxfordshire* in the Mediterranean, caring for casualties from the Italian conflict. A year later she sailed for Australia, where she became part of the Air Evacuation Unit of the RN Auxiliary Hospital in Sydney. Her deployment involved a harrowing crash landing (though fortunately with no injuries) on a Pacific island recently occupied by the Japanese. She also served with the Prisoner of War Reception Unit in Hong Kong before returning to Sydney in November 1945, where Roger encountered her on his way home. 'Charm is also lent to the RN Hospital by the presence of Jill Hippisley',[4] he wrote in a report to the *St Mary's Gazette* reprinted in *Doctors at War*.

George had finally reached New Zealand in April 1943 and was posted to the light cruiser HMNZS *Leander*, but in July his ship was torpedoed and almost sunk off the Solomon Islands. The engine room was destroyed and George was lucky to escape injury. After emergency repairs in Auckland, *Leander* made her way to Boston for a complete refit, arriving in that historic city just before Christmas. Cooling his heels while his ship was in dry dock, George met a beautiful Red Cross volunteer, Pauline Shaw Nesmith. He was charmed by the vivacious Pauline, a divorcée with two little girls. Pauline, in turn, was won over by George's impish sense of humour and bestowed on him her ultimate accolade, 'he makes me laugh'.

On 30 January 1945, Winston Churchill woke up on the island of Malta, with a temperature and feeling unwell. Nonetheless, by the next day he was on his way to a conference with President Roosevelt and the leader of the Soviet Union, Josef Stalin. As always, Charles Wilson was by Churchill's side. Although the youngest of the three leaders, Stalin refused to leave Russia, and so it was the elderly Prime Minister and the ailing President who made the difficult and dangerous journey in the depths of winter to the resort town of Yalta in the Crimea.

Wilson was appalled when he saw the President and privately estimated that he had only months to live. Pictures show Roosevelt wrapped in a shawl against the chill air, looking frail and drawn. Churchill himself was tired and depressed, missing Clemmie very much, and distressed by the deterioration of his American confrère. It was a stark contrast to the two relaxed, laughing leaders photographed two years earlier in Morocco.

Churchill was deeply suspicious of Stalin's designs on those countries of Eastern Europe where the Red Army had gained ground. He believed communism to be as great a threat to individual liberty as fascism. He tried to rein in the Soviet leader's territorial ambitions, but he was overruled by the Americans, who turned a blind eye in their eagerness for Russian assistance in the rapid defeat of Nazi Germany and the final campaign against Japan. Over the course of the next week, these three grumpy old men carved up post-war Europe and sealed the fate of millions, effectively ceding control of much of Eastern Europe and a large chunk of Germany to the wily Stalin. It was especially ironic that Poland was included in the Soviet hegemony, since the spark that had ignited the war in Europe more than five years previously had been the obligation to free that country from a hostile foreign occupation.

Without today's 24/7 TV coverage, the extent of Roosevelt's illness was not apparent to the general public, who were shocked at the announcement on April 12 that the President had died of a cerebral haemorrhage. Churchill mourned his friend, and described his death as a bitter loss to humanity. 'In Franklin Roosevelt,' he told the House of Commons, 'there died the greatest American friend we have ever known, and the greatest champion of freedom who has ever brought help and comfort from the new world to the old.'[5]

For Adolf Hitler, trapped in his Berlin bunker between Allied troops advancing from the West and the Red Army from the East, the end was also close. Although Germany had been utterly defeated, Hitler refused to surrender. On April 28 he married his long-time mistress Eva Braun and on 30 April they both committed suicide. His loyal henchman Josef Goebbels, his wife and six children also took their own lives along with their Fürher. The bodies were burned by retainers to keep them out of the hands of the approaching Russians. A week later the remaining German High Command finally capitulated.

Victory in Europe, V-E Day, was declared on 8 May. Once again all the church bells rang out and there was dancing in the streets.

Annie Miles urged Doris to go into central London with Margaret, Marian and John Gilbert to celebrate with the other young people. Being in a reserved occupation (something very hush-hush to do with radar) John had managed to acquire a little petrol and the three of them set off in John's car. Doris later recalled, 'We parked near the Mall and walked down to Buckingham Palace. Huge crowds shouting and dancing. My sister-in-law Margaret insisted on singing the *Internationale*, to our intense annoyance.'[6]

Among the revellers was the nineteen-year-old Princess Elizabeth in her ATS uniform, and her sister Princess Margaret, fourteen. With a large group of trusted friends they had been given permission to mingle with the people celebrating outside the Palace. In a 1985 BBC interview, the Queen recalled, 'I remember lines of unknown people linking arms and walking down Whitehall, all of us just swept along on a tide of happiness and relief.'[7] After a while Doris and her companions 'thought we had seen enough and walked back to where we had parked the car, only to find it had been stolen!' Luckily Doris had a key to her mother's flat in Paddington, and they decided to stay the night there. There was no public transport running, so they had to walk, and it was a long way. The next day police located John's car in South London where it had been abandoned by joy-riders, undamaged and only the rear view mirror missing.

Twelve thousand miles away in the Pacific, Roger and his shipmates discussed what they would do if they were in London on VE night. In an unpublished essay, Roger wrote that one 'loyal citizen felt he would want to shake Churchill by the hand, while most of us thought that drinking [to] his health in no uncertain fashion would be more satisfactory for all concerned.'

For Winston Churchill, the end of the war was soon followed by a dramatic and unwelcome reversal in his fortunes. In the General Election of July 1945, Clement Attlee and his Labour Party dealt Churchill's Conservatives a resounding defeat. Although

Churchill's heroic stature as a war leader was unquestioned, in the coming peacetime the British people wanted a change. They wanted what Labour was offering – a national health service, a welfare state, and full employment. In a 2001 article in *The Guardian*, Derek Brown wrote:

> The voters wanted an end to wartime austerity, and no return to pre-war economic depression ... Three years earlier, in the darkest days of the war, they had been offered a tantalising glimpse of how things could be in the bright dawn of victory. [The Beveridge Report] had synthesised the bravest visions of all important government departments into a single breathtaking view of the future...
>
> That was the great promise dangled before the British electorate in 1945. Though Churchill had presided over the planning for radical social reform, though he was a genuine hero of the masses – and though, ironically enough, the Tory manifesto pledges were not all that different from Labour's – the people did not trust him to deliver the brave new world of Beveridge.[8]

Even though Churchill knew logically that it was his Conservative Party and not him personally that the voters had rejected, he was stunned by the result, and particularly by the scale of his repudiation. 'Naturally I hoped that power would be accorded to me to try to make the settlement in Europe, to end the Japanese war, and to bring the soldiers home ... I had the world position as a whole in my mind ... I could not believe this would be denied me.'[9] Elisabeth Layton Nel, the Prime Minister's secretary through most of the war, wrote: 'It was more than the hurt. It was not being allowed to lead the Peace, which had been his dream while he was still leading the War. When you have worked for something day in, day out, night in, night out for five years – and held all the strings in your own hand, and seen your carefully planned schemes coming to fruition – then you cannot have that responsibility snatched away without feeling the gaping hole it leaves.'[10]

In Washington, Richard Miles was attending an embassy party when news was received of the Labour victory. When a reporter asked for his reaction, he quipped, 'My country, Right or Left!' – credited as one of the quickest replies ever made by an official spokesman to a very fast question from a journalist.[11] He returned to England for a few months and was a member of the British team at the Potsdam Conference in July. By 1946 he would be back in the States as adviser to the British Delegation to the United Nations and adviser to the UN Atomic Energy Commission, working with Sir Alexander Cadogan, the UK's first Permanent Representative to the United Nations, towards controlling nuclear weapons. By March 1948 the talks were at a stalemate in the face of Russian intransigence. Soviet Deputy Foreign Minister Andrei Gromyko insisted that all existing bombs (i.e. American) must be destroyed before discussions could begin on international controls. Richard pointed out that this would leave the Soviet Union with a free hand to develop its own weapons; 'Miles Tells UN Reds Want US Weapons Destroyed So They Can Make Own', announced the *New York Herald Tribune* on 19 March. The meeting ended with a public spat between Richard and Gromyko as, led by Great Britain, the UN Atomic Energy Commission voted to drop consideration of the Russian proposal. Richard himself wrote the final report.

Richard's tough stance drew widespread support. On 30 March Kay Halle (who would be largely instrumental in obtaining the honorary American citizenship that was conferred on Winston Churchill in 1963), wrote: 'Dearest Richard, fancy my turning on the radio last night to catch Lowell Thomas's 6:45 news to find him saying that "one of the sharpest attacks yet levelled at Gromyko in the UN Atomic Commission group was that of British delegate Richard Miles." Good work Richard.'[12] From Oxford his friend Herbert Nichols, who had served with the British Ministry of Information in Washington during the war and was now a Fellow of Exeter College, wrote:

Dear Richard,
   I find it hard to believe, when I open the centre page of my *Times* and see your name occupying the lead place, in the lead article, that you are going to carry out the threat which you made, that you were going to give it all up and come back to England this summer. If I really thought so, I would hold my epistolary fire until I saw the whites of your eyes. But your duels with Mr Gromyko are so obviously enjoyed by both parties that I refuse to believe you will give them up. I am surprised that you

have not appeared, heavy-jowled [sic], tousled and tough, in the pages of *Time* over some such caption as 'Slugs the Russian Chairman', along with full and colourful details of your youth at Exeter [College].[13]

It is quite possible that Richard's determination in not acquiescing to the Russian plan was more consequential than appeared at the time. In May 1944 an economic warfare expert from the Foreign Office in London was seconded to the British Embassy in Washington. His name was Donald Maclean, and his path frequently crossed Richard's, both socially and professionally. He became First Secretary, and from early in 1947 until the middle of 1948 he was Secretary of the Anglo-American-Canadian Policy Committee on atomic energy matters. In 1951 Maclean was revealed as a Soviet spy who had for many years been passing top secret information to the KGB. He defected to Moscow with fellow-traveller Guy Burgess. It is certain, therefore, that in March 1948 Andrei Gromyko had far more knowledge of the American nuclear programme than Richard and his colleagues could have suspected, and we can only speculate as to what might have happened (for good or bad) had the Russians succeeded in their aim to eliminate the American nuclear arsenal.

Shortly after the armistice in May 1945, George Clayton Greene 'managed to hitch a ride on a destroyer to land in Jersey and to see what our house looked like.'[14] After five years of occupation, the house and furniture were remarkably undamaged. Only the linens had been taken, to be torn up and used as bandages.

His recollection continued:

I attempted to find the trunk of family silver in the vegetable garden, which was quite overgrown. I got a spade, took off my coat and started small holes here and there. Then there was a call from a fence where two boys from the adjacent farm were watching my activities. I went over to them and they said in their Jersey patois, 'We know what you look for, boy. We saw you bury trunk before the occupation. We have it in our cellar'.

I suppose they thought, when they saw me burying it, that I had been burying a body, so they had dug it up. Anyway it was returned to me in good shape.

They told me what a bad time they had had during the occupation. They had heard the progress of the war from BBC broadcasts on small crystal sets (which would be a death sentence if they were found out).

The valuable silver, which these Jersey farmers had guarded so honestly at considerable risk, remains in Doris' and George's families.

The war may have been over in Europe, but in the Pacific the Japanese, vowing never to surrender, fought with increasing ferocity as the American forces battled closer to the Land of the Rising Sun. The cost to both sides was staggering. In a desperate bid to stop the Allied invasion the *Kamikaze*, suicide flyers who used their aircraft as missiles, ramped up their attacks. Thousands of planes and pilots were sacrificed, but barely one in five attacks actually hit a ship, and in only half of these was the vessel crippled or sunk. Roger had been serving in HMS *Quality* with the British Pacific Fleet since late 1944. In his report to the *Gazette* he wrote: '...the Japanese Fleet has ceased to exist and the *Kamikaze* ("Divine Wind" – a delicious expression) Air Force are keener to splay out their Honourable brains on bigger game than us. We have seen a few of these gentlemen on the job and it is difficult to believe that there is a human being in that machine that speeds on towards its target, though often a ball of flame long before it is anywhere near. The resultant explosion is spectacular to a degree although the damage inflicted has been so far negligible.'[15]

The new American President, Harry S. Truman, came to the agonisingly difficult and controversial conclusion that a knock-out blow was the only way to avoid further horrendous losses. On 6 August, the newly developed atomic bomb was unleashed on the city of Hiroshima and a few days later a second bomb was dropped on Nagasaki, both with catastrophic consequences for the civilian population. The next day the Japanese sued for peace. On 15 August Emperor Hirohito made the formal announcement, and on 2 September he signed the articles of unconditional surrender.

Roger was one of a group of British officers who entered Nagasaki and saw first-hand the devastation caused by this terrible new weapon. He wrote a description of the 'appalling scene' for the *Gazette*, ending with '[I] will conclude this sketchy description of the scene by the somewhat Chestertonian remark that it is indescribable, and that any gentleman who is in future desirous of making war should pay a visit to Nagasaki to ensure his recognition of the horror that may be loosed'.[16] His family still possess the samurai sword, traces of dried blood visible on its blade, that he brought home as a souvenir.

It was with profound relief that he was demobbed from the Royal Navy in March 1946 and returned to England, to St Mary's Hospital and to his beloved wife and baby daughter.

Act Four

Roger and Doris did have the four children Doris had planned. After Vicky came Gillian (Jill, the author, 1947), Lesley (1949) and Geoffrey (1951).

Annie and Ted Miles never did move to Torquay. They stayed in Cheam until the ill health that had dogged Ted for many years forced him to retire from the ministry of St Andrew's at the end of 1944. He died of malignant hypertension in November 1947, just three months after I was born. Annie moved in with her younger daughter Margaret and lived with her until her own death in 1977. She remained a regular church-goer, and despite failing eyesight, continued to enjoy literature through the innovation of talking books for the blind. (Annie once remarked that she considered all novelists post-Galworthy as the 'Modern Depressionists'.) Margaret was headmistress of Mayfield Comprehensive School in Putney, a pioneer of comprehensive education, and a vocal and effective advocate of the comprehensive principle that everyone should have an equal chance to learn. Her contributions were acknowledged in 1970 when she was made a Dame of the British Empire. When she retired she converted *Tan-y-Craig* into a year-round residence, moved to Wales and learned to speak Welsh, although with a pronounced BBC accent which was the source of considerable mirth to the locals. Her sister Marion had two more children, Christopher and Elaine.

Roger was fast-tracked as an ex-service registrar, and achieved his Fellowship of the Royal College of Surgeons in November 1946. In 1952 Sir Arthur Porritt, Sergeant-Surgeon to the new Queen Elizabeth II and later President of both the British Medical

Association and the Royal College of Surgeons, recommended him for a position as surgeon and lecturer at the fledgling medical school of the University of the British West Indies in Kingston, Jamaica. Roger accepted the post with enthusiasm. It was quite an adventurous thing to do in those post-war years – and not easy with four small children, the youngest still in nappies. Roger, Doris and the children set off to the Caribbean in the Elders & Fyffe banana boat *Cavina* with all their possessions packed into a large wooden crate. (Well, almost all - I can still remember my dismay when I discovered that they had forgotten to pack my beloved floppy toy dog Molly.)

Roger Pugh also returned to St Mary's as a surgical registrar when he was demobbed in 1946, thereafter becoming a specialist in urological pathology. He and Dorothy had two children and settled in Kent, where Dorothy was a volunteer for the Medical Benevolent Society, the Red Cross and the local hospital. Tony Oddie fully recovered the use of his badly damaged arm. After the war he found the 'nice wife' that Doris had wished for him, and moved back to his home town of Oxford to practice medicine.

Jill Hippisley finally met her Mr Right – or in her case, Dr Right. She had retrained as a secretary after the war and worked for Sir Robert Watson-Watt, the radar pioneer, before moving to Singapore in 1950. It was on a P&O liner returning to England in the summer of 1952 that she met the ship's surgeon, Dr Eric Graham. Eric proposed within a week of meeting her, and they were married that November. They moved to Bexhill-on-Sea in East Sussex where Eric was a GP, and had two daughters.

Richard returned to England in the summer of 1948 to work for HM Treasury in London. In a letter of recommendation Sir Alexander Cadogan, head of the UK Delegation to the UN in New York, wrote: '... he has shown great keenness, intelligence and the gift of getting on well with his colleagues and with people generally. A great deal of his work consisted in representing the Delegation at international discussions, both public and private, of disarmament and the control of atomic energy. He handled this work to my entire satisfaction and with full grasp of the technical problems involved.'[1]

Richard's heartbeat was also eventually stimulated and in 1954 he wed economist Caroline Leslie. They moved back to New

York in 1958 where Caroline worked for the United Nations and Richard was Head of the Economic Section of British Information Services. He maintained his friendship with Eleanor Roosevelt that had begun in Washington during the war. On 13 May 1962 he wrote to his mother Annie from Sutton Place: 'Mrs Roosevelt had us to dinner last week and has since written sweetly to say to tell her when we are back, so that she may have us at Hyde Park.' On 29 August Eleanor wrote:

Dear Richard,
  I was delighted to have a letter from you and I would love to have you and your wife come up to Hyde Park on Friday September 28th for the weekend, leaving right after lunch on Sunday as I have to take a plane for Washington that afternoon.
  It will be wonderful to have news of the Cochrans and to hear your views on the European situation, so I look forward to hearing that I may expect you both.[2]

Eleanor Roosevelt died a few weeks later, and her family invited Richard and Caroline to the interment on 10 November 1962.

They returned to England in 1963 and as a senior civil servant, latterly with the Ministry for Overseas Development, Richard remained in public service all his life.

Doris's brother George resigned from the Royal Navy in 1947. On 14 January 1948 he married Pauline Nesmith, the winsome Bostonian whom he had met during the war while his ship was being repaired, and happily settled in Concord, Massachusetts, as a gentleman dairy farmer tending a herd of Jersey cows. He and Pauline had two children, our cousins Jennifer and Geoffrey.

Arthur Dickson Wright died in 1976. He received unwelcome posthumous attention in 2007 when his younger daughter Clarissa (born in the Lindo Wing just a few weeks after the author), star of the TV cooking show *Two Fat Ladies*, wrote a scathing indictment of her father in her memoir. Doris had enjoyed a warm relationship with Dickson Wright and she was deeply distressed by what she saw as a scurrilous attack on someone she liked and respected, an opinion that was shared by his elder daughter. Doris complained, 'this is not the Dickson I knew.'

Jack Suchet had better luck with his children. He and Joan had three sons who all achieved notable success in their fields: John was 'the face of the evening news' as anchor for ITV News and is now a writer and popular presenter on Classic FM radio, David is one of Britain's best-loved actors, and Peter became a leading advertising executive. Jack himself had a busy private practice in Harley Street, but he also gave his services *pro bono* to St Luke's Hospital for the Clergy. He was NHS consultant to St Andrew's and Poplar hospitals in London's impoverished East End, which meant 'unsung dedication in poorly staffed hospitals,'[3] according to Alasdair Fraser's obituary of Jack in the *British Medical Journal*.

As Leader of the Opposition, Winston Churchill remained a powerful voice in British politics. Just as he had tried to warn the country of the threat of a resurgent Nazi Germany during his time in the political wilderness during the 1930s, now Churchill pointed out a new and present danger in the East. The Soviet Union had maintained a tight grip on the countries of Eastern Europe through which its forces had marched on the westward advance towards Berlin, including half of Germany itself. In March 1946, while visiting Fulton, Missouri, at the invitation of President Truman, Churchill famously declared, 'an Iron Curtain has descended across the continent.'[4] His pessimistic view of the Soviet Union was not widely shared at the time, but his words were to prove prophetic.

Churchill was re-elected as Prime Minister in 1951. By now, however, he was noticeably slowing down. He was tired and ill. He had suffered a mild stroke in 1949, although once again Charles Wilson had concealed the information from the outside world. Churchill was deeply upset by the death of King George VI on 6 February 1952, and although he himself refused to acknowledge the fact, his health continued to deteriorate. In the summer of 1953 he had another stroke, and this time Sir Charles could not conceal it.

Winston Churchill might have invented the mantra 'Keep Calm and Carry On', and that is what he did for almost two more years. (His own preferred expression was 'Keep Buggering On!') He was invested by the young Queen Elizabeth II as a Knight of the Garter, the highest honour that the monarch can personally bestow. But in May 1955 he bowed to the inevitable and resigned as Prime Minister.

Old and unwell he might have been, but Sir Winston Churchill KG was surprisingly tough and resilient. He was ninety years old when he died on 24 January 1965 following a final stroke. His funeral six days later was the largest state funeral ever held anywhere in the world. Millions of people across the globe mourned his passing.

In South Africa his former secretary Elizabeth Layton, now Mrs Nel, was among the mourners. In her book of recollections she wrote: 'I remember, also, to teach [my children] about Winston Churchill and the things he has stood for in his long lifetime. Courage. Strength. Resolution. Steadfast loyalty. Love of country'.[5]

Winston Churchill would still be remembered as an accomplished painter, historian and prolific, best-selling author, even had he never entered politics. He published more words than Shakespeare and Dickens combined. One of his landscapes recently fetched £1.8 million at auction. He was a candidate for the Nobel Peace Prize in 1945, and won the Nobel Prize for Literature in 1953 'for his mastery of historical and biographical description as well as for brilliant oratory in defending exalted human values.'[6] He was named an honorary United States citizen in 1963, and around the world today, from Australia to Zimbabwe, monuments commemorate him. In Amersham churchyard the 'Churchill Tree', an acacia grown from a seed planted by a local resident on the morning of Sir Winston's funeral, now shades a plaque dedicated to the memory of 'that great Englishman'. In a BBC poll in 2002, Churchill was proclaimed to be The Greatest Briton of all Time.

In 1966 Lord Moran published his book *Winston Churchill: The Struggle for Survival 1940–1965*. It caused an immediate controversy, with many people criticising him for publishing so soon after Churchill's death in what they regarded as a violation of patient-doctor confidentiality. Clementine was furious. She had previously written to Moran, when she had heard about the forthcoming book, asking to read the proofs, but had received no reply. 'It shows Winston in a completely false light,'[7] she complained to Mary. Despite her misgivings, however, the book has done little to dent her husband's legend.

Winston Churchill had spent two weeks in Jamaica in January 1953, and visited the University just outside Kingston. Roger was in the crowd with Doris watching as his senior colleagues showed the Prime Minister around the medical school. In 1957 Doris, Roger and their children returned to England after a memorable five years in the West Indies. Roger had obtained a post as consultant surgeon in the venerable city of Chichester, West Sussex, where, fifteen years earlier, Doris had spent a pleasant winter weekend with Dorothy and her sister. Doris's mother May bought a house nearby.

Doris's children loved May, our 'Granny Greene', just as Doris herself had loved May's mother Polly. Along with Polly's strength of character, May had inherited her mother's slightly eccentric streak (Polly had once scandalised the neighbours by prancing along the beach twirling a parasol, clad in what appeared to be her petticoat). She taught her grandchildren to play Scrabble and poker, to sing old music-hall songs while she played the accompaniment on her vintage upright piano. We helped her to make cakes, though an over-exuberant use of cochineal food colouring meant the icing usually ended up a lurid shade of bright pink. We recited along with Granny the American songs and poems that she had learned as a girl in New York. Our favourite was Longfellow's lugubrious lament *The Wreck of the Hesperus*, acted out in full dramatic overdrive.

Doris maintained her wartime friendships with Duncan and Audrey Gregg, Jack and Joan Suchet, and Dorothy and Roger Pugh; she also became good friends with Dorothy's sister Pat Reynish. She stayed close to Jill (formerly Hippisley) and Eric Graham all their lives. From my childhood I remember my pretty, lively 'Aunty Jill' – it was many years before I realised that she was not actually related to me. Doris worked at the hospital as a Red Cross volunteer and played tennis regularly. From its inception she and Roger were supporters of the prestigious Chichester Festival Theatre (H-J's friend John Clements was the Artistic Director from 1966 to 1973).

They bought the sailing dinghy Doris had always wanted, joined the local sailing club, and taught their children to sail (with varying degrees of enthusiasm!). They both loved being on the water, and on any Sunday when Roger was not on call they would be in a race or just pottering about in the boat with the kids. Sometimes they would be joined by Duncan Gregg, now a top clinical radiologist at Addenbrooke's Hospital in Cambridge, who was also a keen sailor. Summer holidays were spent at *Tan-y-Craig* in Wales. We children were thrilled to have our baths in a dammed-up section of the river where the farmers also dipped their sheep.

In the early 1970s, May was diagnosed with a weakened heart. Doris visited her almost every day and they would play a game of Scrabble together. On the afternoon of 6 October 1973, May told her cleaning lady that she was feeling rather tired. She lay down on the sofa and her heart gave out. She was eighty-one years old. Doris was devastated by the sudden death of her beloved mother, who had been such a constant presence in her life. But as always, she continued to 'box on'.

Roger was a gifted and inspiring teacher, and in 1979 he was honoured by the Royal College of Surgeons by being named Penrose May Surgical Tutor, the first such award for ten years. He was only the second surgeon outside of a major London teaching hospital to hold this prestigious post.

The Lindo Wing of St Mary's Hospital where Doris had spent so much of her nursing career, and where I was born, came to the attention of the British public in the early 1980s when Diana Princess of Wales gave birth there to her two sons, William and Harry. Years later William's own children George and Charlotte were also born in the Lindo Wing.

In 1982, the eminent historian Sir Martin Gilbert corresponded with Doris regarding her time with the Prime Minister, and some of her reminiscences are included in his book *The Road to Victory*, part seven of his definitive biography of Winston Churchill.

Neither I nor my siblings ever heard our parents argue or raise their voice to one another. Despite her self-confessed laziness, Doris was a capable, dilligent and loving mother, and their four 'brats' turned out fine. But as he had promised her, Roger nearly always did the washing up!

Epilogue

Roger was diagnosed with Parkinson's Disease shortly after his retirement, and once again Doris became the calm and efficient nurse of the wartime years. She nursed her husband with care and devotion for ten years as the debilitating disease ran its course. Despite the physical ravages of Parkinson's, Roger's mind remained clear and he never lost his dry sense of humour. Shaving became difficult so he grew a beard as he had done in 1942, although this time it was snow-white. His writing deteriorated into micrography, and Doris bought him a light-weight electric typewriter so that he could write letters and funny little rhymes to amuse his family.

My father had become very thin and bony, and the summer before his death I sent him from America a padded lavatory seat (unavailable in England at the time) to make sitting on the toilet less uncomfortable. In his letter to thank me he wrote:

Are you S*itting Comfortably? (to the tune Bless 'em All)

For two days I 'went' not at all,
But I found a big pack in the hall,
An American parcel addressed to my 'Aarrsel'
(old Devonian ... for 'A***hole')
But I'm a large Bummer, so I sent for the Plumber
(A friend of mine, always on call).
Now the padded white seat is an unusual treat,
You just get the notion you're passing a motion
With no discomfort at all!
(Pardon the verse, it could be worse)

With Doris and his two younger daughters (Lesley and me) at his side, Roger died at home a week before his 75th birthday, on 23 April 1990, St George's Day. At his memorial service Lesley read from a testimonial that his old friend Lord Porritt (then Sir Arthur Porritt) had written for Roger in 1947:

> Mr Miles has all the attributes requisite to a first class young surgeon. Hard working, enthusiastic, of equable temperament, tactful and co-operative – he possesses a very sound clinical sense, an admirable manner with patients and both an exceptionally extensive theoretical knowledge of his subject and even more important, the ability to turn that knowledge to good practical purpose.
>
> Added to all of which he has a most delightful personality. He has a keen sense of humour and is a good mixer and has always taken a large part in hospital life from his student days onwards. As a result he is universally and deservedly popular – a fact of which he remains delightfully unaware.[1]

After Roger's death Lord Porritt wrote to my mother: 'That expressed very much what I had thought of him at the time – 43 years ago! – and I had no reason to change my mind in the interim. He was in every way a grand person ... my own life has been made that much the richer for having had Roger as a friend.'[2] In 2010 a new state-of-the-art teaching facility at St Richard's Hospital in Chichester was named the Roger Miles Clinical Skills Suite in recognition of his contribution to medical education.

Doris lived in Chichester for the rest of her life. Just as Winston Churchill had found solace by learning to paint following the trauma of the Dardanelles fiasco in 1915, Doris took up painting after she was widowed and became an accomplished water-colourist. She was an enthusiastic and determined bridge player and enjoyed a rich social life with her many friends. She visited me in Hawaii (where I was living at the time) and we travelled together to the mainland United States, to France and Italy, until a series of mini-strokes severely impacted her mobility. Even restricted to a walker, Doris enjoyed tending to her small patio garden, sitting in a chair to do the pruning, weeding and watering. Her granddaughter remembers Doris taking a phone call from a life insurance salesman.

'Young man,' she told him, 'I'm ninety-five years old and have had a wonderful life. Thank you and goodbye.'

When the Churchill War Rooms Museum was set up in London in 2005, Doris was asked if some of her letters could be included in the exhibit, and she was invited to attend the official opening by Her Majesty Queen Elizabeth II. Among the other guests was Winston and Clementine's daughter Mary Soames, as well as Elizabeth Nel. It was a pleasure and an honour for my mother to revisit the memories of a short but very important time in her long life.

On 3 September 2016, Doris and her family celebrated her 100th birthday in the nursing home where she had lived for nearly four years. A few weeks later, on 14 November, she ate her lunch and then lay down for her afternoon nap. She never woke up.

In the weeks following my mother's death, I wrote these two poems in loving memory of my parents.

Manor Barn Nursing Home, November 14th, 2016

I shall be leaving soon.
Please don't be sad, for I am not;
I've been prepared for this for many years.
I've lived a long, fulfilling life –
Even got a nice card from the Queen
  on my one-hundredth birthday!
I've never suffered hardship, want, abuse.
I had a husband I adored –
  it would be hard to find a better man than he.
Twenty-seven years without him is too long.
Together we raised four fine children,
And I have loved to watch them in their turn
Bear children and grand-children of their own.
What kind of life do I have now?
It's boring here in this dark room at Manor Barn.
There's nothing on TV, just *Antiques Road Show*,
Or suburban couples looking at expensive houses in the
  countryside.
And anyway, I can't hear what they say, and cannot concentrate
  on that small flickering screen.
I gave up painting long ago.
I used to read a lot, but now I cannot hold a book,
Nor can I make sense of all those printed words.
I can do little for myself.
The helpers shuffle me between my chair, the toilet and my bed;
They're kind and caring, but there's no privacy or dignity.
So what I mostly do is sleep.
Sometimes I have visitors, which cheers me up.
I know the faces are familiar, but please forgive me
If I don't remember who you are, or what's your name,
  my brain is full of holes these days.

And so I do not fear 'the undiscover'd country,
  from whose bourn no traveler returns';
Rather, I'm curious to see what's on the other side.
If I really have a maker, then I would like to meet her,
If not, it's of no consequence, I will not know.

The pain that I felt in my legs this morning's disappeared,
My back no longer hurts,
Even my always-reddened eyes aren't sore.
I'm going now ...
   ... I'll close my eyes, go back to sleep ...

It will be teatime soon;
Someone else can have my piece of cake.

Letter to my mother

Dearest Mum,
I hope you are quite comfortable wherever you have gone,
I hope the food is better than the stuff you had at Manor Barn.
Your father died when you were just a girl,
I hope you find him now,
It will be good to get to know him after all these years.
Give my love to Granny Greene;
She was to me as special as her mother Polly was to you.
I wonder if they're dancing on the beach together,
    in their petticoats!
Give Dad a kiss from me; you'll find him on the links
    or at the tennis courts,
Playing a foursome with his siblings, Richard, Marian and
  Margaret.
I know he will be happy you are once more by his side,
I know how much he loved you.
Say that I'm glad we shared those times together in Hawaii,
Say that I'm glad that I was with him at the end.
Tell Lesley ... no, there aren't sufficient words
    to tell her all that's in my heart,
There aren't sufficient tears
    to wash her footprints from my soul.
Give her a hug, and let her know that you are there for her
    as she was always there for you.

Of course I don't believe there is an afterlife,
Death is the end, they all are gone,
Only the memories remain.
But this is what I'd say to Mum
  If I believed.

Biographical Notes

There are many fine books and innumerable articles covering every conceivable aspect of the remarkable man Sir Winston Churchill – he may be the most studied human being in history! This summary of key dates and events in his life, which I have adapted by permission of Richard M. Langworth, ed., from *Churchill in His Own Words* (2012 revised edition), http://amzn.to/2iU8qJK, augments my narrative, although with such a long and storied career it has been hard to keep it short.

I have also included for reference brief biographical details on some of the other significant dramatis personae in Doris and Roger's story.

The Patient:
Winston Leonard Spencer Churchill
Born at Blenheim Palace, Oxfordshire, 30 November 1874, elder son of Lord Randolph Churchill and Jennie Jerome of New York City, grandson of the Seventh Duke of Marlborough. His brother John ('Jack') born February 1880. Educated at Harrow School and the Royal Military College, Sandhurst.
Military career
1895 Commissioned as second lieutenant in the Fourth Queen's Own Hussars. Joins Spanish forces in Cuba to report the revolution. Death of Lord Randolph Churchill.

1897 Joins the Malakand Field Force on India's Northwest Frontier; his book *The Story of the Malakand Field Force 1897* is published the following year.

1898 Attached to the 21st Lancers in the Nile expeditionary force under the command of General Kitchener. Churchill also serves as a war correspondent, and takes part in the cavalry charge at Omdurman; his book *The River War* is published in 1899.

1899 Resigns from the army and travels to South Africa as war correspondent for *The Morning Post*. Captured by the Boers and makes a daring and widely reported escape.

Parliamentary career

1900 Elected Conservative Member of Parliament for Oldham. Is the highest earner of any contemporary journalist. His only novel *Savrola* is published.

1904 Crosses the floor of the House of Commons and joins the opposition Liberal party.

1905 Appointed Under-Secretary of State for the Colonies.

1906 His biography of his father *Lord Randolph Churchill* published. Elected Liberal MP for Manchester Northwest.

1908 Elected MP for Dundee. Appointed President of the Board of Trade. Marries Clementine Hozier (1885–1977) on 12 September.

1909 Advocates for old age pensions, with David Lloyd George.

1910 Becomes Home Secretary.

1911 Appointed First Lord of the Admiralty.

First World War

1915 Dardanelles campaign ends in failure. Churchill resigns as First Lord of the Admiralty and returns to active duty in the army as a Major commanding the 6th Battalion of the Royal Scots Fusiliers.

1916 Returns to the House of Commons..

1917 Appointed Minister of Munitions in the coalition government under Prime Minister David Lloyd George.

Between the World Wars

1919 Appointed Secretary of State for War and Secretary of State for Air.

1921 Appointed Secretary of State for the Colonies. With adviser T. E. Lawrence, works to settle borders of the Middle East.

1922 buys Chartwell in Kent which becomes his family home; after his death his widow gives the estate to the National Trust. Defeated in the November General Election.

1924 Elected as MP for Epping, a seat he will hold until 1964. Appointed Chancellor of the Exchequer in the Conservative Government of Stanley Baldwin, officially rejoining the Conservative Party in 1925.

1929 Conservatives defeated in the General Election. Churchill resigns as Chancellor although he remains as a back-bencher.

1929 to 1939 The 'Wilderness Years'. Publishes many articles and books, including *My Early Life*, *The World Crisis*, *Marlborough: His Life and Times*, and begins work on *The History of the English-Speaking Peoples*. A member of the Amalgamated Union of Building Trade Workers, he builds many walls and cottages at Chartwell, and also indulges his passion for painting, producing approximately half of his lifetime output of more than 500 canvases.

Second World War

1939 Outbreak of war between Great Britain and Germany on 3 September. Churchill appointed First Lord of the Admiralty in the Conservative government of Neville Chamberlain.

1940 On 10 May Churchill becomes Prime Minister and Minister of Defence at the head of a coalition government.

1941 Meets President Franklin Roosevelt in Newfoundland in August, signs the Atlantic Charter. 22 December to 14 January 1942 Washington conference with President Rosevelt; Churchill suffers what Dr Charles Wilson diagnoses as a mild heart attack.

1943 16 February to 15 March, first bout of pneumonia. December, second bout of pneumonia in Tunis.

1944 August/September, third bout of pneumonia. December, intervenes to stop civil war in Greece and to prevent that country from falling under the Soviet hegemony.

1945 Labour Party wins landslide victory in General Election in July. Churchill resigns as Prime Minister and becomes Leader of the Opposition.

The post-war years

1946 Awarded the Order of Merit. At Fulton, Missouri, Churchill warns of the 'Iron Curtain' which has descended across Europe.

1947 Death of his brother Jack.

1948 First volume of *The Second World War* published.

1949 Suffers a mild stroke, which is not made public.

1951 Conservatives win the General Election in October and Churchill again becomes Prime Minister and Minister of Defence.

1953 Suffers another stroke in June, but makes a remarkable recovery. Final volume (of six) of *The Second World War* published. Awarded the Nobel Prize for Literature in December.

1954 Appointment by Queen Elizabeth II as a Knight of the Garter, the most prestigious British order of chivalry.

1955 Resigns as Prime Minister on 5 April, re-elected as an MP on 26 May.

1956 Resumes work on *A History of the English-Speaking Peoples*. The final volume (of four) is published in 1958.

1959 In Marrakesh, paints the last of his over 500 oil paintings.

1963 President John F. Kennedy declares Churchill an Honorary Citizen of the United States.

1964 Retires as an MP in July after more than sixty years in the House of Commons.

1964 Celebrates his ninetieth birthday on 30 November.

1965 Winston Churchill dies at his home in London on 24 January. Following his state funeral, he is buried in St Martin's churchyard at Bladon, Oxfordshire.

Clementine Hosier Churchill

Born in London, 1 April 1885, second daughter of Lady Blanche née Olgilvy, granddaughter of the Earl of Airlie, and Henry Montague Hozier. Educated at home and at Berkhamstead School for Girls. Married Winston Churchill on 12 September 1908. They had five children: Diana (1909– 1963), Randolph (1911–1968) Sarah (1914–1982), Marigold (1918–1921) and Mary (1922–2014). Only two of her children outlived her.

Clementine's volunteer work on behalf of the YMCA during the First World War won her a CBE in 1918. In the Second World War she was President of the YWCA's Wartime Apeal, as well as Chairman of the Red Cross Aid to Russia Fund. In gratitude for her efforts on behalf of the Russians she was invited to Moscow in April 1945 to meet Marshall Stalin. As well as her volunteer work, Clementine provided crucial support to her husband and took care of his constituency business.

She became Dame Clementine Churchill GBE (Grand Cross of the British Empire) in 1946, and Lady Churchill GBE in 1953 when her husband was appointed a Knight of the Garter. Following Sir Winston's death in 1965, she was made a life peer in her own right and took her seat in the House of Lords as Baroness Spencer-Churchill.

Clementine Churchill died at the age of 92 on 12 December 1977, and was buried beside her husband.

Doris's Family:

William Henry Clayton Greene

Born in Wallasey, Cheshire, 3 November 1874, only son of Henry (1846–1881) and Annie (née Penny, 1849–1917) Clayton Greene. Two sisters, Annie Augusta (1876–1928) and Alice Margaret (1878–1971). Educated at Oundle and Rossall schools. BA Corpus Christi College, Cambridge, 1896. Obtained Open University Scholarship and entered St Mary's Hospital Medical School in 1898. Won Kerslake Scholarship in Pathology and Bacteriology. 1901, obtained MB (placing first in surgery) and FRCS. 1902, appointed Surgical Registrar. 1903, appointed Assistant Surgeon to the French Hospital in London. Member of the Hospital Cricket Club. 1905, Surgeon to Outpatients and Lecturer on Anatomy. 1907–1910, Dean of the Medical School. 1911, promoted full Surgeon and Lecturer on Surgery. In 1914 he was anatomy examiner for the FRCS, and also examined in surgery for Cambridge University. During the First World War he was Surgeon to the King George V Hospital and to King Edward VII's Hospital for Officers, and served on the RN hospital ship *Liberty*. Married May Guy 4 November 1915. Awarded CBE in 1919. Resigned in 1924 and moved to Guernsey. Died 29 June 1926.

May Clayton Greene née Guy

Born in Rio Grande do Sul, Brazil, 15 October 1892, only daughter of William Hannaford Guy RNR (1856–1918) and Mary 'Polly' Guy née Naisbett. (1866–1936). Two brothers, Julius (1890–1910) and Lester (c1896 –c1936). Educated in Brooklyn, New York. Moved to Lynton, North Devon in 1911. Trained as a nurse in Tunbridge Wells. Married Harry Clayton Greene 4 November 1915. Two children, Doris (3 September 1916) and George (4 February

1918). Moved to Jersey following Harry's death in 1926. Moved to London following the German Occupation of Jersey in 1940, became a volunteer driver for the St John Ambulance Service, subsequently worked for D. H. Evans department store. Moved to Bognor Regis in 1959. Died in Chichester, West Sussex, 6 October 1973.

George Clayton Greene
Born in London 4 February 1918, only son of Harry Clayton Greene (1874–1926) and May Clayton Greene née Guy (1892–1973). Educated at Britannia Royal Naval College, Dartmouth from 1931 to 1936, and the RN Engineering College, Keyham, Plymouth. 1939, commissioned as Sub-Lieutenant in HMS *Renown*. August 1939, Royal Aero Club Aviators' Certificate. 1940, promoted to Lieutenant. 1943 transferred to HMNZS *Leander*. Resigned 1947, married Pauline Shaw Nesmith (1915–1992) in1948. Two children, Jennifer (1949) and Geoffrey (1951). 1957, became a naturalised US Citizen. Died in Hartford, CT, 23 February 2017.

Roger's Family:
Edwin 'Ted' Griffiths Miles
Born in Aberdare, Glamorgan on 22 February 1881, third son of Richard and Ellen Miles. Graduated from the University of Wales, Aberystwyth, trained in theology at New College, Edinburgh. 1908, ordained as minister of the Welsh Presbyterian Church at Spellow Lane in Liverpool, married Annie Jones (1882–1977) in August. 1912, Minister at Crouch End in north London. Chaplain to the troops in France in the First World War. His book *The Soul of the Ranker* published in 1916. He was a victim of mustard gas and spent some time at a sanatorium in East Africa after the war. In 1919 he became Minister to St George's Presbyterian Church in Felixstowe. In 1928 the family moved to Cheam in Surrey, where Ted spearheaded the building and became the first Minister of the new St Andrew's Church. 1944, retired from the ministry due to ill health. Died 4 November 1947.

Annie Miles née Jones
Born in Bala, North Wales, on 3 April 1882, second daughter (of seven siblings) of William Edward Jones (1838–1908) and Ann

Jones née Edwards (1852–1938). Educated at the University of Wales, Aberystwyth, and qualified as a teacher of French. Married Edwin 'Ted' Griffiths Miles (1881–1947) August 1908. Four children; Marian (1909), Margaret (1911), Roger (1915) and Richard (1917). After her husband's death she moved to Putney and then Kingston-upon-Thames with Margaret. Died 5 June 1977.

Marion Gilbert née Miles

Born in Liverpool, 8 August 1909, elder daughter of Ted and Annie Miles. Educated in Felixstowe and Ipswich. Worked as a children's nurse at the Chailey Heritage School in East Grinstead, then volunteered as an army driver at outbreak of war. Married John Gilbert (1908–1993) in 1941. Three children, Sally (1943), Christopher (1946) and Elaine (1948). Died 11 December 1996.

Margaret Miles

Born in Liverpool, 11 July 1911, second daughter of Ted and Annie Miles. Educated at the county secondary school in Felixstowe and Bedford College, University of London (BA, History). Taught at Badminton School in Bristol, and two years in the Department of Education at Bristol University. 1946–1952, Headmistress of Pate's Grammar School, Cheltenham. 1952–1973, Headmistress of Mayfield Comprehensive School, Putney. Author of *And Gladly Teach* (1965) and *Comprehensive Schooling: Problems and Perspectives* (1968). 1972, Chairman, Campaign for Comprehensive Education, and President 1979–1994. In the 1970s served as chair of the Ministry of Overseas Development's advisory council on development education, and as a member of the Education Committee of the UK's UNESCO Commission. 1970, Dame of the British Empire. After Annie's death Margaret spent her post-retirement years at *Tan-y*-Craig, the family house in North Wales, where she died on 26 June 1994.

Richard Miles

Born in Bala, North Wales, 2 October 1917, younger son of Ted and Annie Miles. Educated at Epsom College and Exeter College, Oxford. September 1939, volunteered for the Royal Navy. 1941, promoted to Sub-Lieutenant. September 1942, represented the Royal Navy at the International Youth Assembly in Washington DC.

November 1942, posted to Naval Attaché's Office, British Embassy, Washington, and promoted to Lieutenant. July 1944, adviser to the British Delegation at the Bretton Woods Conference. July 1945, adviser to the British delegation at the Potsdam Conference. 1946 to May 1948, adviser to the British Delegation to the UN and adviser to the UN Atomic Energy Commission, author of the final report. 1948, member of the British Delegation to UN General Assembly in Paris, and Head of European Recovery Programme (Marshall Aid) Information Office, HM Treasury, London. 1951, Principal Information Officer, Ministery of Materials. 1954, married Caroline Leslie (1929–2006). 1957–1963, Director for Economic Affairs, British Information Services, New York; Caroline worked with the UN Secretariat. 1963, returned to UK and joined Ministry of Overseas Development. Retired in 1977, but maintained an active involvement in many international and local causes. A lifelong member of the Liberal Party, member of the Reform Club, Commodore of Thamesis Yacht Club. Moved to *Tan-y-Craig* following his sister Margaret's death in 1994. Died in Tywyn, Gwynedd, 29 October 1997.

Friends and Colleagues:
Arthur Dickson Wright
Born in Dublin 5 May 1897. Entered St Mary's Medical School in 1914. Served in the RAF from 1915 to 1917, then returned to St Mary's to complete his training, being house surgeon to Harry Clayton Greene. 1922, MB and FRCS. 1924, joined the Colonial Service and spent several years in Singapore as Professor of Surgery at the University of Malaya. 1927, married Aileen Mary 'Molly' Bath (1908–1975). They had one son and three daughters. Returned to St Mary's in the early 1930s as consultant surgeon. On the staff of Maida Vale Hospital for Nervous Diseases. Member of the Council of the Royal College of Surgeons and latterly Vice-President. Served on the Council of the British Medical Association, as Treasurer of the Imperial Cancer Research Fund, and as President of the British Society of Neurological Surgeons and the Medical Society of London. A crack shot himself, Dickson Wright was a strong supporter of the hospital's Rifle Club. Following a debilitating stroke, he died in the Lindo Wing of St Mary's on 6 January 1976.

Duncan Gregg

Born in London 14 August 1915, son of Dr Edward A. Gregg, a prominent London physician. Educated at University College School, and entered St Mary's Medical School in 1935. Qualified in 1941, served as House Physician and Medical Superintendent. 1942, married Audrey Wilkinson; they had four children. Served as Surgeon-Lieutenant in the Royal Navy from March 1943 until the end of the war. Returned to St Mary's and qualified as a radiologist. 1952, appointed consultant at Addenbrooke's Hospital in Cambridge. Worked enthusiastically to keep Addenbrooke's in the forefront of modern imaging technology and became Head of the Department of Radiology. He was a widely respected clinical radiologist, well liked by his friends and colleagues, and a keen sailor. Died 1 January 1969.

Ranald Montague Handfield-Jones

Born in London 12 May 1892, son of Charles and Alice Handfield-Jones. His grandfather Charles Handfield-Jones had been one of the first physicians at St Mary's, and his uncle Montagu was a gynaecologist there. Educated at Weymouth Grammar School and Epsom College. Entered St Mary's Hospital Medical School in 1911 on a scholarship. Served in France as an Army medical officer from 1914 to 1919, rising to the rank of Major and winning the Military Cross for 'exemplary gallantry'. Spent the last six months of the war as a POW. Returned to St Mary's where he was house surgeon to Harry Clayton Greene. Obtained his FRCS and became University Gold Medalist in the MB BS exams. 1922, Assistant Director of the Surgical unit of the Medical School. 1928, appointed as consultant surgeon. Author of *Surgery of the Hand* and co-author, with Arthur Porritt, of *The Essentials of Modern Surgery*. In charge of emergency medical services at St Mary's during the Second World War. He was married twice and had three sons and a daughter before marrying Lilian Tudor-Jones in December 1942. After the War he became Hunterian Professor at the Royal College of Surgeons and Chairman to the Court of Examiners. He was a dedicated Freemason and an enthusiastic cricketer, serving as President of the United Hospital Cricket Club. Died 21 April 1978.

Jill Hippisley

Born in Wells, Somerset, 11 June1917. Educated at Malvern Abbey School. 1937–1941, St Mary's Hospital nursing training. 1942, joined QARNNS, posted to Royal Naval Hospital Haslar, Gosport and Oxford. 1944, appointed to HMHS *Oxfordshire*, in support of the Italian Campaign. 1945, member of the Air Evacuation Unit, RN Auxiliary Hospital, Sydney Australia. 1952, married Dr Eric Graham. Two daughters, Amanda and Juliet. Volunteer, WRVS and Bateman's (National Trust). Died at Bexhill-on-Sea, East Sussex, 21 October 2008.

Douglas MacLeod

Born 9 May 1901. Trained at the Middlesex Hospital, London. 1928, FRCS. Appointed to St Mary's Hospital as consultant gynaecologist. 1933, married Lesley Francis, they had two sons and one daughter. 1939, FRCP and FRCOG. 1939–1945, in the Emergency Medical Service. 1946, Hunterian Professor, Royal College of Surgeons. Author of several textbooks on obstetrics and gynaecology. 1958–1959, President, Obstetric Section, RSM. Died in London 27 January 1970.

Sir Arthur Porritt

Born Wanganui, New Zealand, 10 August 1900. Won a Rhodes Scholarship and studied medicine at Magdalen College, 1924 to 1926. Captain of the NZ team at the 1924 Olympic Games in Paris, won bronze medal in the 100m dash. Appointed by Dean Wilson to St Mary's in 1926, and was a valuable member of the rugby team. FRCS 1930. Captain of the NZ Olympic team, Amsterdam 1928, Manager in Berlin, 1936. Appointed Surgeon to the Duke of York (later King Edward VIII) in 1935 and to the Royal Household in 1936. Author, with R. M. Handfield-Jones, of *The Essentials of Modern Surgery*. Served in the Royal Army Medical Corps during the Second World War, obtaining the rank of colonel. 1943, OBE and 1945, CBE. Married Kathleen (Kay) Peck 1946. One daughter, two sons; his son Jonathon Porrit (1950) is one of Britain's most influential environmental activists. 1946–1952, Surgeon to King George VI. 1952 to 1967, Sergeant-Surgeon to the Queen. 1950 KCMG. 1957 KCVO. 1967 GCMG. 1970 GCVO. 1962, President of both the BMA and the Royal College of Surgeons.

1966, President of the RSM. 1967–1972,Governor-General of New Zealand. Made a life peer, Baron Porritt, in 1973. An active Freemason. Died 1 January 1994.

Dorothy Pugh née Cooper

Born 3 April 1919. Worked at a children's home in Paddington before joining St Mary's as trainee nurse in 1938. 1942, married Dr Roger Pugh (1917–1999). Nursed Winston Churchill 18 February to 3 March 1943 (with Doris Miles), and August 29 to September 26 1944, when she accompanied him on the *Queen Mary* to the Quebec Conference. Moved to Bromley, Kent, after the war where her husband became a urological pathologist. Two children, Robert and Sara. Voluntary work included League of Friends Middlesex Hospital, Medical Benevolent Society, Red Cross and Beckenham Hospital. Died 13 December 2013.

Jack Suchet

Born Johannesburg, South Africa, 10 May 1908. Pre-clinical studies at the University of Cape Town. 1932, emigrated to England. 1933, entered St Mary's Medical School on a 'rugby scholarship'. 1935, MRCS, LRCP. Registrar in department of obstetrics, then director of the department of venereology. During the war he was adviser in venereology to the War Office, and worked closely with Sir Alexander Fleming on the use of penicillin in the treatment of venereal disease. Military service in Egypt and Palestine with the Royal Army Medical Corps. Returning to St Mary's after the war he specialised in obstetrics and gynaecology. FRCOG. Private practice in Harley Street, NHS consultant to Poplar Hospital and St Andrews, Bow. Married Joan Jarché 23 January 1943. Three sons, John, David and Peter. Retired to Torquay. Died 9 September 2001.

Sir Charles Wilson, 1st Baron Moran

Born in Yorkshire 10 November 1882. Entered St Mary's Medical School in 1901. 1908, MB. 1913, MD. 1910, Editor of SMH *Gazette*, member of the hospital's rugby team. 1914 to 1918, Medical officer in the Royal Army Medical Corps. 1916, MC. 1917, Italian Silver Medal of Military Valour, twice mentioned in despatches. 1919, married Dorothy Dufton (1895–1983), two sons. Dean of St Mary's Medical School 1920–1945, responsible for substantial expansion. Knighted in 1938. 1938–1939, Chairman of the Wilson Committee to develop wartime casualty hospital scheme for the London area. May 1940, appointed personal physician to Winston Churchill, a position he held until Churchill's death in 1963. 1941–1950, President of the Royal College of Physicians. 1943, created Baron Moran. 1945, publication of his book *The Anatomy of Courage*, based on essays about his experiences in the First World War. 1945–1951, a close ally of Minister of Health Aneurin Bevan in the post-war development of the National Health Service. 1966, publication of his controversial book *Winston Churchill: The Struggle for Survival*. Died 12 April 1977.

Notes

Author's Note

1. Boris Johnson, *The Churchill Factor: How One Man Made History* (New York: Riverhead Books, 2014), p. 5

Act One

1. Dominique Enright, ed., *The Wicked Wit of Winston Churchill* (London: Michael O'Mara Books, 2001), p. 61
2. Headmaster's report from St George's School, Ascot, April 1881, in *Winston Churchill 1874–1965: Facsimiles of historical documents and papers* (London: Michael O'Mara Books)
3. Winston Churchill, 'The Truth about Hitler', *Strand Magazine*, November 1935
4. *Winston S. Churchill, The Second World War: Volume I, The Gathering Storm. 1948.* Reprint. (New York: Houghton Mifflin Company, 1985), p. 207
5. *Home Office, The Protection of Your Home against Air Raids* (London: HM Stationary Office, 1938), p. 1
6. Andrew Roberts, *The Storm of War: A New History of the Second World War (1st US ed.).* (New York: HarperCollins, 2011), p. 45
7. Lord Normanbrook in John Colville et al, *Action this Day: Working with Churchill* (London: Macmillan, 1968), p. 19
8. Roberts, *The Storm of War,* p. 45
9. Churchill, *The Gathering Storm,* p. 601
10. Winston Churchill, House of Commons, 4 June 1940. Churchill's speech is widely quoted and available online: www.winstonchurchill.org/resources/speeches/1940-the-finest-hour/we-shall-fight-on-the-beaches/

11. Winston Churchill, quoted in Richard Langworth (editor), *Churchill by Himself: the Definitive Collection of Quotations* (New York: PublicAffairs, 2008), p. 572
12. Zachary Cope, *The History of St Mary's Hospital Medical School* (London: Heinemann, 1954), p. 149
13. Richard Lovell, *Churchill's Doctor: A biography* (London: Royal Society of Medicine Services, 1992), pp. 10–11
14. Ibid., p. 32
15. E. A. Heaman, *St Mary's: The History of a London Teaching Hospital* (Montreal: McGill University Press, 2003), p. 161
16. Cope p. 64
17. Lovell p. 130
18. Oscar Craig and Alasdair Fraser, *Doctors at War* (Stanhope: The Memoir Club, 2007), pp. 330–331
19. Lovell, p. 136
20. Ibid., p. 137
21. *St Andrew's, Cheam*, 1968. 2nd ed. (Cheam: Published with approval of the Elders' Meeting of St Andrew's United Reformed Church, 1990), p. 12
22. Winston S. Churchill, *My Early Life: A Roving Commission. 1930* (London: Macmillan 1941), p. 385
23. *Bradfield College Chronicle*, p. 1489
24. Cope, p. 67

Act Two

1. Hand-written unsigned notation on Doris's hospital contract, November 1941
2. Letter from Doris to Roger, 6 January 1943

July 1942

1. Winston Churchill, House of Commons 13 May 1940, quoted in Langworth, p. 4

August 1942

1. Winston S. Churchill, *The Second World War: Volume IV, The Hinge of Fate. 1950.* Reprint. (New York: Houghton Mifflin Company, 1985), p. 400
2. Ibid., p. 411
3. Lord Moran, *Churchill at War 1940–45. 1966.* (Abr. Rev. ed). (London: Constable & Robinson, 2002), p. 57

4. Craig and Fraser, pp. 289–291
5. Churchill, *The Hinge of Fate,* p. 428
6. Ibid., p. 446
7. Moran, p. 83
8. Dacre Balsdon, Sub-Rector, Exeter College, Oxford, 1938

September and October 1942

1. Eleanor Roosevelt, 'My Day, September 2, 1942', *The Eleanor Roosevelt Papers Digital Edition (2017)* accessed 7/7/2017, https://www2.gwu.edu/~erpapers/myday/displaydoc.cfm?_y=1942&_f=md056280.
2. Anne Steward, *The Seattle Post-Intelligencer,* 4 October 1942, p. 14
3. Ibid.
4. William Manchester and Paul Reid, *The Last Lion: Winston Spencer Churchill, Defender of the Realm 1940–1965* (New York: Little, Brown, 2012), p. 571
5. Kathleen Hey, *The View from the Corner Shop: The Diary of a Yorkshire Shop Assistant in Wartime,* ed. Patricia and Robert Malcolmson, (London: Simon & Schuster, 2016), p. 182
6. Roberts, *The Storm of War,* p. 111
7. Langworth, p. 34
8. Cynthia Helms, *An Intriguing Life: A Memoir of War, Washington, and Marriage to an American Spymaster* (Lanham, MD: Rowman & Littlefield, 2013), p. 50

November 1942

1. Winston Churchill, speech at the Mansion House, London, 10 November 1942, quoted in Langworth p. 8
2. St Andrew's, Cheam, p. 23
3. Letter from Robert Pugh to the author, 10 October 2017
4. Heaman, p. 437
5. Ibid., p. 439
6. Ibid., p. 305
7. Ibid., p. 431

December 1942

1. William Beveridge, *'Social Insurance and Allied Services',* 20 November 1942, p 458.
2. *St Mary's Hospital Gazette 48/9 (1942),* p. 152

January 1943

1. Franklin D. Roosevelt, *'State of the Union Address'*, 7 January 1943, http://www.presidency.ucsb.edu/ws/index.php?pid=16386
2. *Dorothy Pugh Diary* (unpublished, 1943), 17 January 1943
3. Roy Jenkins, *Churchill, a Biography* (London: Macmillan, 2001), p. 705
4. Moran, p. 94
5. Churchill, *The Hinge of Fate,* pp. 604–605
6. Jean Edward Smith, *FDR* (New York: Random House, 2007), p. 500
7. Smith, p. 501
8. Langworth, p. 371
9. Moran, pp. 95–96

February 1943

1. Manchester, pp. 639–40
2. Churchill, *The Hinge of Fate,* pp. 650–651
3. John Colville, *The Fringes of Power: Downing Street Diaries 1939–1955 (*London: Hodder and Stoughton, 1985), p. 758
4. A. J. Vale and J. W. Scadding, 'Sir Winston Churchill: treatment for pneumonia in 1943 and 1944'. *J R Coll Physicians Edinb 2017;* 47: pp. 388–94
5. Letter from Doris Miles to Sir Martin Gilbert, 14 January 1982
6. Ibid.
7. *Dorothy Pugh Diary,* 20 February 1943
8. Mary Soames, *A Daughter's Tale: The Memoir of Winston Churchill's Youngest Child* (New York: Random House, 2011), p. 233
9. Craig and Fraser, p. 22
10. Letter from Doris Miles to Sir Martin Gilbert, 14 January 1982
11. Ibid.
12. Anthony Seldon, *10 Downing Street: The Illustrated History* (London: HarperCollins, 1999), p. 84
13. Soames, *A Daughter's Tale,* p. 168
14. Elizabeth Nel, *Mr. Churchill's Secretary* (London: Hodder and Stoughton, 1958), p. 55
15. Dorothy Pugh Diary, 22 February 1943
16. Churchill, *The Hinge of Fate,* p. 651
17. Ibid., p. 655
18. Ibid., p. 651

19. Ibid.
20. Norma Major, *Chequers: The Prime Minister's Country House and its History* (London: HarperCollins , 1996), p. 198
21. Langworth, p. 543
22. Soames, *A Daughter's Tale*, p. 230
23. Smith, p. 544
24. Ibid., p. 543
25. Langworth, p.537
26. Sonia Purnell, *Clementine: The Life of Mrs Winston Churchill* (New York: Viking, 2015), p. 193
27. Letter from Doris Miles to Sir Martin Gilbert, 14 January 1982
28. Ibid.
29. Colville, *The Fringes of Power*, p. 126
30. Letter from Doris Miles to Sir Martin Gilbert, 14 January 1982
31. Soames, *A Daughter's Tale*, p. 165
32. Frontispiece, *Memoirs of General Lord Ismay*, 1960
33. Langworth, p. 511
34. Johnson, p. 126

March 1943

1. Martin Gilbert and Larry P. Arnn, eds., *The Churchill Documents, vol. 17, One Continent Redeemed January-August 1943* (Hillsdale, Mich.: Hillsdale College Press, 2015), pp. 64–65
2. Major, p. 70
3. Ibid., p. 75
4. Ibid., pp. 94–95
5. Ibid., p. 247
6. Letter from Doris Miles to Sir Martin Gilbert, 14 January 1982
7. Ibid.
8. Churchill, *The Hinge of Fate,* p. 662
9. Churchill, *My Early Life,* p. 30
10. Ibid.
11. Letter from Doris Miles to Sir Martin Gilbert, 14 January 1982
12. Colville, *Action this Day,* p. 69
13. Johnson, p. 97
14. Major, p. 190
15. Letter from Doris Miles to Sir Martin Gilbert, 14 January 1982
16. Ibid.
17. Moran, p. 289
18. Soames, *A Daughter's Tale,* p. 145

19. Mary Soames, *Clementine Churchill: The Biography of a Marriage*. 1979. (Rev. ed.). (New York: Mariner Books, 2003), pp. 32–33
20. Ibid., p. 39
21. Purnell, p. 32
22. Soames, *Clementine Churchill*, p. 41
23. Ibid., p. 52
24. Soames, *A Daughter's Tale*, p. 5
25. Soames, *Clementine Churchill*, p. 72
26. Ibid.
27. Churchill, *The Hinge of Fate*, p. 662
28. Moran, p. 107
29. Letter from Doris Miles to Sir Martin Gilbert, 14 January 1982
30. Soames, *A Daughter's Tale*, p. 235
31. Winston Churchill, 'A Four Year Plan for England', broadcast from London over BBC 21 March 1943, http://www.ibiblio.org/pha/policy/1943/1943-03-21a.html; the subsequent excerpts in this section are all taken from the same speech.

April 1943
1. Churchill, *The Hinge of Fate*, pp. 663
2. http://hansard.millbanksystems.com/commons/1943/apr/20/church-bell-ringing-removal-of-ban#S5CV0388P0_19430420_HOC_250

May 1943
1. Churchill, *The Hinge of Fate*, p. 700
2. Ibid., p. 714
3. Langworth, p. 43

Act Three
1. Address to the Royal College of Physicians, London, 2 May 1944, quoted in Langworth, p. 468
2. Colville, *Action this Day*, p. 115
3. Johnson, p. 252
4. Craig and Fraser, p. 325
5. Winston Churchill, Parliamentary Debates, 17 April 1945 http://www.ibiblio.org/pha/policy/1945/1945-04-17a.html
6. Interview with Doris Miles in a magazine article (title and date unknown)

7. Harry Mount, *Daily Telegraph, 25 April 2015.* http://www.telegraph.co.uk/culture/film/11561880/The-Queens-Big-Night-Out-what-really-happened.html

8. Derek Brown, '1945–51: Labour and the creation of the welfare state', *The Guardian,* 14 March 2001

9. Winston S. Churchill, *The Second World War: Volume VI, Triumph and Tragedy. 1953.* Reprint. (New York: Houghton Mifflin Company, 1985), p. 512–13

10. Nel, p. 184

11. *Times* (London), 1957, undated

12. Letter from Kay Halle to Richard Miles, 30 March 1948

13. Letter from Herbert G. Nichols to Richard Miles, 5 May 1948

14. George Clayton Green, *Thistle*, Vol 23, No. 3, Fall 2008

15. Craig and Fraser, p. 324

16. Ibid., p. 323

Act Four

1. Letter of reference for Richard Miles from Sir Alexlander Cadogan, Permanent UK Representative to the UN, 8 July 1948

2. Letter from Eleanor Roosevelt to Richard Miles, 29 August 1962

3. Alasdair Fraser, BMJ 2001 Nov 24; 323 (7323):1255

4. Winston Churchill, 'The Sinews of Peace', speech at Fulton, Missouri, 5 March 1946. See www.winstonchurchill.org/resources/speeches/1946-1963-elder-statesman/the-sinews-of-peace/

5. Nel, p. 188

6. www.nobelprize.org/nobel_prizes/literature/laureates/1953/

7. Soames, *Clementine Churchill, p. 558*

Epilogue

1. Arthur Porritt CBE, letter of reference for Roger, 23 December 1947

2. Letter to Doris from Lord Porritt, 11 May 1990

Bibliography

Churchill, Winston S., *The Second World War: Volume I, The Gathering Storm*. 1948. Reprint (New York: Houghton Mifflin, 1985)

Churchill, Winston S., *The Second World War: Volume IV, The Hinge of Fate*. 1950. Reprint (New York: Houghton Mifflin, 1985)

Collingham, Lizzie, *The Taste of War: World War II and the Battle for Food* (London: Penguin, 2012)

Colville, John, et al, *Action this Day: Working with Churchill* (London: Macmillan, 1968)

Colville, John, *The Fringes of Power: Downing Street Diaries 1939–1955* (London: Hodder and Stoughton, 1985)

Cope, Zachary, *The History of St Mary's Hospital Medical School* (London: Heinemann, 1954)

Craig, Oscar and Alasdair Fraser, *Doctors at War* (Stanhope:The Memoir Club, 2007)

D'Este, Carlo, *Warlord: A Life of Winston Churchill at War 1874–1945* (New York: HarperCollins , 2008)

Gilbert, Martin, *Winston S. Churchill Vol. VII: Road to Victory 1941–1945* (London: Heinemann, 1986)

Hager, Thomas, *The Demon Under the Microscope* (New York: Harmony Books, 2006)

Halle, Kay, *The Irrepressible Churchill: Winston's World, Wars & Wit*. 1985. Reprint. (London: Conway, 2010)

Heaman, E.A. *St Mary's: The History of a London Teaching Hospital* (Montreal: McGill University Press, 2003)

Helms, Cynthia, *An Intriguing Life: A Memoir of War, Washington, and Marriage to an American Spymaster* (Lanham, MD: Rowman & Littlefield, 2013)

Hutton, Mike, *Life in 1940s London* (Stroud: Amberley Publishing, 2014)

Jenkins, Roy, *Churchill, a Biography* (London: Macmillan, 2001)

Johnson, Boris, *The Churchill Factor: How one man made history* (New York: Riverhead Books, 2014)

Langworth, Richard (editor), *Churchill by Himself: the Definitive Collection of Quotations* (New York: PublicAffairs, 2008)

Langworth, Richard (editor), *The Churchill Companion: A Concise Guide to the Life & Times of Winston S. Churchill*, 2nd ed. Kindle ed. (Moultonborough: Dragonwyck, 2012)

Lovell, Richard, *Churchill's Doctor: A biography* (London: Royal Society of Medicine Services, 1992)

Major, Norma, *Chequers: The Prime Minister's Country House and its History* (London: HarperCollins , 1996)

Malcolmson, Patricia and Robert (editors), *The View from the Corner Shop: The Diary of a Yorkshire Shop Assistant in Wartime, by Kathleen Hey* (London: Simon & Schuster, 2016)

Manchester, William and Paul Reid, *The Last Lion: Winston Spencer Churchill, Defender of the Realm 1940–1965* (New York: Little, Brown, 2012)

Moran, Lord, *Churchill at War 1940–45. 1966. (Abr. Rev. ed).* (London: Constable & Robinson, 2002)

Nel, Elizabeth, *Mr. Churchill's Secretary* (London: Hodder and Stoughton, 1958)

Partington, S.V.(editor), *Mrs' Miles's Diary: The Wartime Journal of a Housewife on the Home Front, by Constance Miles* (London: Simon & Schuster, 2013)

Rex, Christina, *Doodlebugs, Gas Masks and Gum: Children's Voices from the Second World War* (Stroud: Amberley Publishing, 2008)

Roberts, Andrew, *Masters and Commanders: How Four Titans won the War in the West, 1941–1945* (1st US ed.). (New York: HarperCollins, 2009)

Roberts, Andrew, *The Storm of War: A New History of the Second World War* (1st US ed.). (New York: HarperCollins, 2011).

Seldon, Anthony, *10 Downing Street: The Illustrated History* (London: HarperCollins, 1999)

Smith, Jean Edward, *FDR* (New York: Random House, 2007)

Soames, Mary, *A Daughter's Tale: The memoir of Winston Churchill's youngest child* (New York: Random House, 2011)

Soames, Mary, *Clementine Churchill: The Biography of a Marriage*, 1979. (Rev. ed.). (New York: Mariner Books, 2003)

Soames, Mary, *Speaking for Themselves: The personal letters of Winston and Clementine Churchill* (London: Doubleday, 1998)

Vale, A. J. and J. W. Scadding, 'Sir Winston Churchill: treatment for pneumonia in 1943 and 1944'. *J R Coll Physicians Edinb* 2017; 47: 388–94